PRIVATE SECURITY TRENDS

1970 TO 2000

THE HALLCREST REPORT II

William C. Cunningham
John J. Strauchs
Clifford W. Van Meter

HALLCREST SYSTEMS, INC.
McLean, VA

Butterworth-Heinemann
Boston   London   Singapore   Sydney   Toronto   Wellington

Recognizing the importance of preserving what has been written, it is the
policy of Butterworth-Heinemann to have the books it publishes printed
on acid-free paper, and we exert our best efforts to that end.

Library of Congress Catalog Card Number: 90-084229
ISBN: 0-7506-9179-4

Butterworth-Heinemann
A division of Reed Publishing (USA) Inc.
80 Montvale Avenue
Stoneham, MA 02180

Printed in the United States of America

CONTENTS

TABLES AND FIGURES ix

PREFACE xiii

CONTRIBUTORS xiv

ABOUT THE AUTHORS xv

CHAPTER 1 INTRODUCTION 1

    BACKGROUND 1
    NATIONAL RESEARCH ON SECURITY 2
    PROJECT SCOPE 4
    METHODOLOGY 6
    ORGANIZATION OF THE REPORT 12

PART I: ECONOMIC CRIME

CHAPTER 2 AMERICA'S PRICE TAG FOR ECONOMIC CRIME 17

    GENERAL CRIME TRENDS 18
    WHAT IS ECONOMIC CRIME? 19
    DATA LIMITATIONS 22
    REPORTING PROBLEMS 25
    UPDATED ESTIMATE 28
    INDIRECT COSTS 32
    LIABILITY 34

CHAPTER 3 SELECTED CRIME CONCERNS 45

ETHICS AND VALUES 47
CORPORATE ETHICS 49
DRUG ABUSE AND PROTECTIVE SERVICES 52

    THE SCOPE OF THE PROBLEM 52
    IMPLICATIONS FOR PRIVATE SECURITY 54
    LAW ENFORCEMENT AND DRUGS 55
    DRUG ABUSE IN INDUSTRY 56

COMPUTER SECURITY AND ELECTRONIC INTRUSION 60

    OVERVIEW OF THE THREAT 60
    ELECTRONIC BULLETIN BOARDS 64
    CRIMINAL HACKERS 66
    COMPUTERS AND INDUSTRIAL ESPIONAGE 66
    DIMENSIONS OF COMPUTER CRIME 67
    THE COMPUTER SECURITY INDUSTRY 71
    OTHER GROWING CONCERNS 74
    COMPUTER SECURITY MANGEMENT PROBLEMS 75

THE SECURITY & TERRORISM INTERFACE 78

    THE "HYPE" FACTOR 79
    THE QUESTION OF A MEASURED RESPONSE 79
    DEFINING RISK AND TERRORISM 83
    THE BUSINESS OF COUNTERTERRORISM 86
    EFFECTS ON CORPORATE AMERICA 90
    EFFECTS ON PUBLIC LAW ENFORCEMENT AND GOVERNMENT 92
    LOOKING TO THE YEAR 2000 94
    NEW DEFENSES 95
    SUMMARY 96

PART II SECURITY RESOURCES

CHAPTER 4 DIMENSIONS OF PROTECTION 109

    THE POLICE ROLE: CRIME CONTROL 110
    CITIZEN CRIME PREVENTION 113
    PRIVATE SECURITY ROLE: ASSET PROTECTION 115
    SHIFT IN TURF 116
    COMPOSITION OF PRIVATE SECURITY 122
    MAJOR PRIVATE SECURITY COMPONENTS 127

CHAPTER 5 SECURITY PERSONNEL ISSUES 137

    PERSONNEL CHARACTERISTICS 137
    PERSONNEL SCREENING 141
    ATTRITION 142
    ARMED PERSONNEL 143
    TRAINING AND EDUCATION 144
    STANDARDS AND REGULATION 150
    COMPENSATION 156
    SUMMARY 158

PART III MARKET ANALYSIS

CHAPTER 6 SECURITY MARKET ANALYSIS 163

    INTRODUCTION 163
    SOURCES 164
    VARIANCES AMONG SOURCES 166
    DATA TREATMENT 168
    METHODOLOGY 169
    OVERVIEW OF KEY MARKET INDICATORS AND EMPLOYMENT 173
    SERVICE SECTOR 181

          Armored Car 182
          Alarm Companies 183
          Contract Guards 184
          Private Investigators 185
          Consultants/Security Engineers 187
          Locksmiths 188
          Manufacturers and Distributors 189
          Other 190

    SERVICE REVENUES 1980 to 2000 191
    NUMBERS OF PRIVATE SECURITY COMPANIES 1980 to 2000 195
    PRIVATE SECURITY EMPLOYMENT 196
    HOW AMERICA USES SECURITY SERVICES 198
    VALUE OF SECURITY SHIPMENTS 198
    ORIGINAL EQUIPMENT MANUFACTURERS AND DISTRIBUTORS 206
    ELECTRONIC SECURITY PRODUCTS AND SERVICES 208
    PROPRIETARY SECURITY 209
    COMPARISON OF HALLCREST 1985 AND 1990 PRIVATE SECURITY DATA 214
    THE EFFECT OF LARGE COMPANIES ON INDUSTRY STATISTICS 217
    THE "UNAMERICAN" GROWTH OF THE INDUSTRY 219
    DEPARTURES AND VARIATIONS FROM THE 1985 HALLCREST REPORT ... 220

**CHAPTER 7 COMPARISONS OF PRIVATE SECURITY AND LAW
ENFORCEMENT EMPLOYMENT AND EXPENDITURES** 227

    PRIVATE SECURITY SUMMARY 227
    LAW ENFORCEMENT SUMMARY 228
    COMBINED PROTECTIVE SERVICES SUMMARY 228
    HALLCREST'S 5-SITE TEST 229
    PRIVATE SECURITY PROFILE 232
    LAW ENFORCEMENT PROFILE 233
    COMBINED PROTECTIVE SERVICES PROFILE 234
    REASONS FOR PRIVATE SECURITY GROWTH 235
    PRIVATE SECURITY AND LAW ENFORCEMENT
    EMPLOYMENT COMPARISONS 236
    COMPARISON OF PRIVATE SECURITY AND
    LAW ENFORCEMENT EXPENDITURES 237
    SUMMARY OF NATIONAL DATA 240

PART IV PUBLIC AND PRIVATE SECTOR ISSUES

CHAPTER 8 RELATIONSHIPS AND COOPERATIVE PROGRAMS 243

    SECURITY AND POLICE RELATIONSHIPS (Before 1980) 243
    HALLCREST'S FINDINGS - EARLY 1980s 244

COOPERATIVE PROGRAMS (MID-1980s to 1990) 245

    NATIONAL PROGRAMS 246
    STATE/LOCAL PROGRAMS 255
    CORPORATE AND OTHER INITIATIVES 262
    SUMMARY 266

CHAPTER 9 MAJOR SECURITY AND POLICE ISSUES 269

PRIVATIZATION OF LAW ENFORCEMENT ACTIVITIES 270

    TRANSFER OF POLICE TASKS 271
    CONTRACTING OUT 272
    RECENT TRENDS (1985 AND 1990) 273
    THE FUTURE OF PRIVATIZATION 281

FALSE ALARMS 282

    GROWTH OF ALARM FIRMS AND SYSTEMS 282
    CONTRACTING OUT ALARM RESPONSE 283
    ALARM RESPONSE - A PIVOTAL ISSUE 284
    DEFINITIONAL ISSUES 284
    EFFECTIVENESS OF ALARM SYSTEMS 286
    MANAGING THE PROBLEM 286
    A NATIONAL STRATEGY NEEDED 287
    RECENT DEVELOPMENTS 288

POLICE MOONLIGHTING IN PRIVATE SECURITY 289

    BACKGROUND 289
    RECENT TRENDS IN MOONLIGHTING (After 1985) 293

PRIVATE JUSTICE 296

    NONREPORTING OF CRIME 296
    BYPASSING PUBLIC CRIMINAL JUSTICE 298
    CHARACTERIZING PRIVATE JUSTICE 301

PART V AGENDA FOR CHANGE

CHAPTER 10   FINDINGS, RECOMMENDATIONS, FORECASTS AND
RESEARCH NEEDS 311

FINGINGS, RECOMMENDATIONS, AND FORECASTS 312

GENERAL AND ECONOMIC CRIME 312
SELECTED CRIME CONCERNS 315
DIMENSIONS OF PROTECTION 319
SECURITY PERSONNEL ISSUES 320
SECURITY SERVICES AND PRODUCTS 323
COMPARISONS OF PRIVATE SECURITY AND LAW ENFORCEMENT 326
RELATIONSHIPS AND COOPERATIVE PROGRAMS 328
MAJOR SECURITY/POLICE ISSUES 328

RESEARCH NEEDS 330

SELECTED BIBLIOGRAPHY

SELECTED BIBLIOGRAPHY 335

GOVERNMENT PUBLICATIONS 337
PERIODICALS 342
BOOKS 351
OTHER 353

INDEX

INDEX   357

TABLES AND FIGURES

PART I

CHAPTER 2

TABLES:

2.1	Estimated Costs of Crime Against Business (1967-1976)	24
2.2	Estimates of Losses From Various Categories of Economic Crime	29
2.3	Total Economic Loss to Victims of Personal and Household Crimes (1986)	31
2.4	Indirect Costs of Employee Crime, By Type of Crime	34

FIGURES:

2.1	General Crime Trends	18
2.2	Estimated Costs of Economic Crimes	30

CHAPTER 3

TABLES:

3.1	Honesty and Ethical Standards for Selected Occupations	48
3.2	Percent of Companies with Drug Programs (1987-1988)	57
3.3	Use of Computer Security Technology (1985 & 1991)	63
3.4	Computer Threat Incident Rates	68
3.5	Summary of National Costs of Computer Crimes	69
3.6	Summary of Computer Crime Victims	69
3.7	Summary of Rates of Computer Crimes	70
3.8	Terrorist Incidents Against United States (1981-1985)	82

FIGURES:

3.1	Terrorist Incidents in the U.S. (1983-1987)	78
3.2	International Terrorist Incidents (1968-1989)	81

PART II

CHAPTER 4

TABLES:

4.1	Respondents' Opinions of Life Without Private Security	
4.2	Law Enforcement Executive Ratings of Law Enforcement Functions	
4.3	Law Enforcement Executive Ratings of Response Priorities	
4.4	Security Manager Rankings of Private Security Functions	
4.5	Private Security Contributions to Crime Prevention and Control	

FIGURES:

| 4.1 | The Security Continuum | 116 |

CHAPTER 5

TABLES:

5.1	Characteristics of Private Security Personnel, St. Louis (1959-1989)	138
5.2	Starrett Personnel Characteristics	139
5.3	Police Recruit Profile	140
5.4	Challenges Facing Private Security	145
5.5	State-Imposed Training Requirements	147
5.6	Higher Education in Private Security	150
5.7	State Regulation of Private Security Firms	153
5.8	Average Base Salary of Top Corporate Security Executives (1989)	157

PART III

CHAPTER 6

TABLES:

6.1	Comparison of Various Estimates for Alarm Industry Annual Revenues	167
6.2	Hallcrest Estimates and Projections, Private Security Gross Annual Revenues/Expenditures (1980-2000)	175
6.3	Private Security Industry, Hallcrest Projection of Number of Companies (To the Year 2000)	175
6.4	Private Security Industry, Hallcrest Projection of Number of Employees (To the Year 2000)	176
6.5	Hallcrest Estimate of Average Annual Revenues per Company and Average Employment per Company (1990)	178
6.6	The Service Sector in 1990	180
6.7	Employment Change in Selected Industries: 1988-2000	181
6.8	Security Service and Manufacturing Sector (1980)	192
6.9	Security Service and Manufacturing Sector (1990)	193
6.10	Security Service and Manufacturing Sector (2000)	194
6.11	Security Service and Manufacturing Sector, Hallcrest Projections of Number of Companies to 2000	195
6.12	Security Service and Manufacturing Sector, Hallcrest Estimates of Private Security Employment (1990)	196
13	Security Service and Manufacturing Sector, Hallcrest Projections of Number of Employees to 2000	197
	Hallcrest Estimate, Distribution of Private Security Services Among Consumer Groups (1990)	198
	Hallcrest Estimates of Gross Annual Equipment Sales Revenues (1980)	202

6.16	Hallcrest Estimates of Gross Annual Equipment Sales Revenues (1990)	203
6.17	Hallcrest Estimates of Gross Annual Equipment Sales Revenues (2000)	205
6.18	Hallcrest Estimates and Projections of Number of Original Equipment Manufacturers and Distributors	207
6.19	Hallcrest Estimates and Projection for Electronic Security Products and Services, Annual Revenues (1980-2000)	208
6.20	Hallcrest Estimates and Projections, Proprietary Security (1980-2000)	209
6.21	Hallcrest Estimates and Projections, Composition of Proprietary Security Organizations (1982-2000)	210
6.22	Hallcrest Estimates and Projections of Average Annual Operating Budgets for Security Organizations (1980-2000)	211
6.23	*Security* Estimates of Average Annual Operating Budgets for Security Organizations (1988-1990)	213
6.24	Comparison of Hallcrest 1982 to 1990 Data, Proprietary Security Employees	215
6.25	Comparison of Hallcrest 1982 to 1990 Data for Service and Manufacturing Employees	216
6.26	Ten Largest U.S. Security Guard and Patrol Companies	217
6.27	Comparison of Total Guard Segment, Averages for 1988 Annual Revenues and Employment per Company if Top 40 Companies Not Considered	218

FIGURES:

6.1	Security Product and Service Revenues	177
6.2	Distribution of Private Security Revenues/Expenditures (1990)	194
6.3	Security Equipment Revenues (1990)	204

CHAPTER 7

TABLES:

7.1	Hallcrest Estimates and Projections (1980-2000), Summary of Private Security and Law Enforcement Employment and Expenditures	229
7.2	Comparison of Private Security and Law Enforcement Employment (1989)	230
7.3	Five-Site Test Data	231
7.4	National Projections Based on 5-Site Test Data	231
7.5	Hallcrest Projections from Other Sources and Comparisons with 5-Site Test Data Projections	232
7.6	Private Security Contrasts with National Populations (1990)	232
7.7	Private Security Contrasts Projection (2000)	233
7.8	Law Enforcement Contrasts (1990)	233
7.9	Law Enforcement Contrasts (2000)	234
7.10	Combined Private Security and Public Law Enforcement Contrasts (1990)	2

7.11   Combined Private Security and Public Law Enforcement
        Contrasts (2000)   235
7.12   Hallcrest Estimates and Projections of Law Enforcement
        Expenditures (1970-2000)   238
7.13   Hallcrest Estimates and Projections of Private Security
        Revenues/Expenditures (1970-2000)   238
7.14   National Employment Data Summary   240

FIGURES:

7.1   Projected Protective Employment (2000)   236
7.2   Private Security and Law Enforcement Employment   237
7.3   Private Security and law Enforcement Spending   239

PART IV

CHAPTER 9

TABLES:

9.1   Possibility of Transferring Responsibility to Private Security   272

PREFACE

This publication, *The Hallcrest Report II: Private Security Trends (1970 to 2000)*, presents the results of a descriptive research project performed in 1989 and 1990 by Hallcrest Systems, Incorporated, of McLean, Virginia, under a grant (89-IJ-CX-0002) from the National Institute of Justice, U.S. Department of Justice. The principal investigators for this research project were William Cunningham, John Strauchs, and Clifford Van Meter.

The major purposes of this research project were to

- profile the growth and changes in the private security industry over the past 2 decades;

- identify emerging and continuing issues and trends in private security and its relationships with public law enforcement; and

- present recommendations and future research goals in the interests of greater cooperation between private security and law enforcement.

Major research tasks included literature searches, field and focus group interviews with private security and law enforcement professionals, and analysis of employment and security market trends. Published in 1985, *The Hallcrest Report: Private Security and Police In America*, reported an extensive, 30-month research effort performed by Hallcrest also under a grant from the National Institute of Justice. This work involved several national surveys and emphasized the relationships between law enforcement and private security operations. Several sections of the updated document, *The Hallcrest Report II*, rely upon and summarize the earlier research published in *The Hallcrest Report* (1985).

Opinions stated in the current document are those of the authors and do not necessarily represent the official position or policies of the National Institute of Justice, U.S. Department of Justice.

CONTRIBUTORS

The authors gratefully acknowledge the assistance of George Shollenberger, grant monitor for the National Institute of Justice, and each of the following contributors to this research:

Carlos Alvarez	Raymond Fjetland	Ken Nicholas
Norman Bates	R. J. Fries	Robert Oatman
Nicholas Beltrante	Mike Fullman	Garret Ochalek
David Bergsma	Vicky Heibeck	Peter Ohlhausen
Richard Blay	Greg Hill	Lynn Oliver
Charles Botkin	Rawley Hobbs	John Paul
Gloria Boyd	Wanda Hunt	Jonathan Peck
James Brodie	Jack Ingersoll	James Pierce
Bruce Brownyard	Harriett Isenberg	Anthony Potter
James Calder	Ed Jackson	Pat Rivers
Susan Call	Brian Jenkins	Richard Roth
George Campbell	Larry Joiner	Geno Schnell
Michael Carlson	Lee Jones	Theresa Schumacher
Carl Carter	Patrick Jones	Phyllis Scott
Joseph Carter	Radford Jones	Michael Shanahan
Thomas Cernock	Carol Kaarlela	Lewis Shealy
Michael Chapman	Jim Kallin	Barbara Sheldon
Meredith Cohn	David Kassenbaum	Robert Shellow
Charles Connolly	Norman Kates	Lawrence Sherman
E. J. Criscuoli, Jr.	James King	George Silvestri
William Cumming	Richard Kobetz	John Simmons
Ronald Cundiff	Richard Krueger	George Slicho
Minot Dodson	Richard Kuhblank	Ira Somerson
Lawrence Doria	Douglas Laurain	Thomas Sutak
Sarah Dowdey	Charles Lavin	Karyn Thomas
Kevin Dunbar	Barry Levy	Louis Tyska
Joseph Duych	Kai Martensen	Thomas Wathen
Patrick Egan	Mary Mattimore	Timothy Williams
Rosemary Erickson	Frederick Matz	Marla Wilson
Anthony Fague	Robert McCrie	Terence Wood
Kenneth Fauth	Ronald McLanahan	Richard Worch
Albert Fisher	Allen Muntz	Bill Zalud

Finally, the Hallcrest staff thanks the other 106 people who took the time to grant us interviews. Many of these security and law enforcement practitioners who were interviewed were exceptionally helpful, and the authors would like to acknowledge them publicly. However, anonymity was an important part of the research; therefore, Hallcrest simply expresses its thanks to all interviewees.

ABOUT THE AUTHORS

The authors have extensive and relevant experience on a wide variety of security and law enforcement research and consulting assignments over the past 2 decades. They have been involved in earlier national studies of private security and efforts to develop security-related standards.

William C. Cunningham, president of Hallcrest and project director for this research, has more than 20 years of research and management consulting experience in both law enforcement and private security. Between 1975 and 1978, he served both LEAA-appointed national private security groups, as senior consultant to the Private Security Task Force (PSTF) and as research director of the Private Security Advisory Council (PSAC). From 1980 to 1983, he was the principal investigator on the NIJ-sponsored national study of private security and police relationships, which resulted in the publication of *The Hallcrest Report: Private Security and Police In America*, along with a National Institute of Justice (NIJ) Executive Summary and a 1984 NIJ *Research in Brief*, "The Growing Role of Private Security."

While serving as the chief executive officer for 2 national consulting firms, he has directed research and consulting assignments for federal, state, and local law enforcement agencies and numerous *Fortune* 500 companies. Earlier, he served as director of personnel for the St. Louis Metropolitan Police Department. He has authored more than a dozen articles and monographs and has been a frequent speaker on police and security issues. A Certified Protection Professional (CPP), he is a member of the American Society for Industrial Security, the International Association of Chiefs of Police, and the U.S. Chamber of Commerce. He also serves on the editorial board of *Security Journal* and on the Prentice-Hall Review Board of *The Human Resources Yearbook*. Mr. Cunningham attended Davidson College, received a BS degree in industrial security administration from the School of Police Administration at Michigan State University, and has done graduate work toward an MBA.

John J. Strauchs, principal associate for Hallcrest Systems, Inc., and president of Systech Group, Inc., has more than 20 years of domestic and international experience in security and intelligence. He is a nationally recognized authority on security systems engineering. He is a frequent lecturer at universities, professional associations, and seminars, and he has written extensively on security issues for numerous professional journals. Prior to founding Systech Group, Inc., a security systems design firm, in 1985, he was a principal with Gage-Babcock & Associates responsible for security engineering.

Mr. Strauchs has completed over 450 security design, consulting, and market research projects over the past 15 years for various corporations, local, state, and federal governments, and foreign clients. Formerly with the U.S. Central Intelligence Agency, Mr. Strauchs was chairman of the American Society for Testing and Materials (ASTM) subcommittee (F12.10) on standards for security systems and services. A Certified Protection Professional (CPP), he is a member of the American Society for Industrial Security (ASIS), is a past chairman of a national ASIS standing committee, and received the ASIS President's Award of Merit in 1987. He is a technical consultant for the ASIS/Bell Atlantic *Security Industry Buyers Guide*, and he served on the advisory board of Datapro/McGraw-Hill as a specialist on technical security systems. He received his BA degree from Lehigh University and his MA degree from The George Washington University.

Clifford W. Van Meter, principal associate for Hallcrest Systems, Inc., and director of the Police Training Institute (PTI) at the University of Illinois, has more than 20 years of experience in education and in security and law enforcement research. Dr. Van Meter has been PTI Director since 1976; previously he was chairman of the Department of Law Enforcement Administration at Western Illinois University (WIU); director of Safety and Security at WIU; and assistant director of training for the St. Louis Metropolitan Police Department. He was an officer in the U.S. Army, Military Police Corps.

Dr. Van Meter served as executive director of the Private Security Task Force, National Advisory Committee on Criminal Justice Standards and Goals, and was on the National Advisory Panel for the earlier NIJ research project that resulted in *The Hallcrest Report: Private Security and Police In America*. He is 1 of 3 authors of *Principles of Security*, and he has authored several other texts and journal articles.

Dr. Van Meter holds a BS degree in industrial security administration from the School of Police Administration at Michigan State University, an MA in history from Western Illinois University, and a PhD in higher education administration from Southern Illinois University (Carbondale). Dr. Van Meter is a member of several law enforcement boards and advisory committees in Illinois and holds membership in the International Association of Chiefs of Police and the Academy of Criminal Justice Sciences.

Hallcrest Systems, Inc., headquartered in the Washington, D.C., suburb of McLean, Virginia, provides a group of highly experienced consultants who assist corporations and law enforcement agencies in applying security technology and management science to achieve cost-effective protection programs. Typical client services include corporate risk assessment; strategic planning; security systems design; policy and procedures development; market research; security awareness and other training programs; and job analysis, compensation planning, and other personnel management services. For the past 15 years, the Hallcrest staff has conducted research and consulting services for numerous large corporations, federal agencies, state and local governments, and several foreign clients.

CHAPTER 1
INTRODUCTION

BACKGROUND

The study of private security is a relatively recent phenomenon. Only in the past 20 years have the research, professional, and government communities begun to explore the extent, role, and contribution of the private sector to crime and loss prevention. Still, with very little hard data and not-yet-forged agreement even on the parameters of the "industry," recognition has developed that private security represents a sizable and powerful ally to the nation's publicly provided law enforcement efforts.

Technological advancements over the past 20 years have generated new and valuable kinds of assets to be protected and techniques required to protect them. These advancements also have generated innumerable opportunities for more sophisticated and more costly kinds of crime. Public law enforcement cannot be expected to provide protection against computer crimes, employee theft and fraud, and other complex economic crimes. Police cannot patrol corporate plants, office buildings, or computer facilities; they must await requests for police response or legal cause to become involved. Too often, the call comes long after the damage has been done. It is virtually certain that without internal private safety nets for detection of workplace crimes, most would go completely undetected.

Despite the fledgling nature of research in this field and the scarcity of reliable source data, agreement on the general trend is virtually unanimous: Private security is a large and growing industry, with considerable and often sophisticated resources to deter crime and to prevent other losses. With the enormous increases in crimes committed against businesses, private security resources have multiplied to help control economic crimes and to provide safer work environments. Further, individual citizens are increasingly relying upon private

1

security products and services such as alarms, locks, fencing, and security patrols for protection.

In addition to their fear of direct victimization by violent or property crimes, citizens are increasingly aware that they pay the price of crime (1) by feeling unsafe on their neighborhood streets and often at their workplaces, (2) by facing rising costs--e.g., pilferage-inflated retail prices, higher costs of insurance, etc., and (3) by enduring countless other economic side effects of crime losses in business and in homes. Everyone has a vested interest in the success of any effort, public or private, to protect personal as well as business assets.

NATIONAL RESEARCH ON SECURITY

Prior to this project, 4 national study efforts on private security have been undertaken over the past 20 years by the Rand Corporation (1970-72), the Private Security Advisory Council (1972-77), the Private Security Task Force (1975-76), and Hallcrest Systems, Inc. (1980-83). The first major study to focus solely on private security in the United States was conducted by James Kakalik and Sorrel Wildhorn (1971).[1] Their seminal work for the Rand Corporation (commonly known as the "Rand report") provided the first in-depth look at the dimensions of private security, with an emphasis on contractual security. The Rand report provided a glimpse of the size and growth trends of private security. Two distinct impressions were left by the Rand report--neither of which was well received by the security community. First, the vast resources and programs of private security were overshadowed by characterizations of the "average security guard"--underscreened, undertrained, undersupervised, underpaid, and in need of licensing and regulation to upgrade the quality of personnel and services. Second, private security was depicted as "private policing" and "policing-for-profit" to meet the needs of special interest groups, as opposed to public policing, which serves the larger community.

The growth of private security, its potential for interaction with law enforcement, and the problems listed by the Rand report led to 2 other major study efforts. A Private Security Advisory Council (PSAC) to the Law Enforcement Assistance Administration (LEAA) was established in 1972 and produced advisory reports until 1977. In 1975, a Private Security

2

Task Force (PSTF) was added to the National Advisory Committee on Criminal Justice Standards and Goals. The creation of these bodies recognized the pervasive involvement of private security in safety and protection, succinctly stated by the chairman of the National Advisory Committee in his foreword to the PSTF report: "There is virtually no aspect of society that is not in one way or another affected by private security."[2]

The membership of both bodies was multidisciplinary, including members from the academic, law enforcement, business, and security communities. Problems related to the interaction and cooperation of law enforcement and security resources were tangentially addressed by both groups. In general, the members of both groups felt that establishing standards would help upgrade the quality of private security and prevent abuses and unethical practices. This would increase the probability for a greater contribution by private security to crime prevention and control. The standards developed by the Task Force in 1976 were designed, in part, to motivate private security to begin upgrading its various components.

Among the publications prepared by the PSAC and published by the LEAA were model statutes for burglar alarms, and for state licensing of security guards; a code of ethics for security management and operating personnel; and standards for armored car and armed courier services. Additionally, the PSAC published documents outlining the scope of legal authority of security personnel and areas of conflict between law enforcement and private security.[3]

In 1980, Hallcrest Systems, Inc., was selected by the National Institute of Justice (NIJ) to conduct a 3-year, national study of the roles and resources of private security as well as the nature, extent, and growth of security markets. This research also included a national assessment of law enforcement and private security relationships. The results were published in *The Hallcrest Report* in 1985.[4]

In the traditional academic sense, security is not a body of knowledge girded with a strong research base, although the field of security itself constitutes a specialized area of knowledge. Indicative of a sparse research base, most of the publications on security listed by the National Criminal Justice Reference Service and the American Society for Industrial Security (ASIS) Information Resources Center catalog useful information and technical knowledge for the practitioner. But they yield little empirical data or theory on security, asset protection, loss prevention, or economic crime. In addition, the publications of other disciplines (especially management and social sciences) focus minimal attention on security-related topics--e.g., the tremendous impact of crime in the workplace and the development and impact of security-related technology. Thus, the Rand, PSTF, PSAC, and Hallcrest research efforts, along with a few market research reports and security directories, provide the only real baseline data. Most other empirical research has been sketchy and tends to yield "soft" numbers rather than "hard" data on the nature and size of private security. Therefore, it is extremely difficult to construct tight research hypotheses in a normal research environment that can then be accepted or rejected on the basis of empirical testing.

PROJECT SCOPE

Goals

The present research effort intends (1) to profile trends and issues in private security over the past 2 decades, (2) to provide relevant projections to the year 2000, and (3) to consolidate and compare the various findings of earlier private security research efforts. A contribution will be made by our research if students of and professionals in private security and law enforcement gain broader knowledge of available and needed data, and if they move toward consistency in how these data are used to describe and measure change in the security industry.

Hallcrest's contacts and interviews with experts, practitioners and associations in the private security and law enforcement communities, along with analysis of market research, media, literature, and government data, enabled us to identify and review significant issues and trends in the security field.

Areas of Research

The National Institute of Justice (NIJ), U S. Department of Justice, funded Hallcrest Systems, Inc., in January, 1989, to undertake descriptive research to explore issues and trends in the private security industry. Through a review and update of extant literature and data, national reconnaissance and focus group interviews, and site visits, the present research addresses the following areas:

Description of private security and law enforcement relationships. National reconnaissance and focus group interviews (also referred to as field interviews) and literature searches were used to examine a wide variety of private security issues and trends.

Presentation of updated profile of the private security industry. Data from the Rand Corporation, Private Security Task Force, and Hallcrest Reports published in the 1970s and in 1985 are reexamined and used as baselines for comparison with the results of current literature and data searches, reconnaissance interviews, and market analysis of the private security industry. Aspects of this analysis include the following:

- Comparative analysis of the data encompasses revenues, expenditures, employment, and industry trends and developments in various mixes of technology and security services

- The potential for alternative use configurations of public and private protective resources, such as special taxing districts and privatization are explored

- An updated profile on the economic impact of crimes against businesses is presented

Exploration of progress in the professionalization of private security. Literature reviews and reconnaissance interviews with a cross-section of security, police, and regulatory personnel examine the training, operations, licensing, and regulation of private security.

METHODOLOGY

The major tasks of literature and data review, site reconnaissance interviews, focus group interviews, and market research were undertaken simultaneously from the project's inception.

Literature and Data Review

A comprehensive literature review was conducted during the earliest phases of the project. A sustained effort to monitor and regularly review the major security-related literature and journals continued throughout the duration of the research.

The National Criminal Justice Reference Service provided multiple custom searches of its literature and research database, covering the subjects of private security, asset protection, economic crime, and related security and police subject areas. A total of 438 abstracts were reviewed during the selection of material most relevant to the present research.

The largest security association, the American Society for Industrial Security (ASIS), provided the information and referral capabilities of its library and other staff to broaden coverage of relevant literature and ongoing research. Other security associations and numerous individuals contributed information and additional referrals to ongoing work and contacts with others active in the security field.

Literature and data review did not end with examination of relevant reports or articles. In many instances, authors and expert sources were personally contacted for further information.

Market Analysis

The present research is descriptive and qualitative in nature and, for the most part, did not provide for the development of new, independent source data. Nearly 20 relevant security market research and law enforcement statistical reports were analyzed to develop a supporting framework for updating information regarding industry parameters and growth and market trends. For the first time, various market trendlines over a 2-decade period are presented along with projections to the year 2000.

Data analysis and update included publicly provided sources, including the Bureau of Justice Statistics, Bureau of Labor Statistics, and the U.S. Department of Commerce. The U.S. government remains, as it was a decade ago, the only source of large-scale, regularly collected, national, state, and local census and survey data descriptive of both private and public sectors of the security and law enforcement industries. Such data are nevertheless severely limited in their coverage of the many components of the private security industry.

The security market analysis was expanded by an extensive, computer-based analysis of recent market research performed in the private sector. This material provided valuable security industry business perspectives as well as independent data to amplify and support government data. Due to the for-profit, proprietary nature of this market research, however, some of these studies were unavailable for review by the Hallcrest staff.

Other indicators of industry size and growth trends, such as association memberships, conference and exposition attendance, and insurance information, contributed to our analysis. General business and economic data and trends were reviewed for relevant information and cross-checking with specific industry data. Finally, the reconnaissance or field interviews and focus group sessions provided yet another source of expert industry information and guidance as to the current and projected size and growth characteristics of the security industry, its components and markets.

The 1985 *Hallcrest Report* emphasized the following problems involved in classifying, defining, and obtaining consistent and comparable measures of security industry size, growth, market segments, and trends using government and private market research data:

1) Grouping of security product types within categories is inconsistent among various market research reports

2) Citations and source references are often absent in the literature describing industry size and growth statistics

3) Growth rates reported are often inconsistent, and efforts are rarely made to compare them

4) Failure to relate categories to the Department of Commerce's Standard Industrial Classification (SIC) codes, although they offer a partially acceptable standard in forecasting industrial and consumer goods market sizes, is frequent

These problems remain and in fact have become exacerbated in the 1980s by significant changes in methods and categorizations even within government data sources.

A major goal of the security industry market analysis, therefore, has been to improve the accuracy and specificity of the various and, in many ways, incompatible data. Also, projections to the year 2000 are presented for virtually every component of private security; and contrasts with public law enforcement employment, expenditures, and numbers of agencies are made.

Reconnaissance/Focus Group Interviews

Interviews were conducted in the following 12 metropolitan areas during this 1989-1990 research effort:

- Baltimore, MD
- Boston, MA
- Chicago, IL
- Detroit, MI
- Ft. Myers (Lee County), FL
- Los Angeles, CA
- Louisville, KY
- Miami (Dade and Monroe Cos.), FL
- Nashville, TN
- Salt Lake City, UT
- Seattle/Tacoma, WA
- Washington, D.C. Area

The number of people interviewed during the field or reconnaissance phase varied in each metropolitan area. During this research effort interviewees include the following:

- corporate security directors/managers
- executives of national and local security companies
- sheriffs, police chiefs, and command officers
- association executives, staff, and committees
- federal law enforcement agents
- police officers and deputy sheriffs
- security guards and private investigators
- news/trade journalists

- security systems engineers and installers
- security equipment manufacturers
- trainers, educators, and researchers
- insurance underwriters/brokers
- state regulatory agencies

Interviews with more than 150 people conducted throughout the project have contributed a nationwide perspective on the current delivery systems for private security services and their interrelationships with law enforcement in crime prevention and control. The major objectives of these interviews have been to:

- update information presented in the earlier research by the Rand Corporation, Private Security Advisory Council, Private Security Task Force, and Hallcrest

- identify trends over the past 2 decades in private security services and modes of delivery

- indicate the principal market issues arising from these changes

Interview content for law enforcement personnel included the following:

- trends in police agency budget and staffing levels

- shifts in tasks assumed and shed over the past 2 decades, and the effect on private security

- attitudes toward private security--personnel selection, training, regulation, and working relationships

- perception of the protective roles and contributions of private security

- views on "problem" areas such as false alarms, moonlighting, job performance, and conduct of private security personnel

- plans for cooperative programs such as contracting out certain noncrime, police tasks; special task forces for white-collar crime, etc.

- opinions about the "best" strategies for using private security technology and personnel to control crime

- projections about the future of public law enforcement vis-a-vis private security

Topics in the interviews with private security executives and practitioners included the following:

- nature of security business/organization

- types of security services provided

- rank order of clients served by business type, growth trends in security revenues or expenditures, and employment

- personnel size, characteristics, and training

- security markets--current and future

- law enforcement/private security interrelationships and conflict areas

- law enforcement tasks shed and assumed by private security

- cooperative programs with law enforcement

- attitude toward privatization of selected police tasks

- extent of and attitudes toward licensing and regulation

- economic crime problems--frequency and severity

- identification of major issues impacting private security and law enforcement

- projections about the future of private security and public law enforcement

In addition to the interviews with law enforcement and security practitioners, the research team reviewed the relevant topics listed above with representatives of 6 major national associations:

- Academy of Security Educators and Trainers
- American Society for Industrial Security
- Committee of National Security Companies
- National Burglar and Fire Alarm Association
- National Council of Investigation and Security Services
- International Association of Chiefs of Police

Further, contact was made with a variety of selected police and security researchers whose research experience provided information and perspectives for the Hallcrest project. Finally, several small focus groups with security and law enforcement practitioners were held to gain the groups' perspectives on current and future issues and trends in private security.

Study Limitations

By far, the greatest limitation of this project was our inability to conduct national survey research to collect and analyze current data from a representative sample of security businesses as well as law enforcement agencies. Time and funding restrictions prevented repeating or extending the 5 levels of national surveys undertaken by Hallcrest in the early 1980s. Therefore, for the most part, the Hallcrest staff was dependent upon secondary analysis of relevant, extant data instead of obtaining original empirical information.

ORGANIZATION OF THE REPORT

This report is divided into 4 parts, comprising a total of 10 chapters. Chapter 1 presents introductory material about prior security industry research and describes the scope, methodology, and limitations of this research. Part I (Chapters 2 and 3) addresses economic crime--its pervasiveness and its direct and indirect costs--and explores several topical crime areas such as drug abuse, terrorism, and computer crime. In Part II (Chapters 4 and 5) the dimensions and components of protective services are described, as well as security personnel issues.

Part III presents a comprehensive analysis of the protective market--its size, growth, revenues, expenditures, and projections to the year 2000. Specifically, Chapter 6 contains a detailed market analysis of the private security industry, and Chapter 7 compares various aspects of law enforcement and private security spending and employment in addition to other comparisons.

Part IV (Chapters 8 and 9) reviews police and security relationships and describes a number of cooperative programs that have recently emerged. Also, this part addresses topical security and police issues such as privatization, false alarms, moonlighting, and private adjudication of workplace crime.

Finally, Part V (Chapter 10) presents the major findings, recommendations, forecasts, and research needs. This final chapter is an action list:

- to improve private security's crime and loss control capability

- to achieve greater cooperation between law enforcement and private security

- to better understand the market for security products and services, and

- to learn more about economic crimes, private justice systems, privatization and other public and private sector security issues.

END NOTES

1.   James Kakalik and Sorrel Wildhorn, *Private Police In The United States*, 5 Vols., (Washington, D.C.: Government Printing Office, 1971.)

2.   *Report of the Task Force on Private Security*, National Advisory Committee on Criminal Justice Standards and Goals, (Washington, D.C.: Government Printing Office, 1976.)

3.   *A Report on a Model Hold-Up and Burglar Alarm Business Licensing and Regulatory Statute*; *A Report on the Regulation of Private Security Guard Services, Including a Model Private Security Licensing and Regulatory Statute; Terroristic Crimes: An Annotated Bibliography; Potential Secondary Impacts of the Crime Prevention Through Environmental Design Concept; Private Security Codes of Ethics for Security Management and Security Employees; Prevention of Terroristic Crimes: Security Guidelines for Business, Industry and Other Organizations; Law Enforcement and Private Security Sources and Areas of Conflict and Strategies for Conflict Resolution; Scope of Legal Authority of Private Security Personnel; Model Security Guard Training Curricula; Standards for Armored Car and Armed Courier Services; Guidelines for the Establishment of State and Local Private Security Advisory Councils*, by the Private Security Advisory Council to the Law Enforcement Assistance Administration, U.S. Department of Justice, 1973-1977.

4.   William Cunningham and Todd Taylor, *The Hallcrest Report: Private Security and Police In America*, 1985.

PART I

ECONOMIC CRIME

CHAPTER 2
AMERICA'S PRICE TAG FOR ECONOMIC CRIME

A customer who buys a $20 shirt in a retail clothing store pays $3 more for that shirt because earlier a shoplifter stole one just like it.[1] Driving home from the store, that same customer hits a pot hole that the city was unable to repair because it had paid out $300 on a fraudulent welfare claim. He will not be able to get his car repaired at the neighborhood garage because it has been forced out of business by recurrent vandalism. The impact of economic crime on American citizens is pervasive and inescapable.

The cost of economic crime is astronomical. American business loses $114 billion or more a year to crime--the equivalent of what is annually spent by all American corporations on business travel and entertainment.[2] Businesses and citizens currently spend another $52 billion annually for security products and services to combat crime and prevent losses. Federal, state, and local governments spend billions more in their effort to help control economic crime.[3] The nature of the problem is such that economic crime can never be eradicated, but present business and governmental efforts do not seem to be controlling the increasing frequency or cost of economic crime.

The public's perception of crime, along with that of many criminal justice practitioners, is based largely on the FBI Uniform Crime Reporting (UCR) of index crimes and on victimization studies undertaken as part of the National Crime Survey (NCS). Although these 2 sources, UCR and NCS, measure crime differently, they form a useful method for the public to gauge street and household crime trends.

In the business world, however, there are no generally accepted definitions, measures, or reporting mechanisms for most categories of economic crime. Therefore, accurate measurement and precise assessment of costs are presently impossible. Further, neither government nor business organizations are attempting to accurately measure economic crime--the cost of which may exceed 2% of the gross national product (GNP).

This chapter reviews general crime trends, provides a working definition of economic crime, presents a variety of estimates of business crime costs, suggests an updated cost estimate of economic crime in 1990 and for the year 2000, and suggests various indirect costs of workplace crime, including the increase in lawsuits relating to crime and security.

GENERAL CRIME TRENDS

FIGURE 2.1

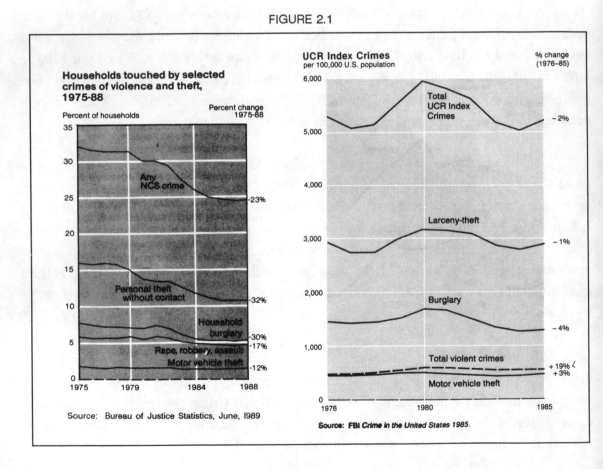

According to the NCS victimization studies, the percentage of households touched by crime has declined between 1975 and 1988.[4] **Figure 2.1** shows an overall 23% decrease over the 13-year period. Also, as depicted in **Figure 2.1**, total UCR Index Crimes reported to the police between 1976 and 1985 declined 2% per 100,000 population according to the FBI, although violent crimes increased 19% during this period.[5] Yet, according to 1988 UCR, the rate of index crimes increased 13% between 1984 and 1988. According to some criminologists, this decline in household crime rates reflected in **Figure 2.1** has occurred because of (1) community crime prevention activities such as Neighborhood and Block Watch programs, (2) incarceration of larger numbers of career criminals, and (3) fewer teens and young adults, who are the most crime-prone age group.[6]

Conspicuously absent from virtually all the literature which attempts to explain the stabilization of crime rates over the past decade is the role of private security products and services. Crime prevention and proactive approaches to crime and loss control have long been a major thrust of private providers of security equipment (locks, alarms, security lighting and fencing, etc.) and security services (guards, neighborhood and business patrols, armored car services, alarm monitoring, and security engineering). Surely the increasing use of the varied and growing resources of the security industry by millions of individuals, property owners, and businesses has contributed to the prevention and decline of property crime. Thus, to the other theories mentioned above to explain recent declines in crime rates, add the massive use of private security resources--equipment and personnel--selected and paid for by individuals, neighborhoods, and businesses.

WHAT IS ECONOMIC CRIME?

Choose any standard definition of economics, and it will contain some generalized description of how resources are used to produce goods and services for distribution and consumption. Economic crime is crime that keeps the economy from operating in accord with legitimate business, social, and political expectations.

Though there are many valid and useful ways to define economic crime,[7] the 2 Hallcrest working definitions presented here suggest its breadth and pervasiveness:

Economic crime is illicit behavior having as its object the unjust enrichment of the perpetrator at the expense of the economic system as a whole and its individual components. The consequences of economic crime are increased costs that are passed on to consumers and taxpayers and that place a financial burden upon business, the government, and, ultimately, the public. This working definition of economic crime is intended to encompass the terms of white-collar crime, crimes against business, management fraud, ordinary workplace crimes, and fraud against the government, business, and consumers.

Another working definition might be:

Economic crime is financially motivated crime that has a direct impact on the economy. Such crime destroys public and private assets or diverts them from legitimate channels, thereby imposing higher costs on all consumer goods and services. It especially affects private business and government contracting programs.

These definitions accommodate crimes against both business and government, thereby recognizing the major role public expenditures play in the economy.

Most economic crimes fall into the category of crimes against property. Among others these include arson, burglary, and various forms of fraud or theft--both external and internal. Crimes against business at first glance would not seem to include crimes against persons, but some people become the victims of crime because of their connection with a business enterprise. For example, terrorism has involved the kidnapping of business executives for ransom to be paid by their companies, and bank officers and their families have been held hostage as part of bank robberies.

As early as 1949, Edwin Sutherland, in his pioneering book, *White-Collar Crime*, sought to document the existence of crime committed by otherwise noncriminal stereotypes. Law enforcement agencies directed virtually no resources to investigation and prosecution of what is now colloquially referred to as "crime in the suites" as opposed to "crime in the

20

streets." Today, the existence of white-collar crime--largely acts of fraud and embezzlement--is unquestionably accepted by researchers and law enforcement agencies. Although state and local law enforcement agencies have relatively few resources assigned to economic crime investigation, the Federal Bureau of Investigation (FBI) labeled it "the crime of the 1980s" and assigned nearly 25% of its agents to detecting such crimes.[8]

Yet, no consensus exists among researchers, the business community, and law enforcement on definitions, classification, and measurement of economic crime. For example, Simon Dinitz provides an excellent analysis of white-collar crime issues, including a content analysis of important business periodicals and an evaluation of leading authors in the field of white-collar crime.[9] However, focusing only on white-collar crime ignores the sizable economic impact of "ordinary crime"[10] against business, especially small business.

For the past 20 years, the 2 major components of economic crime have been *white collar* and *ordinary crime*. The common elements of most white-collar crime definitions can be summarized as:

- crimes committed in the course of one's lawful occupation (e.g., a bank employee who embezzles funds while carrying out normal bank duties)

- a violation of trust

- a lack of physical force to accomplish the crime

- money, property, or power and prestige as the primary goals of the crime

- intent to commit the illegal act

- an attempt to conceal the crime[11]

Some examples of the types of crimes generally categorized as "white-collar crime" are consumer fraud, embezzlement, tax evasion, bankruptcy fraud, corporate bribery (kickbacks and payoffs), computer crime, securities fraud, political corruption, and government procurement fraud. Ordinary workplace crime has, for many years, included

21

arson, bad checks, burglary, credit card fraud, employee theft, robbery, shoplifting, and vandalism.

Sophisticated contemporary technologies require that several crimes be added, such as automatic teller machine (ATM) fraud, telecommunications fraud (telephone and computer hackers), money laundering, and theft of intellectual property (computer software, trade secrets, etc.). In addition, drug trafficking and use in the workplace are thought to be rampant. Whether these and other workplace crimes are white-collar or ordinary business crimes is not always clear. It is clear, however, that they are economic crimes in the fullest sense of our working definitions.

Legitimate business enterprises are concerned not only about crime perpetrated directly against their businesses, but also about forms of crime represented to the public as regular businesses. Every form of fraud on the consuming public has a strong impact on legitimate businesses trying to sell the same product. For example, product counterfeiting of Rolex watches, Chanel perfume, Gucci bags, Nike athletic shoes, and many other legitimate products deprives the consumer of the genuine item he thinks he is buying and the business of its rightful sales opportunity. The U.S. International Trade Commission estimates that U.S. businesses lose between $8 billion and $20 billion annually to makers of counterfeit products.[12]

DATA LIMITATIONS

As previously noted, neither government nor the business community has generally accepted measures of economic crime. The lack of standard classifications and definitions, coupled with limited reporting of workplace crime, contributes to the problem of measurement. Over the past 15 years, no fewer than 5 study efforts on business and white-collar crime have identified the need for indices to accurately measure economic crime and its true impact on society. Yet, there is still no single, centralized compilation of economic crime statistics similar to the statistics on street crime compiled by the FBI in its annual Uniform Crime Reports.

The most frequently quoted figure for the cost of crimes against business during the 1970s and much of the 1980s is $40 billion a year, which has sometimes been expressed as 1% of the gross national product (GNP). Economic crime cost statistics usually come from 1 of 6 sources:

- *Crimes Against Small Business*, Report of the Small Business Administration, 1969

- *The Economic Impact of Crimes Against Business*, U.S. Department of Commerce, 1972 (updated in 1974 and 1976)

- *Handbook on White Collar Crime*, Chamber of Commerce of the United States, 1974

- *Costs of Crime*, A Study of the Joint Economic Committee, Congress of the United States, 1976

- *Background, Findings, and Recommendations, Crimes Against Business Project*, American Management Associations, 1977

- *The Hallcrest Report: Private Security and Police In America*, Hallcrest Systems, Inc., 1985

Table 2.1 sets forth the statistics derived from 4 of these projects for estimated crime costs, by type of crime. These estimates are not entirely comparable since they covered different time periods, used different methodologies, and did not consider the same offenses. For example, only 2 of the listed crimes, check fraud and employee theft, were considered by all 4 groups, and the number of crimes studied ranged from 6 to 11. The Small Business Administration (SBA) study focused on ordinary crimes against business (burglary, robbery, shoplifting, etc.), whereas the Joint Economic Committee was concerned primarily with white-collar crime (fraud, embezzlement, bribery, etc.). Although the estimates differ because the goals and methodologies of each study were different, the data are presented here to illustrate the increasing costs of crimes against business.

TABLE 2.1 ESTIMATED COSTS OF CRIME AGAINST BUSINESS 1967-1976				
	SOURCES *(Figures in billions of dollars)*			
TYPE OF CRIME	SMALL BUSINESS ADMIN. (1967-68)	CHAMBER OF COMMERCE OF THE U.S. (1974)	AMERICAN MANAGEMENT ASSOCIATIONS (1975)	JOINT ECONOMIC COMMITTEE (1976)
Arson			1.3	
Bankruptcy Fraud		0.08		.103
Bribery, Kickbacks, Payoffs		3.00	3.5-10.0	3.85
Burglary	.958		2.5	
Check Fraud	.316	1.0	1.0-2.0	1.12
Computer-related		0.10		.129
Consumer Fraud		21.00		27.0
Credit Card Fraud		0.1	0.5	.500
Embezzlement		3.0	4.0	3.86
Insurance Fraud		2.00	2.0	2.50
Pilferage/ Employee Theft	.381	4.0	5.0-10.0	4.84
Robbery	.077			
Securities Theft/Fraud		4.00	5.0	.291
Shoplifting	.504		2.0	
Vandalism	.813		2.5	
Receiving Stolen Property		3.50		
TOTAL $*	3.05	41.7	29.3-41.8	44.2

*(Total cost estimates may not be exact due to rounding.)

The studies do have 1 theme in common: the lack of consistency among data sources, preventing the development of a sound data base. Each of the major study efforts, or reviews thereof, identified this issue as a shortcoming of the estimates of economic crime.

Committee on the Judiciary, Subcommittee on Crime, U.S. House of Representatives

> *Since so little data exist, any estimate of white-collar crime can only be a ball park figure.*

Crimes Against Business Project, American Management Associations

> *There are little or no hard data on losses to business due to nonviolent crime, either at the macro or micro levels.*

Committee on Economic Crimes, American Bar Association

> *The data which have been gathered are of questionable validity because there are no uniform standards for collecting economic crime statistics.*

The Cost of Crimes Against Business, U.S. Department of Commerce

> *The most serious difficulty associated with analyzing the impact of crimes against business continues to be the sparseness and sporadic nature of the data available.*

Employer Perceptions of Workplace Crime, Michael Baker and Alan Westin, Bureau of Justice Statistics

> *It is generally recognized that most cost estimates are, at best, informed guesses.*

REPORTING PROBLEMS

In part because of these efforts to assess business crime in the 1970s, considerable attention was directed toward influencing business, federal government agencies, and trade associations to improve economic crime reporting and statistics. A Federal Interagency Committee to Assess the Impact of Crimes Against Business was established in 1974 and continued until 1977, and included representatives of 10 federal agencies. Additionally, between 1975 and 1978, other federal task forces, along with committees of the U.S. Chamber of Commerce and the American Management Associations (AMA), raised some key issues concerning the inadequacy of economic crime data--issues that are still viable more than a decade later.

The deputy director of business research and analysis for the U.S. Department of Commerce, in congressional testimony, urged a reporting process for business crime:

> *Government must focus its attention and initiatives on filling the data and information gaps...Any proposal for improving data on a national level suffers from the necessity to impose reporting requirements on the private sector.*[13]

Stopping just short of actually recommending that private sector crime reporting be mandated by law, he recommended that "most importantly, the private sector must develop comprehensive crime loss measurement."[14]

AMA's Crime Against Business Council recommended the establishment of a National Economic Crime Center to serve as a business crime research and statistical clearinghouse. Despite consensus by virtually all study groups in the 1970s that economic crime loss measurement was vital to the assessment of its magnitude and to the formulation of strategies to reduce those losses, little or no progress can be found toward that goal in the 1980s.

Four major obstacles prevent development of an ongoing program of reporting crime and loss data by business and industry: (1) no accepted definitions exist,[15] (2) there is no data base upon which to build and measure trends, (3) businesses have not developed effective methods of collecting or reporting crime-related losses, and (4) organizations are generally reluctant to release financial loss data that could reflect adversely on them.

Two reports published by the U.S. Department of Commerce on crimes against business, *Crime in Retailing* and *Crime in Service Industries*, highlight the problem of industry reporting of crime. In the *Crime in Retailing* report, over 50% of the survey respondents in the food retailing sector stated that they did not even keep records of loss experiences--they were unable to determine whether inventory shrinkage was due to shoplifting, internal theft, shorted shipments of merchandise, accounting errors, or other causes. Yet, this industry is among the most vulnerable to crime through shoplifting and employee theft. The introduction to this report noted the problems of nonreporting:

> *Most crimes against retail store operators are not reported to law enforcement officers, and therefore do not appear in statistical reports on the incidence of crime. In the case of shoplifting or theft of merchandise by employees, the crime is often not discovered until an inventory is taken.*[16]

In *Crime in Service Industries*, significant mention was made of underreporting of crime and the lack of reporting systems:

> *For some entire industries, there is a complete lack of figures. Known crime in the services sector is merely the 'tip of the iceberg.'*[17]

Often in business there is concern for public embarrassment, adverse publicity, and decline in sales from reporting losses due to crime. The lodging industry, for example, tends to minimize knowledge of its crime losses for fear of adversely affecting occupancy rates. Researchers for the service industry report found that the only industries computing and reporting losses at that time were the transportation and financial sectors, where some reporting is mandated by federal regulations. Even in these sectors, it is difficult to get accurate reporting.

In cargo transportation services, for example, carriers regulated by the Interstate Commerce Commission (ICC) transport only one-third of all manufactured product tonnage in the United States. Crime loss figures could not be computed for the private carriers, shippers, manufacturers, or merchants using their own vehicles to carry goods.

Michael Baker and Alan Westin in their research on workplace crime concluded that "...most companies do not know and usually cannot measure accurately the losses they suffer from different types of crime by employees or outsiders.[18] The authors further note:

> *The professional business literature contains many accounts indicating that when companies do gather the necessary data, they are often surprised at the magnitude of losses they have been sustaining.*[19]

During Hallcrest's 1989 reconnaissance interviews with dozens of corporate security executives in various industries throughout the country, the staff found a major impediment to collecting economic crime loss data. Repeatedly, and often with embarrassment, security executives told the Hallcrest research staff that their companies' incident or crime loss reporting system was incomplete or nonexistent. Many security managers have great difficulty persuading management of various operating divisions and at different locations to completely and accurately report crimes and other security violations. Perhaps this results from a lack of corporate management support for and insistence on complete and accurate incident reporting. It appears that many plant and business managers feel that reporting the occurrence of fraud, drug use, theft of trade secrets, or employee theft in their work unit might adversely reflect upon their competence. Consequently, and all too often, they handle the situation "their way" and avoid reporting or notifying upper management, corporate security, or public law enforcement. As a security executive in one of the nation's largest corporations said, "We probably know of only about 1 fraud out of every 10 that is occurring or has occurred."

Therefore, only when top corporate management declares nonreporting of workplace crime to be unacceptable behavior for all employees--especially supervisors--will meaningful corporation-wide measurement of economic crime costs begin. Then, perhaps, accurate crime loss measurement by various industry segments or groups can be accomplished, providing, in turn, more accurate assessments of the economic impact of workplace crimes. Economic crime prevention and control strategies can then be realistically developed.

UPDATED ESTIMATE

Although about 15 years have passed since the major studies on business crime were completed, the $40 billion total business crime loss estimate shown in **Table 2.1** on **page 24** is frequently quoted. Other than the estimate of at least $67 billion for 1980 (*The Hallcrest Report*, 1985), no updating of total direct economic crime loss has been documented. Numerous sources have estimated the annual cost for various types of economic crime such as computer crime ($200 billion), theft of intellectual property ($40 billion), product counterfeiting ($8 billion to $20 billion), employee theft ($15 billion to $25 billion), and check fraud ($7 billion to $10 billion).

Table 2.2 presents a list of various economic crime types with estimates of annual cost to businesses and to the public, along with the source for each estimate. However, few of the sources explain how their crime cost figures were derived. If just a few of these crime cost figures are plausible, then the impact of economic crime is, indeed, profound and represents a cancer in the economy. Some of the following loss estimates are almost unbelievable; in fact, the Hallcrest research staff members doubt that any of these estimates are based upon empirical research.

Estimates of economic crime in the 1970s most frequently included inflationary indexing. Further, some earlier research--Department of Commerce (1975) and AMA (1976)--indicates that the 2 major segments of economic crime (white-collar crime and ordinary crime) are about *equal* in direct cost to business and to society.

TABLE 2.2
ESTIMATES OF LOSSES
FROM VARIOUS CATEGORIES OF ECONOMIC CRIME

Crime/Loss	Amount
Employee theft, "time theft," and drug abuse on the job	$320 billion annually[20]
White-collar crime	$ Hundreds of billions annually[21]
Computer crime	$200 billion annually[22]
Time theft (bogus sick days, late arrivals, early departures, excessive socializing on the job, etc.)	$170 billion annually[23]
Lost worker productivity due to drug use	$130 billion annually[24]
Business property theft	$100 billion annually[25]
Savings and loan (S&L) fraud	$100 billion[26]
Worldwide product counterfeiting	$100 billion annually[27]
[U.S. product counterfeiting	$8-20 billion annually][28]
Federal income tax evasion	$81.5 billion annually[29]
Workplace drug abuse	$60-100 billion annually[30]
Income of organized crime	$$46.6 billion annually[31]
Theft of intellectual property	$40 billion annually[32]
Retail theft	$30 billion annually[33]
Retail shrinkage	$16-24 billion annually[34]
Employee theft	$15-25 billion annually[35]
Bank crime	$17-21 billion annually[36]
[check fraud	$7-10 billion annually]
[loan fraud	$6-7 billion annually]
[embezzlement	$2.1 billion annually]
[credit card fraud	$1.2 billion annually]
[ATM fraud	$70-100 million annually]
[bank robbery	$60-70 million annually]
Commercial bribery (kickbacks)	$3.5-10 billion annually[37]
Telephone fraud	$500 million annually[38]
Business failures due to economic crime	20% - 30%[39]
Underwriting losses on bonds guaranteeing employee honesty	112% increase[40] (1979-1984)

The 1980 estimate of at least $67 billion was derived by applying the *FBI Uniform Crime Report* (UCR) index crime increase for nonviolent crimes and the increase in consumer price index (CPI) over the previous 5 years to arrive at an estimate of annual loss due to ordinary crime. Based upon the 1976 AMA finding that white-collar crime equals the cost of ordinary business crime, the Hallcrest research staff estimate of $33.5 billion for ordinary business crime plus a $33.5 billion cost for white-collar crime equals $67 billion as a "best estimate" for losses in 1980.

This same technique has been used to derive a 1990 estimate of direct economic crime cost. The *FBI Uniform Crime Report* index crime rate for property crimes rose only an estimated 3% from 1980 to 1990, while the consumer price index rose 65.7% during the same period. Applying these increases to the 1980 ordinary business crime figure results in an estimated $57.1 billion direct cost in 1990.

If, as estimated earlier by AMA, white-collar crime losses are at least equal to ordinary business crime losses, then a best estimate for 1990 for the direct cost of economic crime is at least $114 billion ($57.1 ordinary + $57.1 white collar). If this trend continues, the direct cost of economic crime will be at least $200 billion per annum by the year 2000. Amazingly, the 1990 estimated loss of $114 billion to economic crime is the same as the annual expenditure for public works to repair the nation's infrastructure (i.e., bridges, highways, tunnels, etc.).[41] **Figure 2.2** presents a summary of economic or business crime cost estimates from various studies beginning in the late 1960s and ending with a projection for the year 2000.[42]

FIGURE 2.2

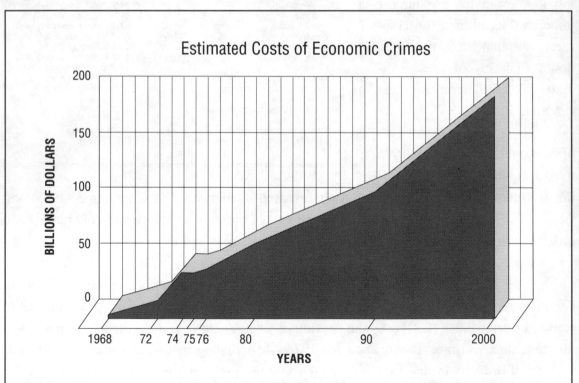

The Hallcrest best estimate of $114 billion as the annual cost of economic crime in 1990 is admittedly conservative compared to the total of various crime categories in **Table 2.2** on **page 29**. Further, the Hallcrest staff members have seen estimates of $200 billion per year and more, but no descriptions were offered for the methods of arriving at such estimates.[43] Whatever the figure, annual economic crime costs seem to be at least 8 times higher than the total personal and household crime costs. **Table 2.3** depicts the costs to crime victims by offense, totaling about $13 billion for personal and household crimes.

The important point to consider is that estimated costs of crime not only are subject to an inflationary factor, they are an inflationary factor in the economy! The cost of crime is passed on to the consumer, adding as much as 15% or more to the costs of goods paid by the consumer at the retail level. The total costs of crime, however, are much greater than those absorbed by the retail consumer, or the sole loss of an asset by business. The scope of the problem increases significantly when secondary or indirect costs of crime are added to the direct losses from workplace crime.

From the available crime cost data, it appears that the costs of economic crime are not precisely known. The literature provides estimates that are, to a large degree, based upon earlier estimates adjusted for inflation. Even using similar crime index and inflation-adjusting techniques, the direct cost of economic crime was at least $114 billion in 1990, and other estimates, though not as thoroughly substantiated, would place economic crime at $200 billion to $300 billion. The cumulative direct and indirect costs are much greater, and valid estimates are necessary if public and private organizations are to allocate their resources cost-effectively. But gross estimates of overall costs are useful only for gross

TABLE 2.3 TOTAL ECONOMIC LOSS TO VICTIMS OF PERSONAL AND HOUSEHOLD CRIMES, 1986	
TYPES OF CRIME	**GROSS LOSS (MILLIONS)**
All Crimes	$ 13,039
Personal Crimes	3,592
of Violence	1,000
Rape	18
Robbery	567
Assault	414
of Theft	2,592
Personal Larceny:	
With Contact	72
Without Contact	2,521
Household Crimes	9,447
Burglary	3,442
Household Larceny	1,372
Motor Vehicle Theft	4,633

Note: Details may not add to totals shown because of rounding. Losses include those from property theft or damage, cash losses, medical expenses, lost pay because of victimization (including time spent with the police in investigation and in court and time spent in replacing lost property), and other crime-related costs.

Source: *Criminal Victimization in the United States*, 1986.
See *BJS Data Report*, 1988, Bureau of Justice Statistics, U.S. Department of Justice, April 1989.

31

policy decisions. Truly effective programs for specific crimes or specific industries or each corporation must rest on accurate data pertaining to those crimes and businesses.

Clearly, there is a substantial amount of crime in the community that affects business and institutions but that may not be visible to law enforcement agencies because of their primary concern with violent crime and order maintenance. Any strategies for improving public and private resources in addressing economic crime must be based upon a much more accurate description of the entire economic crime problem.

INDIRECT COSTS

The problems of arriving at the direct costs of economic crime are surpassed by trying to assess the secondary or indirect costs. Attempting to establish a dollar cost is simply impossible, given the data limitations and lack of reporting of economic crime. Yet, the indirect impact or costs of economic crime can be grouped into 3 categories: costs to business, government, and the public.

The effects on business include:
- increased costs of insurance
- costs of security and internal audit activities to detect crime
- costs of investigation and prosecution of suspects measured in terms of lost time of security and management personnel
- reduced profits
- increased selling prices and weakened competitive standing
- lower employee morale
- loss of productivity
- damage to business reputation/image
- deterioration in quality of service
- threats to the survival of small business
- higher overhead due to theft (reordering, reshipping, restocking, etc.)

The effects on government include:

- costs of investigating and prosecuting suspects
- increased costs of prosecuting sophisticated (e.g., management fraud) and technology-related (e.g., computer) crime
- costs of correctional programs to deal with economic crime offenders
- costs of crime-prevention programs
- costs of crime reporting and mandated security programs
- loss of tax revenue (e.g., loss of sales tax, untaxed income of perpetrator, and tax deductions allowed business for crime-related losses)

The effects on the public include:

- increased costs of consumer goods and services to offset crime losses
- loss of investor equity
- increased taxes
- reduced employment due to business failures

These effects are only those related to nonviolent economic crime, but if the total crime environment of institutions (schools, hospitals, museums, etc.) were also considered, the effects on institutions would include:

- declining enrollment, attendance, or occupancy due to crime-related incidents
- employee turnover and recruitment costs due to fear of crime incidents
- increased costs of services
- increased costs of insurance and security protection

Michael Baker and Alan Westin, in their national survey of perceptions on workplace crime, found that while the respondents recognized the significance of secondary costs of workplace crime, they had difficulty in assigning priorities among the costs in lower morale, damage to public image, or damage to market position.[44] Their survey results on indirect costs of workplace crime are shown in **Table 2.4**.

TABLE 2.4
INDIRECT COSTS OF EMPLOYEE CRIME, BY TYPE OF CRIME

		Percent of respondents indicating that most significant indirect cost is				
CRIME CATEGORIES	NUMBER	EMPLOYEE MORALE	PRODUCTIVITY LOSSES	PUBLIC IMAGE DAMAGE	REGULATORY EXPOSURE	MARKET POSITION DAMAGE
Major Theft	181	25%	19%	30%	7%	18%
Major Fraud	176	23	16	37	14	11
Violence/ Intimidation	171	68	13	16	1	2
Sabotage	171	29	42	14	3	13
Information Theft	171	16	14	11	5	54
Petty Theft of Supplies/ Tools	178	63	28	3	2	4
Petty Fraud	173	65	20	7	5	4
Abuse of Company Services	176	51	38	5	6	2
Kickback/ Bribe Schemes	178	19	17	33	19	13

Source: *Employer Perceptions of Workplace Crime*, Bureau of Justice Statistics, 1987

LIABILITY

Perhaps the largest indirect cost of economic crime has been the increase in civil litigation and damage awards over the past 20 years. This litigation usually claims inadequate or improperly used security to protect customers, employees, tenants, and the public from crimes and injuries. Most often these cases involve inadequate security at

34

apartments and condominiums; shopping malls, convenience and other retail stores; hotels, motels, and restaurants; health care and educational institutions; office buildings; and the premises of other business or governmental facilities. Frequently, private security companies are named as defendants in such cases because they incur 2 basic types of liability: (1) negligence on the part of the security company or its employees and (2) criminal acts committed by the security company or its employees.

A review of news articles, television documentaries, and magazine stories suggests widespread abuses in the security industry, including fatal shootings, physical abuse of alleged shoplifters, and guards who burglarize their clients. In California, a security guard and an accomplice were charged with the theft of $3.2 million in computer chips. In New York, an investigative commission heard allegations that alarm firm employees staged burglaries to demonstrate the need for their services. In Pennsylvania, a security guard assigned to patrol the county courthouse was sent to prison for stealing drugs and money from the Chester County detectives office.

Such abuses are probably not common. In hearings in Illinois, the security director of a retail chain stated that in the previous year, 14,000 people had been stopped for shoplifting and 1,800 cases of employee dishonesty had been uncovered, but only about 30 lawsuits were filed against the store as a result. Thus, serious incidents would seem to be infrequent compared to the volume of detentions and arrests.

Of the security employees in the 1982 Hallcrest survey in Baltimore County, Maryland, and Portland, Oregon, less than 50% said they had ever had occasion to detain a person at any security job they had performed, and only slightly more than 50% said their company policy expected them to detain suspects. Less than 10% said they had ever used force, whether in defending themselves, evicting trespassers, preventing vandalism or assault, or conducting lawful search, detention, or arrest. While 66% said that their companies expected them to use force to protect themselves, fewer than 25% were expected to use force in protecting property; 20% were expected to search a suspect; and 15% were expected to arrest a suspect. In general, therefore, the policies of security companies seem to discourage employee detention, search, and arrest, due to fear of lawsuits and higher insurance premiums. Surprisingly, only 11 states require security firms to carry general liability insurance.

Compounding the problem is the fact that most general liability coverage is written for risk on a business's own premises. Specialists in security firm insurance recommend that liability coverage also include independent contractors and completed operations coverage, as well as specific endorsements for assault and battery, personal injury, broad-form property damage, errors and omissions, theft, and contractual and punitive damages coverage.

One scholar has estimated that "U.S. corporations pay more than $20 billion a year to litigation attorneys."[45] When one considers recent major cases such as the disaster litigation following the Union Carbide chemical accident in Bhopal, India, or the 150-plus civil lawsuits relating to Exxon's supertanker oil spill in Alaska,[46] liability cases and damages involving crime and security may seem rather pale by comparison. Perhaps, but all indications point to more security-related lawsuits and more $1 million-plus awards than ever before.

Indeed, liability issues and concerns have increasingly been addressed in the security and legal periodicals and newsletters since the early 1980s.[47] In fact, at least 4 informative newsletters devoted to security law and liability issues have emerged during the past decade: *Security Law Newsletter*, Eva Sherman, Esq., editor; *Private Security Case Law Reporter*, R. Keegan Federal, Jr., editor; *The Spain Report*, Norman and Judith Spain, JD, editors; and *Civil Liability Alert*, Norman Bates, Esq., editor.

Growing concern over lawsuits was expressed by virtually all of the corporate and contract security managers in the Hallcrest 1989 reconnaissance interviews in 12 metropolitan areas. Further, this concern is manifest in a variety of security management issues such as hiring, training, equipment (armed vs. unarmed), personnel deployment, crime incident response, supervision, and security systems (locking, lighting, fencing, access control, etc.). The list is extensive, covering nearly all aspects of private and public security.

Lawrence Sherman and Jody Klein (1984) conducted significant research on security-related lawsuits reported to the American Trial Lawyers Association.[48] These researchers found that while a fairly steady increase in security-related litigation awards had been occurring for 20 years (between 1958 and 1978), the real explosion in cases and awards began about 1979.[49] Other major findings from this research include the following:

- security and crime-related lawsuits have risen 17 times higher than the inflation rate

- by 1982, the average, major award of reported cases had risen to more than $1 million

- most lawsuits were filed by victims of crime (or families of victims) against operators (private and public) of premises open to the public such as retailers, residential landlords, hotels, and government facilities

- in descending order, the greatest number of security-related lawsuits occurred in Florida, New York, California, District of Columbia, Pennsylvania, and Texas[50]

In announcing this research report, Professor Sherman suggested, "The increase of major awards in inadequate security lawsuits comes at the confluence of 4 major social trends: the rise in violent crime, the growth of private security, the crime victim's rights movement, and the general rise in major personal injury awards."[51]

For 1990 and beyond, leading students of, and expert witnesses in, security-related lawsuits agree that more cases will be filed and more million-dollar punitive damage awards will be ordered (perhaps increasing 25% per year). At least two-thirds of these cases are expected to claim inadequate security. The types of crimes most frequently leading to lawsuits will continue to be sexual assaults, simple assaults and battery, wrongful deaths, and a variety of torts and crimes committed by security workers and employees.[52]

Again, the "experts" and security practitioners predict that liability cases involving crime and security incidents will most frequently involve:

- shopping malls, convenience stores, and other retailers

- apartments and condominiums

- hotels, motels, casinos, bars, and restaurants

- health care and educational institutions

- security service and equipment companies

- transportation operators such as common carriers, airports, and rail and bus stations

37

- governmental and privately-owned office buildings and parking lots

- sports and special event centers

Case law regarding a duty to protect customers, tenants, etc., foreseeability of crime or risk, negligent hiring and retention, and other tort actions will likely continue to evolve throughout the 1990s.

Perhaps during the 1990s, as a secondary outcome of litigation, we will see evaluative research into the crime prevention effectiveness of security guards, alarms, locks, cameras, lighting, and employee training. Significant research by W. J. Crow and Rosemary Erickson of Athena Research Corporation to assess the effectiveness of various security measures in preventing robberies and violence in convenience stores is an example of the type of research that, most importantly, may save lives and, secondarily, may help avoid litigation.[53] The litigation explosion may also be the catalyst for long overdue security standards and/or codes which should help reduce the claims of inadequate security and ultimately may improve security services and products.

ENDNOTES

1.   An estimated 15% of the retail costs of U.S. goods is due to theft, according to studies entitled *Crime in Retailing*, by the U.S. Department of Commerce, 1975, and *Crimes Against Business: Recommendations for Demonstration, Research, and Related Programs Designed to Reduce and Control Non-Violent Crimes Against Business*, by the American Management Associations, December 1977, p. 88.

2.   "Business Travel Management in the Nineties," *Fortune*, March 26, 1990, p. 196.

3.   D. Peloso in "Future Role of Local Police in Economic Crime," California Commission on Peace Officer Standards and Training, 1985, estimates that about 1% of local law enforcement resources are allocated to combating economic crime. Yet, several federal law enforcement agencies (FBI, Secret Service, Customs, among others) allocate 20% or more of their resources to crimes that adversely affect the economy and legitimate businesses.

4.   "Households Touched By Crime, 1988," by the Bureau of Justice Statistics, U.S. Department of Justice, June 1989, p. 1.

5.   *Report to the Nation on Crime and Justice*, 2d ed., by the Bureau of Justice Statistics, U.S. Department of Justice, March 1988, NCJ-105506.

6.   Ibid.

7.   Edelhertz offers an excellent definition of white-collar crime: "An illegal act or series of illegal acts committed by nonphysical means and by concealment or guile, to obtain money or property, to avoid the payment or loss of money or property, or to obtain business or personal advantage." See Herbert Edelhertz, *The Nature, Impact, and Prosecution of White Collar Crime*, National Institute of Law Enforcement and Criminal Justice, 1970, p. 3.

8.   W. Steve Albrecht, et. al., *How to Detect and Prevent Business Fraud* (Englewood Cliffs, N.J.: Prentice-Hall, 1982), p. 24.

9.   Simon Dinitz, "Multidisciplinary Approaches to White-Collar Crime," *White-Collar Crime: An Agenda for Research*, eds. Herbert Edelhertz and Thomas Overcast, Lexington Books, 1982.

10.   "Ordinary crime" was defined by the Small Business Administration in 1967 as the crimes of burglary, robbery, vandalism, shoplifting, employee theft, and bad checks. The U.S. Department of Commerce subsequently added arson and credit card fraud in 1972 and 1975, respectively.

11.   *White Collar Crime: The Problem and The Federal Response*, Committee on the Judiciary, House of Representatives, Ninety-Fifth Congress, Library of Congress, June 1978, p. 7.

12.   Bill McAllister, "Counterfeit Shoe Ring Uncovered," *The Washington Post*, December 30, 1989, p. B1.

13.   Robert Francis, Sr., "Testimony before the Subcommittee on Special Small Business Problems," House Small Business Committee, U.S. House of Representatives, June 16, 1977, p. 23-24.

14.   Ibid.

15.   For a discussion of definitional and measurement issues of white-collar crime, see Marvin Wolfgang, *National Survey of Crime Severity* (Philadelphia: Center for Studies in Criminal Law, University of Pennsylvania, 1980).

16.   U.S. Department of Commerce, *Crime in Retailing* (Washington, D.C.: Government Printing Office, 1975), p. v.

17.   U.S. Department of Commerce, *Crime in Service Industries* (Washington, D.C.: Government Printing Office, 1977), p. 5.

18.   Michael Baker and Alan Westin, *Employer Perceptions of Workplace Crime*, Bureau of Justice Statistics, U.S. Department of Justice, May 1987, p. 12.

19.   Ibid.

20.   Ryan Kuhn, "The Attack On Employer's Rights," *Security Journal*, Vol. 1, No. 2, 1990, pp. 74-75

21.   Richard Thornburgh, Attorney General of the United States, *The Police Chief*, April 1989, p. 10.

22.   *The Lipman Report*, November 15, 1988, indicates "some experts put the loss" at this amount.

23.   Robert Half International (annual "time theft" survey), reported in *Nation's Business*, Vol. 75, No. 6, June 1987, p. 23.

24.   Kuhn, 1990, p. 75. The author cites an address by Assistant Attorney General Richard Willard before the National Center for Public Interest, September 1987, as the source of this estimate.

25.   *Forbes*, August 7, 1989, p. 106.

26.   General Accounting Office, as reported in *The Miami Herald*, January 28, 1989.

27.   "Financial Times," *Security Management*, January 1990, p. 15. Amount equals about 4% of world trade.

28.   "U.S. International Trade Commission," *The Washington Post*, December 30, 1989, p. B8.

29.   Internal Revenue Service, 1981.

30.   Drug Enforcement Administration, U.S. Department of Justice, May 1988, and Institute for a Drug-Free Workplace, January 1990.

31.   "President's Commission on Organized Crime and Wharton Econometric Forecasting Associates, Inc.," *The Washington Post*, April 2, 1986, p. A3.

32.   International Trade Commission as reported in *The Wall Street Journal*, March 16, 1989, p. 1.

33.   *Forbes*, November 14, 1988, p. 258.

34.   "Retailers on the Defensive," *Chain Store Age Executive*, February 1983, p. 16, as reported by H. Gregory Zendek and Steven Werner, "The Specific Case Inventory: Measuring Respondents' Information for Single-Theft Investigators," *Security Journal*, Vol. 1, No. 2, 1990, p. 81. See also, Francine Schwadel, "Chicago Retailers' Sting Aims to Put Shoplifting Professionals Out of Business," *The Wall Street Journal*, June 5, 1990, p. B1. This article claims that shoplifting is the fastest-growing crime of larceny.

35.   Bureau of National Affairs as reported in *The Wall Street Journal*, August 30, 1988, p. 1.

36.   Carl Brown, "Crimes of the Vault," *Security Management*, January 1990, and *Report to the Nation on Crime and Justice*, 2d ed., Bureau of Justice Statistics, U.S. Department of Justice, March 1988, p. 10. See also, James Adams, "The Bank Dicks' Dirty Linen," *The Wall Street Journal*, February 15, 1989, p. A14, which addresses a potential for an "epidemic" of fraud in the banking and thrift system. This article also quotes Florida's former chief bank and thrift supervisor as follows: "I haven't found a single bank failure that didn't involve a conscious conspiracy to defraud."

37.   *Crimes Against Business: Background, Findings and Recommendations*, by the American Management Associations (AMA), October 1977, p. 3.

38.   Communications Fraud Control Association, McLean, VA, January 20, 1990, Presentation to International Association of Chiefs of Police, Private Sector Liaison Committee.

39.   *Crimes Against Business*, AMA, 1977, p. 1.

40.   Harry Bacas, "To Stop A Thief," *Nation's Business*, June 1987, p. 16.

41.   "New Streets, Paved With Gold," *Business Week*, October 16, 1989, p. 92.

42.   The estimated costs of economic crime were taken from studies by the following agencies/organizations: Small Business Administration (1968); U.S. Department of Commerce (1972); Chamber of Commerce of the U.S. (1974); American Management Associations (1975); and *The Hallcrest Report* (1985). Trendline projections for 1990 and the year 2000 were made by the Hallcrest staff.

43.   The Peat, Marwick, Mitchell Foundation in a report entitled *How to Prevent and Detect Business Fraud* estimated the total cost of just white-collar crime and fraud in 1981 to be $200 billion.

44.   Michael Baker and Alan Westin, *Employer Perceptions of Workplace Crime*, Bureau of Justice Statistics, U.S. Department of Justice, May 1987.

45.   John Allison, "Five Ways To Keep Disputes Out of Court," *Harvard Business Review*, January-February 1990, p. 166.

46.   Kara Swisher, "Lawyers Coordinate Myriad Suits Against EXXON," *The Washington Post*, January 30, 1990, p. C9.

47.   A number of useful articles have appeared in recent years, among them:

- Robert McCrie, "The Growing Crisis in Civil Liability," *Security Letter*, Vol. XVI, No. 21, Part II, November 3, 1986.

- Michael Silver, "Negligent Hiring Claims Take Off," *American Bar Association (ABA) Journal*, May 1987, pp. 72-78.

- Norman Bates, "Reducing Liability's Toll," *Security Management*, October 1988, pp. 75-77.

- Andrew Anthony and Frederick Thornburg, "Security on Trial," *Security Management*, February 1989, pp. 41-46.

- Robert Meadows, "It's 1990 - Do You Know How Liable You Are?" *Security Management*, January 1990, pp. 55-62.

- Lucien Canton, "Limiting Liability Exposure: Have We Gone Too Far?" *Security Management*, January 1990, pp. 71-72.

- "Security Survey: Liability Issues Lead To Growing Concern," *Security*, January 1990, p. 12.

48. Lawrence Sherman and Jody Klein, *Major Lawsuits Over Crime and Security: Trends and Patterns, 1958-1982*, Institute of Criminal Justice and Criminology, University of Maryland, September 1984.

49. Ibid, p. 14.

50. Ibid, pp. 2, 3, 16.

51. "News Release," *Major Lawsuits Over Crime and Security*, University of Maryland, September 15, 1984, p. 1.

52. Norman Bates, Esq., (Sudbury, MA) telephone interview February 13, 1990.

53. W. J. Crow, Rosemary Erickson, and Lloyd Scott, "Set Your Sights on Preventing Retail Violence," *Security Management*, September 1987, pp. 60-64. Also, see W. J. Crow and Rosemary Erickson, *Cameras and Silent Alarms: A Study of Their Effectiveness As A Robbery Deterrent*, Athena Research Press, 1984.

CHAPTER 3
SELECTED CRIME CONCERNS

Chapter 3 reviews certain economic crimes that have either a direct or indirect influence on the economic well-being of the nation. The initial section in this chapter discusses business ethics because of its relevance to business-related crime and security issues. Ensuing sections focus on the relationships between drug abuse and protective services, computer security and computer crimes, and the effect of terrorism on private security in the United States.

The first section reviews business ethics and demonstrates the importance of ethical conduct in corporate America. This overview attempts to illustrate why more than 1 out of 5 major corporations in the United States have been guilty of at least 1 legal transgression in the past decade. The section on drug abuse summarizes the extent of the problem and considers the effects of drug abuse on private security and law enforcement. This section also reviews whether the business community has been effective in its efforts to curb drug abuse in the workplace and postulates that drug prevention and drug treatment programs may not be as widespread as the news media has implied in its coverage of the drug war in America.

The section on computer security reviews the nature of the computer crime threat and focuses on electronic intrusion vulnerabilities. This section suggests that the tools to effectively combat computer crime are available, but that industry and government have not yet learned how to implement the necessary countermeasures, and, in some cases, may not understand the nature of the threat. The computer security section predicts the risk levels for computer crime will increase for the first few years of this decade, but that by the end of the 1990s it will be a diminishing problem for protected computer networks and systems. In addition, this section assesses the size of the computer security industry and predicts the value of this market segment to the year 2000.

"The Security and Terrorism Interface" section presents a number of controversial issues related to international terrorism, but entirely within a United States geographic frame of reference. The discussion speculates that current perceptions of risk are largely out of proportion to the actual threat of international, political terrorism and that the United States has not practiced a policy of measured responses to the risk. Further, this section proposes the argument that much of the climate of public fear of terrorism is a product of contemporary hype. Also included is a short overview of the business of counterterrorism and its influences on private security, law enforcement and the corporate community.

ETHICS AND VALUES

One writer recently noted: "There's good and there's evil, and the moral manager knows the difference."[1] The "evil or bad news" is that Wall Street has experienced insider trading scandals,[2] that industrial espionage and bribery have been committed by major defense contractors,[3] that pharmaceutical company officials have lied to the Food and Drug Administration,[4] that medical wastes have been dumped into the Atlantic,[5] and that sugar water has been packaged as apple juice for babies.[6] A recent costly example of unethical business practice is the fraudulent management of many U.S. savings and loan institutions, resulting in catastrophic losses.

The "good" news is that many leading business schools now recognize that they must teach ethics to students;[7] and a majority (69%) of business managers agree that corporate ethics should be as important as the pursuit of profits.[8] The Ethics Resource Center exists and offers assistance to business and government in establishing ethical guidelines for organizational activity.[9] Additionally, a Touche Ross survey reveals that more than 80% of polled professional and business persons believe that American businesses are reasonably ethical.[10] During the past decade, individual and corporate greed as well as breaches, unparalleled in recent history, of ethical behavior by business and government officials have soared; a *U.S. News and World Report* survey of government records found that 115 of the 500 largest corporations have been convicted in the past decade of at least 1 major crime or have paid civil penalties for "serious misbehavior."[11] Unethical and illicit behavior not only causes economic crime losses for businesses, governments, and consumers, but also contributes to the increasing use of, and expenditures for, private security.

The term "ethics" is defined as the discipline dealing with what is right and with moral duty and obligation; as a set of moral values; or as the principles of conduct governing an individual or group. The term "values" has been defined as "...the beliefs that guide an organization and the behavior of its employees."[12]

Ethics has developed as man has reflected upon the intentions and consequences of his actions. Ethical philosophy began in the fifth century BC, with the appearance of philosophical scholars whose self-appointed mission was to awaken others to the need for rational criticism of their values and practices. In the centuries that followed, the interests of ethical scholars shifted from theoretical to practical ethics, that is, to new conceptions of the goals of human life and to new codes of conduct.[13]

According to the public's perception of honesty and ethical standards as measured by a Gallup Poll, both business executives and politicians were poorly regarded.[14] **Table 3.1** presents the entire list of 25 occupations, ranked according to the total percentage of combined "very high" and "high" ratings. In fact, as seen in **Table 3.1**, fewer than 20% of those surveyed rated business or government officials highly on honesty and ethics. In the 25 occupations shown in the table, it is interesting to note that police officers ranked in the upper third and that virtually all of the professions in the upper third have long-established codes of ethics.

The public's rather dim view of business ethics might be reinforced by the results of a survey of business persons conducted by *Business Month*, which ranked 5 corporate "offenses" as follows:

- "Taking credit for someone else's accomplishment" was picked by 57% as the most egregious infraction

- "Playing dirty tricks on a competitor" was chosen by 27% as the number-one offense

TABLE 3.1 HONESTY AND ETHICAL STANDARDS FOR SELECTED OCCUPATIONS	
Occupations	Ratings
Druggists, Pharmacists	66%
Clergymen	60%
College teachers	54%
Medical doctors	53%
Dentists	51%
Engineers	48%
Policemen	**47%**
Bankers	26%
Funeral directors	24%
Journalists	23%
TV reporters, commentators	22%
Newspaper reporters	22%
Building contractors	22%
Senators	19%
Lawyers	18%
Business executives	16%
Congressmen	16%
Local officeholders	14%
Labor union leaders	14%
Real estate agents	13%
Stockbrokers	13%
State officeholders	11%
Insurance salesmen	10%
Advertising	7%
Car salesmen	6%

SOURCE: "Who Do We Trust," *Gallup Report*, December, 1988

- "Cheating on an expense report" was selected by 23% as the primary offense

- "Lying to protect a friend" received the top pick by 15% of respondents

- "Paying bribes in a country where it's the accepted custom" was the least offensive peccadillo with 14%[15]

Almost half of those who strongly agreed that ethics are as important as profits were not very troubled about paying bribes abroad.[16] Perhaps they simply forgot--or did not care--that it is a federal offense!

As Wasserman and Moore point out in "Values in Policing," high-performance organizations have one thing in common: "They operate with a core set of values that guides conduct throughout the organization."[17] These authors cite Federal Express and W. L. Gore as high-performing corporations with explicit value statements that reflect the pursuit of excellence in product, customer service, and work environment for all their employees.

CORPORATE ETHICS

Usually, corporations with strong values and ethical statements have a more proactive attitude toward workplace security and asset protection. Management and employee support for ethical behavior, security awareness, and loss prevention is most frequently found in organizations where top management and boards of directors have established corporate codes of ethical principles and practices. As the president of the ASIS Foundation, Ira Somerson, observed after an Ethics Resource Center conference: "When busy CEOs take time to discuss ethical issues in their work, the message soon filters down."[18]

Studies on internal theft and business ethics point to lower theft rates and better business practices when top management undertakes "responsibility to assure integrity at the top and throughout the organization, and to communicate a strong moral commitment to do what is right."[19] John Clark and Richard Hollinger (1982), in a 3-year study of approximately 10,000 employees in selected U.S. cities, found that organizations with clear policies against theft and strong internal controls experienced less theft than those without.[20] Policy statements are considered more comprehensive than simple employee-manual prohibitions against stealing. The important connection between business ethics and effective security was well described by a corporate officer of a *Fortune* 500 company:

> *The best security people in the world can't be effective if they have to function in a climate where integrity and honesty are the exception rather than the rule. It's up to management to establish the highest ethical standards for business conduct and to see that those standards are adopted throughout the company.*[21]

Many businesses that are committed to creating or maintaining an ethical corporate culture are also concerned about instilling ethical behavior into America's youth. Professor Max Thomas, who teaches business ethics, observes:

> *There is a tragic conviction among students that business has no ethical responsibilities beyond the duty to make money. They are often alarmingly naive, assuming that businesspeople are as unconcerned with ethics as astronomers are with commodity prices. They don't even see business ethics sardonically as a contradiction in terms, but innocently, as completely mismatched ideas.*[22]

This cynicism about the business world is caused in large part by media reports of economic crimes such as stock frauds, bribery, money laundering, and crimes against the environment. For these and other reasons, business ethics has become an "in" subject on campuses.

Although 12,000 courses in ethics are being taught in graduate and undergraduate schools, many critics consider them unrelated to real-life business applications. A University of Washington professor calls the courses "the equivalent of giving students a quick dunk in a morality bath."[23] Yet, many academics and business executives agree that ethical standards of conduct must be taught to America's future business leaders.

Does a business that lives within the law have no further obligation to conduct its operations in a way that promotes an ethical workplace and society? Perhaps, but laws cannot be so complete as to reach every aspect of business activity. Businesses need ethical standards to make decisions on sensitive issues affecting their interests as well as the interests of their shareholders and customers.

Take Mobil, for example, which spends $670 million annually in its worldwide effort to protect and improve the environment. Mobil established formal policies to control environmental and health hazards in 1956--before the launching of the environmental movement in the 1960s and before the creation of the Environmental Protection Agency in 1970.[24] All Mobil employees are instructed to comply fully with all environmental laws and regulations. But, according to Mobil's chairman, "[We] go *beyond* compliance by stating that Mobil and its affiliates will continue to conduct their worldwide activities [in 100+ countries] with full concern for safeguarding public health and protecting the environment even in the absence of local laws to that effect."[25]

In the late 1980s, an increasing focus on ethical concerns resulted in codes of ethics being written, ethics ombudsmen being hired by many businesses, and more workshops on ethics for employees than ever before. The motivation for this growing emphasis on ethics is multifaceted. As Robert McCrie, editor of *Security Letter*, reports:

> *Some executives claim that ethical behavior is morally proper and that's why they believe in it. Others would agree, and discreetly add that voluntary ethical standards decrease public censure and chances of unwelcome litigation and legislation. But there's more to it than that. Perhaps the biggest factor behind the wave of ethical enlightenment is that such behavior is good business. Put differently, if only one part of an organization is perceived as being unethical, the entire organization can be tainted by it, and potentially devastated.*[26]

Data from the staff's reconnaissance interviews with a number of corporate security executives support McCrie's observation that, increasingly, corporate security personnel will be involved in testing adherence to ethical policies.[27] Some security executives and consultants are even involved in developing corporate ethical codes and policies. Further, some businesses, such as the Harris Corporation, warn their personnel that failing to report ethical violations by others could bring discharge.[28]

DRUG ABUSE AND PROTECTIVE SERVICES

Drug abuse is a costly and pervasive problem in America today. Considering the omnipresent media coverage of drugs in our society, most Americans have a fairly sophisticated appreciation of the substance abuse crisis. Evening television news programs regularly include something about drugs, drug wars, and drug czars. The news media, especially print media, are replete with insightful data and statistics charting the depth of the problem.

The problems caused by drug abuse in our cities and factories are also well documented. Survey after survey has found that government and industry regard drug and alcohol abuse as one of their highest priority concerns, but has this concern been translated into action? The impact of the "drug wars" on law enforcement is well known, but what has been the effect on private security? The social and monetary costs of drug use are clear, but what is the profit side of the problem? How much revenue is being earned by companies providing drug testing and treatment programs? These and similar questions are examined in this section. The objective is not to study drug abuse, but rather to investigate its influence on private security, law enforcement, and the American business community.

THE SCOPE OF THE PROBLEM

According to a 1989 Gallup Poll, 1 in 4 American workers has personal knowledge of coworkers using illegal drugs on the job.[29] According to the White House Conference for a Drug-Free America, in 1988 approximately 37 million Americans had used an illegal drug in the past year--almost 1 in 7 Americans.[30] The 1988 National Household Survey on Drug Abuse, conducted by the National Institute on Drug Abuse (NIDA), resulted in a somewhat lower, but still alarming, estimate.[31] That survey found that about 28 million people in the United States aged 12 and up had used illicit drugs in the prior year. An estimated 14.5 million people had used illicit drugs in the prior month. A nationwide poll conducted by *The Wall Street Journal* and NBC News during September 1989 found that 73% of registered voters were directly affected by the drug abuse crisis.[32]

While the estimates of drug abuse vary, it is evident that illicit drugs take a great toll each year. The annual price tag was $59 billion in 1987 for drug abuse in the United States, a statistic frequently quoted by the White House Conference for a Drug-Free America and by many others. This was the cost of lost productivity, absenteeism, added health care costs, accident rates, crime, treatment, prevention programs, and other factors.[33] In 1988, this estimate was raised to $100 billion,[34] and in 1989 the estimate was raised to $114 billion annually.[35]

How much was earned by criminals? The global underground market may earn as much as $300 billion in drugs, of which the U.S. criminal community may share $110 billion, about 35%.[36] The $110 billion is twice the combined profits of the 500 largest companies in the United States.[37] * About 60% of the world's production of illegal drugs is consumed in the United States. Every day, 5,000 Americans try cocaine for the first time; 2,700 boats and airplanes smuggle drugs across our borders; and almost 2,000 persons are arrested for drug-related crimes.[38] President Bush's 1990 drug strategy, led by William Bennett, will be targeting about $7.9 billion toward the war on drugs, some of which will clearly trickle into the private sector.[39] Approximately $5.7 billion will be spent for law enforcement and drug supply reduction programs.

There is some indication that drug use is declining. Not every authority agrees, but according to a study conducted by the National Institute on Drug Abuse, the use of illicit drugs continued a decline (as of 1988, the date of the survey) which began in 1979, but declined most during the period of 1985 to 1988. The study reported: "Current drug use declined significantly in all age categories, among both men and women, and for blacks,

---

* Yet other sources place the figure much lower. The U.S. Internal Revenue Service estimates the market at $25 billion, while a Wharton study prepared for the President's Commission on Organized Crime places the figure at $58.6 billion. The retail value of just South American cocaine in North America and Western Europe is estimated to be about $20 billion, as reported in "The Cocaine Economies: Latin America's Killing Field," *The Economist*, October 8, 1988. p. 21.

whites, and Hispanics. The decline also was seen in all regions of the United States and for all levels of educational attainment."[40]

IMPLICATIONS FOR PRIVATE SECURITY

There is a profit side to the drug-abuse problem. As more companies and public agencies become involved in employee drug testing, increasing revenues will be earned by private security companies (and others) involved in the administration of this testing. A study conducted by Market Intelligence Research Company assessed the value of the drug-testing market at about $80 million in 1986.[41] According to some forecasts, the value of drug-abuse testing is expected to grow at an average annual rate of 11.4%.[42] At this rate the drug-testing market would be $123 million in 1990; and if the rate is sustained, it would reach $363 million by the end of the decade. Other sources project higher estimates. *Security* recently reported that 1990 revenues for drug testing will be $340 million, an increase of 48% over their 1989 estimate.[43] If this estimate grows at an average annual rate of only 12%, by the year 2000 the revenues would exceed $1 billion. The Hallcrest research staff could not determine which estimate is more accurate or how much of either could be claimed as revenue by the private security sector.

Yet other revenue sources include private investigation companies placing more people undercover for investigation and surveillance purposes. As the drug problem worsens, revenues of private security companies that provide any type of drug-related services will increase commensurately. Some companies have become involved in profitable drug prevention and treatment programs, such as drug-abuse awareness seminars, security officer training, counseling, and other services. Drug detection has been a boon to companies that provide "drug-sniffing" dogs. In the area of equipment sales and manufacturing, the search for electronic narcotics detection is ongoing. The first company that develops such sensors that are inexpensive and reliable is virtually guaranteed great profits. There are also spin-off technologies. As one example, GTE has developed a software product, called VT-Narco©, which is intended to assist in the analysis and investigation of narcotics cases and organized crime. The overall value of the entire anti-substance abuse market is not known, and it is doubtful that data are available upon which to base an estimate.

The downside of the drug problem to private security is much clearer. Both proprietary and contract security guard forces are likely to face demands for ever-increasing involvement in drug abuse surveillance and enforcement duties--areas which many may not be particularly suited to manage. The potential requirement for private security to address drug abuse in the workplace comes quite close to toppling the delicate balance between prevention and enforcement; the latter is more properly the domain of public law enforcement. Many corporate security departments are not equipped to manage the growing problem of substance abuse on the job. They often lack the training and resources. Some security directors also are not motivated to tackle a problem that they view as more properly a law enforcement responsibility.

There are many other dimensions to the effect of drug abuse on private security. If, for example, the war on drugs worsens significantly, the resulting demands on law enforcement agencies may accelerate a shift of more and more duties to the private sector, both contract and proprietary segments. Another dimension of the crisis private security shares with law enforcement is the need for private security companies to ensure that their personnel do not abuse drugs. Considering that private security has far more difficulty in conducting thorough and reliable background investigations of its personnel than do public law enforcement agencies (because of limited, or nonexistent, access to arrest and conviction records), the incidence of private security personnel being drug abusers is potentially an acute problem. Further, will the private sector be able to afford 100% drug testing of its employees? Will these added costs be passed on to clients? No one knows the answers to these questions, but the potential impact of the drug-abuse problem in America on private security is not trivial.

LAW ENFORCEMENT AND DRUGS

Based on recent data from the National Institute of Justice Drug Use Forecasting, at least 45% of arrestees charged with violent or income-generating crimes tested positive for use of drugs.[44] More startling, the same study looked at arrests for serious offenses in 20 major cities between October and December 1988 and found that testing for illicit drugs was positive in 54% to 83% of the cases. Overall, two-thirds to three-quarters of people arrested on non-drug-related charges tested positive for illegal drugs at the time of their arrest.[45] It is evident that a high correlation exists between drug abuse and crime trends in America and that the relationship is directly proportional. A 1986 survey of inmates of state correctional facilities indicated that 43% of the inmates reported having used illegal drugs on a daily or near daily basis a month prior to their offense.[46] Clearly, then, if America's war on drugs progresses with some success, one might reasonably expect crime rates to go down. Should America be able to substantially reduce either the availability or the use of drugs, law enforcement agencies would likely see meaningful mitigation of their overburdened workload.

Another aspect of drugs and law enforcement is the theoretical correlation between the severity of the drug crisis and consequent drug abuse by police officers. As more and more police officers are assigned to narcotics-related duties, one may also assume that the opportunities for corruption will increase. Statistics pertaining to drug abuse by police officers were not collected by the Hallcrest research staff, but data obtained during field interviews suggest a strong interest in this potential problem by law enforcement administrators.

For example, a 1986 study conducted for the National Institute of Justice surveyed 33 police departments and found that 24 (73%) had programs to test all applicants.[47] Conversely, 27% of the departments did not test applicants. While this study noted that 21% of the departments were considering mandatory drug testing of all officers, it was not noted how many were actually doing so. The San Francisco Police Department went so far as to disseminate a departmental general order concerning policies related to the use of drugs by sworn officers.[48] In friendlier times, most people would have taken it for granted that police officers would not use illicit drugs by virtue of their duty to enforce the law, thus a policy statement to that effect would be superfluous.

DRUG ABUSE IN INDUSTRY

One way of gauging the extent of involvement in drug-abuse programs by corporate security departments is to assess how involved their companies are. While the press continues to feature news reports about the growth of drug testing in American business, the trend may not be as representative of the business community as many believe. Numerous national surveys of the business community clearly establish that American companies regard drug abuse as one of their highest priority concerns and strongly support either drug-prevention or drug-testing programs. It is not yet evident, however, that these intentions are being commensurately implemented. The data suggest that, while the largest firms are extremely active in such programs, small companies appear to be comparatively inactive. This finding is significant because the majority of the workers in America work for smaller companies. A 1989 Department of Labor study found that only 10% of employees in America work for a company that is considering implementing a drug-testing program.[49]

If it is true that most small companies do not provide drug-prevention or drug-testing programs, the reasons may be (1) they do not believe that they have a drug-abuse problem, or (2) they don't think that they can afford such programs. Pressures upon companies to avoid or delay drug testing arise from employee and union concerns about rights of privacy, serious concerns about accuracy, fears about consequent exposure to civil lawsuits, and the $25- to $100-per-employee costs for testing. Before judging small businesses too harshly, it is important to recall that the current national campaign to curtail drug and substance abuse is still in its incipient stages. Small businesses may simply need more time to become involved. If the cost is prohibitive for small businesses, it may be that more governmental or other outside support for such programs is warranted.

A comparison of estimates of how many companies have drug programs is presented in **Table 3.2**, as reported by the Department of Labor and by a Gallup Poll. The discrepancies are the result of problems of definition as to what constitutes a drug program. A side-by-side comparison dramatizes how unclear data pertaining to drug abuse are, since the variance between the surveys is significant.

TABLE 3.2
PERCENT OF COMPANIES WITH DRUG PROGRAMS 1987-1988

Size of Company (employees)	Dept. of Labor Survey	Gallup Survey
5000 +	60%	28%
1501 to 5000*	43%	13%
500 to 1500	N/A	10%
Less than 50	N/A	2%

*Department of Labor criterion is "more than 1000 employees."

There is considerable evidence that the larger a company is the more likely it is to have some form of substance abuse prevention program in place. A survey by the Department of Labor in 1988 found that of companies with 1,000 or more employees, approximately 43% had drug testing. Of companies with 5,000 or more employees, about 60% had some form of drug-testing program. Nearly all of the nation's 500 largest corporations have implemented some type of drug program,[50] (of which a significant portion may only include counseling).[51] In contrast, in 1983, only 3% of the country's 500 largest companies had drug-testing programs, according to Richard Lesher, president of the U.S. Chamber of Commerce.[52] It is evident that the national campaign to fight drug abuse has been reflected in America's largest companies.

While the major companies have been extremely active in drug-prevention programs, the same profile is not as evident for small companies. According to a 1987 study on drug abuse in the workplace conducted by the U.S. Labor Department (reported at the time to be the most extensive study ever conducted), only 20% of American workers were employed by companies that tested for drug use.[53] Based on a survey of 7,500 establishments, only 1 employee in 100 was actually tested in a 12-month period, and of that 1% tested, about 12% tested positive[54] (a portion of which may have involved legal prescription drugs). Moreover, 91% of employers did not have testing or counseling programs, and of those that did have programs, two-thirds tested workers only when they were suspected of drug abuse. Only 4% of employers without programs were considering establishing one in the following year.

Different statistics were reported by a 1988 Gallup Organization survey, but the same pattern is indicated. The Gallup survey reported that only 28% of companies with more than 5,000 employees had drug-testing programs. Of companies with 1,501 to 5,000 employees, 13% had drug testing; and of companies with 500 to 1,500 workers, only 10% had testing. Only 2% of companies with fewer than 50 employees had testing programs.[55] It is also noteworthy that only 4% of the companies surveyed that did not have drug-testing programs planned to consider such programs in their next fiscal year. Although it is still early in the war on drugs, the perception of drug testing in the workplace may be outracing the reality.

The opinions of industry leaders are also representative of the business community's attitudes about drug-abuse programs. About 88% of 265 chief executive officers surveyed in 1989 thought that substance abuse was a very significant problem; only 22% believed that drug abuse was very significant in their own organizations.[56] Similarly, a 1989 study done by Arthur Andersen & Company surveying 4,500 chief executives found that only 64% favored a drug testing program for their employees; how many actually had a program was not noted.[57] It is too early to accurately predict whether drug testing will meet private security revenue growth projections over the next decade.

COMPUTER SECURITY AND
ELECTRONIC INTRUSION

*"This is for all that good info on beating bell at there {sic} own game...Well, this is LD, but fun. The **** Credit Union's PBX is on ***-***-****, 300 baud, 7 and 2. Password is ****. At the > enter Login. have fun...Here is a VAX system I got into, even have a password! When you connect, making sure CAPS lock is ON, enter *** ***, hit enter and the (sic) input the same thing again. User name is ****, password is ****. Also make sure you are emulating a VT100 or VT200 terminal...Well, ****, I guess a phone number would help on that VAX too! ***-***-****. hehehehehe...Heres (sic) a working auth code for MCI. Of course the dial up is 950-1022 or 1-800-950-1022!! The code is *** *** **** ****. Don't abuse so it will last!"*

This is a printout [expletives and compromising information are deleted] from a December 1, 1989, message section of an electronic conference called "**** Ma Bell" on a notorious "hackers" computer bulletin board. This message is indicative of a growing concern for security and data processing departments: electronic intrusion into corporate and governmental communications and computer systems. This section reviews computer security in general, but electronic intrusion in particular.

OVERVIEW OF THE THREAT

Electronic intrusion is probably not the most serious threat facing computerized information systems. On a statistical basis, "insider" attacks by dishonest or disgruntled employees represent the greatest risk, accounting for up to 80% of incidents. The internal threat is well recognized, but the electronic intrusion threat is not always perceived and may be silently growing in the background. Most management information system managers are fully aware of the measures needed to mitigate their vulnerabilities to internal threats, or, at least, to the extent that this type of threat can be mitigated. On the other hand, some computer network managers, and many security managers, may not fully comprehend external, electronic intrusion risks.

Many managers are unaware of the nature and capabilities of outside threat sources. Some managers do not regard electronic intrusion as credible--and it may not be--and others believe that the chances that they would be victimized by outside attacks are too low to worry about. It is the incredible nature of electronic intrusion that makes it an increasing concern, at least in the short term. Sophisticated computer networks with adequate counter-measures to thwart or detect insider threats have been penetrated occasionally by outsiders with little more than a computer and a modem. Currently, network defenses sometimes only provide minimal safeguards against such attacks.

While some computer security experts believe that electronic intrusion attacks against computer systems presently represent a low statistical risk, other authorities believe that it is the improbable nature of this threat that makes it so potentially dangerous. Electronic intrusion has been successfully used for governmental and industrial espionage; it is not limited to juvenile hackers. The ideal attack penetrates a computer system to extract, delete, or modify data without leaving any indication that the intrusion has occurred. If such highly competent attacks are occurring, then it is unlikely that anyone can say with certainty how prevalent electronic intrusion is in the nation today.

Most large governmental and corporate security systems containing critical information are well protected against expert attacks, particularly for computer networks containing classified and highly proprietary information. In a real-world sense, classified and restricted-access governmental and military computer systems are virtually impregnable, unless network operators have been negligent or there has been an "insider" conspiracy. However, for those computer networks which disregard electronic intrusion as a realistic threat, vulnerability is high. Moreover, there are tens of thousands of small computer systems and networks, both in government and private industry, which are connected by modems with little or no protection against outside attacks. Some networks have marginal protection, such as the use of simple passwords or call-back modems. When computer system users believe such measures are sufficient, their false sense of security also makes them highly vulnerable.

Part of the computer security problem today is caused by the increasing portability and ease of use that makes microcomputers so attractive for use at home and at work. The days when computers were limited to the data processing department are long gone. Desktop computers can be found throughout most offices, and portable computers are going into homes, linked to office computers by modem. Many modems are brought into the workplace privately by employees; companies frequently are entirely unaware of the existence of many modems in their offices. Various communications software programs are available that allow an employee to operate his or her office computer from home exactly as if he or she were at work. Portable cellular telephones are now common in cars and briefcases. Facsimile machines are as commonplace as copiers. Employees are bringing floppy disks with personal data and programs to process at work, and they're taking company disks home for work on home computers. They may spread a computer virus into the office system, and they may compromise company proprietary information on their home computers. The modern security manager faces a monumental problem when it comes to computer security, since the extent of the threat is often not understood or appreciated. And, it is likely that it could become much worse before it becomes better by the year 2000.

As noted, the current defenses against electronic intrusion are formidable, and should become increasingly so, provided they are used. The technologies utilized to thwart electronic intrusion include: electromagnetic shielding and containment, optical disk storage, data encryption, local area network work stations without local storage capabilities, computer-managed password software, audit trail software, increasingly sophisticated "call-back" modems, fiber-optic cabling, enhanced call-tracing capabilities by telephone companies, call-in telephone number identification signals, biometric identification access to terminal hardware, and many others. These defenses represent expensive augmentation for many smaller companies and agencies. Small organizations often lack the in-house expertise to install and manage some of these defensive technologies. Moreover, most security directors would readily admit they are in over their heads when it comes to computers; many view computers as tools for the next generation, not for the "old guard." The threat will not wait, however, for the next generation of security managers to take the helm.

Any communications or computer network connected to telephone lines, microwave links, modems, facsimile machines, or similar apparatus is hypothetically vulnerable to external, electronic intrusion. Protective procedures, software, and hardware already available can make external penetration improbable, as long as the threat is viewed as credible. Although excellent countermeasure tools are now available, they are often not being fully used or are being improperly implemented. Computer security specialists generally believe that external electronic intrusion will not be a major risk by the end of the decade as countermeasures are fully implemented by most computer networks and systems. While risk levels may increase for a few years, external electronic intrusion is, theoretically, a diminishing problem.

Table 3.3 presents National Center for Computer Crime Data (NCCCD) estimates and projections on the use of computer security technology.[58] By 1991, NCCCD predicts that the most frequently used technologies will be access control (75% of all users), secure networks (61%), secure data base management systems (57%), audit analysis aids (54%), and anti-virus products (53%). In terms of the greatest rates of growth, anti-virus product use will increase by 5300%, followed by advanced encryption (967%), smart cards (720%), secure networks (610%), and secure data base management systems (518%). The lowest rate of growth is predicted to be for access control, at 123%. In fact-- and not depicted on the table--NCCCD estimates that access control technologies were used by 86% of computer systems in 1988 and predicts that use will decrease to 75% by 1991. Despite that decrease, access control products will continue to be the most widely used technology for computer security, according to the study by NCCCD.

TABLE 3.3 USE OF COMPUTER SECURITY TECHNOLOGY 1985 AND 1991			
Technology	Percent of Users 1985	Percent of Users 1991	Percent of Increase
Mainframe/Mini Access Control	61%	75%	123%
Smart Cards	5%	36%	720%
Call-Back Modems	17%	43%	253%
DES (Data Encryption Standard) Encryption	19%	47%	247%
Advanced Encryption (Other than DES)	3%	29%	967%
Intrusion Detection Expert Systems	8%	31%	388%
Audit Analysis Aids	19%	54%	284%
Secure Operating Systems	19%	57%	300%
Secure Networks	10%	61%	610%
Secure Database Management Systems	11%	57%	518%
Anti-Virus Products	1%	53%	5300%
SOURCE: NCCCD and RGC Associates Security Survey			

In larger companies, numerous security managers currently rely on their in-house data processing departments to take care of computer security. Many security directors have little personal knowledge about computers or computer security. It is likely, however, that in the coming years security managers will be expected--perhaps required--to become increasingly knowledgeable about computer security. Moreover, as computer systems proliferate within security departments--both as management information tools and as a part of electronic security systems--these systems, too, may become targets.

In summary, some of the key factors security managers must consider are the following:

- Electronic intrusion is currently a minimal threat that has the potential of growing to significant risk levels in the next few years before it finally dissipates by the end of the decade

- Most security managers are presently ill-equipped, personally and organizationally, to counter the computer security threat, particularly external, electronic intrusion

- As security departments increasingly rely on computers, their vulnerability to electronic intrusion will commensurately increase

ELECTRONIC BULLETIN BOARDS

By some estimates, at present there are about 15,000 electronic bulletin board systems (BBSs) in use in the United States.[59] Even at a modest rate of growth, such as 5% per year, this group would increase to more than 25,000 by the year 2000. For the tens of millions of computers in America, this is still a relatively small number. Most of these bulletin boards are benign, and many are useful, supporting various special-interest groups. Some are even operated by various levels of government. The City of Santa Monica, CA, for example, maintains a bulletin board for its citizens to present and discuss local issues. Through the Overseas Security Advisory Council--a joint private and federal organization established in response to the overseas terrorist threat--the U.S. Department of State is running an electronic bulletin board designed to inform the business community about security threats overseas.[60]

A small number of these bulletin boards, however, are deliberately malicious, perhaps as few as 20 to 30 BBSs, representing an underground network of 200 to 300 "criminal hackers." Their existence is a problem that private security and law enforcement, in particular, will have to contend with for the next decade. And it is a problem that most private security directors and practitioners presently have little background in coping with, or even understanding.

Criminal hackers represent a very small percentage of the overall computer security threat. By some estimates, presently less than 1% of all computer security incidents can be attributed to criminal hackers, and yet they always seem to generate considerable press interest.[61] Some press accounts have called malicious hacking terrorism; and hackers, like terrorists, can manifest themselves in destructive ways, particularly for large corporations and government institutions, their favorite targets. The infamous "Friday the 13th" computer virus was reported on national and local TV news for days prior to the target date of October 13, 1989. Nothing really happened on Friday the 13th, but the nation was on edge waiting for it. There were fewer than 10 verified sightings out of tens of millions of personal computers targeted.[62]

Some statistics help put the computer security threat in perspective. In 1989, about 50 million corporate personal computers were in use; by 1991, there may be more than 90 million computers. Moreover, in 1988, about 5 million microcomputers were sold in the United States to businesses and individuals.[63] If this rate were maintained to the end of the current decade--and it is likely to increase--there would be an additional 50 million computers in use by the year 2000, totaling more than 200 million computers.

It is evident that the ratio of the number of computer virus incidents to the number of all computers is rapidly diminishing as the number of computers increases. Based on virus incidents reported in 1988 to the Computer Virus Industry Association, there were 400 incidents involving 90,000 computers.[64] The association estimated that an equal or greater number of virus attacks were unreported. On these bases, about 0.2% to 0.4% of all business computers were involved, a very small number. It is likely that the ratio of virus incidents to all computers--government, business and private--is currently virtually nil. On the other hand, as the number of computers in use grows, the number of potential targets of viruses will commensurately increase. While it seems likely that computer viruses will

65

never amount to a significant problem, it is a well-established security industry maxim that as vulnerability increases, so too must risk increase. More than 53% of commercial systems with modem communications are expected to have some form of computer virus protection.[65] Just as for terrorism, it is the perception of threat, not necessarily the reality of the threat, that compels people to implement countermeasures in response to a few vandals.

CRIMINAL HACKERS

Minuscule in number, criminal hackers have been able to intimidate a national system of electronic communications by victimizing only a few such systems. With names such as "The Legion of Twilight," these fringe groups have been involved with theft of telephone service, vandalism of computer systems, larceny of protected and privileged information, sabotage of government systems and records, alteration of vital medical records, credit card fraud, and manipulation of credit records--the list goes on. Computer security specialists likely would agree that these groups are relatively insignificant in terms of real impact on national interests and corporate security. They are, nevertheless, a factor most corporate security directors and management information systems managers need to contend with. Unattended and undefended modem communications is a thing of the past. Short and simple "modem hunting" computer programs, often called *WarGames* programs (taken from the motion picture of the same name), can readily dial thousands of telephone numbers, seeking out vulnerable modems and looking for "handshakes," the characteristic squeals and tones of modem communications. The acts of criminal hackers are usually fairly easy to accomplish. They do not generally break into well-protected computer systems. That type of attack is largely a news media myth. Hackers are successful only against the undefended and the careless. They remotely prey on the easiest victims they can find.

COMPUTERS AND INDUSTRIAL ESPIONAGE

There are few hard data to indicate that industrial espionage, and particularly electronic eavesdropping, is a realistic threat. It may be that electronic intrusion is not presently a problem in corporate America. Documented incidents are scarce, and when they are reported, details are intentionally minimal. However, security managers say privately that many discoveries of electronic intrusion go unreported because of fear of embarrassment or loss of client confidence.[66] Many computer network managers lack the technical means or competence to detect that an intrusion has occurred.

One way to sound the true depth of the problem is to approach it obliquely. How willing are companies to engage in industrial espionage? A 3-year study completed by Washington Researchers in 1984 resulted in startling findings.[67] In brief, the study concluded the following:

- **Fifty-four percent of company market researchers were willing to call a competitor's suppliers, posing as journalists doing a study of the industry, to obtain information about a competitor's sales.**

- **Thirty-five percent were willing to masquerade as students to gather information from recruiters and personnel directors.**

- **While 39 percent of those polled said they would plant informants to spy on competitors, 74 percent believed that rivals were already doing so anyway.**

Although this study does not prove in any way that most companies would be willing to engage in electronic spying against competitors, it does raise concern about the willingness of some firms to consider it. Since professional electronic intrusion is designed to conceal any sign that it has occurred, there is no reliable way to determine whether it is, or is not, a meaningful problem today.[68]

DIMENSIONS OF COMPUTER CRIME

A study conducted by the Florida Department of Law Enforcement surveyed 900 businesses and all law enforcement agencies in the state.[69] This study determined that 1 out of 4 businesses was the victim of some form of computer crime. In cases where offenders were identified, 84% were employees, slightly higher than a Datapro Research Corporation estimate of 70% to 80%.[70]

According to a Datapro report, computer threats fall into the incident and rate categories depicted in **Table 3.4**. [71] The Florida study results differ from the data in the table, when it comes to law enforcement agencies. These agencies reported that only 50% of their computer crime incidents were perpetrated by employees but Datapro reports only 20%. Whereas the Datapro report estimates that only 1% to 3% of incidents can be attributed to outside human threats, the Florida study reported that for law enforcement agencies 19% of the incidents were from outside hacker attacks.

| TABLE 3.4 COMPUTER THREAT INCIDENT RATES ||
CATEGORY/Subcategory	PERCENT OF TOTAL/[Subtotal]
HUMAN INSIDER THREAT	70% to 80%
Human errors/accidents	[50% to 60%]
Dishonest employees	[10%]
Disgruntled employees	[10%]
HUMAN OUTSIDE THREATS	1% to 3%
NON-HUMAN PHYSICAL THREATS	20% to 25%
Fire	[10% to 15%]
Water	[10%]
Source: Datapro Research Corporation and NCCCD	

An article published in a National Institute of Justice *NIJ Report* categorized types of computer crimes as follows:[72]

- **Internal Computer Crimes**: Trojan horses, logic bombs, trap doors, and viruses

- **Telecommunications Crimes**: Phone phreaking *[sic]*, hacking, illegal bulletin boards, and misuse of telephone systems [theft of services]

- **Computer Manipulation Crimes**: Embezzlements and frauds

- **Support of Criminal Enterprises**: Data bases to support drug distributions, data bases to keep records of client transactions, and money laundering

- **Hardware/Software Thefts**: Software piracy, thefts of computers, and thefts of trade secrets

A computer crime survey was reported by *Data Processing & Communications Security* in the spring 1989 issue; the data presented in this article appear to have been derived from the Second Statistic Report of the National Center for Computer Crime Data (NCCCD).[73] The article did not identify how many organizations were surveyed for the study. The study predicted the national, annual computer crime statistics depicted in **Table 3.5**. Although the national, direct cost to organizations is estimated to be almost $560 million, the NCCCD estimates that the total direct cost of computer crime may be as much as $1 billion each year if the value of lost personnel time is also considered. As discussed further in this section, other sources estimate the total direct and indirect costs of computer crime to be as much as $200 billion. If this estimate is valid, it is evident indirect costs represent the bulk of the estimate and would

TABLE 3.5 SUMMARY OF NATIONAL COSTS OF COMPUTER CRIMES	
Total Annual Person-Years Lost	930
Total Annual Computer-Years Lost	15.2
Average Annual Loss per Organization	$109,000
National Cost for Computer Crimes to Organizations	$555,000,000
SOURCE: National Center for Computer Crime Data	

include, for example, the losses resulting from illegal electronic fund transfers, white-collar crime, and similar activities in which a computer crime is an integral element but not the primary objective of the crime.

Table 3.6 presents NCCCD data pertaining to the percentages of computer crime experienced by specific categories or organizations.[74] It is noteworthy that the share of attacks from 1986 to 1989 increased for all categories except for banks, whose share decreased from 18% to 12%. Further, the table does not intend to imply that there were no attacks against individuals and universities in 1986, but rather that there was inadequate reporting prior to 1989 to include incident data for this category for 1986. As an increasing number of home computer systems acquire modems, attacks against individuals are likely to increase over the next decade.

TABLE 3.6 SUMMARY OF COMPUTER CRIME VICTIMS		
Type of Organization	Percent of Attacks: 1986	Percent of Attacks: 1989
Commercial Organizations	23%	36%
Banks	18%	12%
Telecommunications Companies	15%	17%
Governmental Agencies	14%	17%
Individuals	*not reported*	12%
Universities	*not reported*	4%
SOURCE: National Center for Computer Crime Data		

The 1989 NCCCD study also reported the percentage of all incidents that each type of computer crime represented. This is depicted in **Table 3.7**. It is significant that money theft, information theft, damage to software, and deceptive alteration decreased from 1986 to 1988. The rate of malicious alteration incidents remained the same. It is significant that theft of services, harassment, and extortion increased over the period. This may be indicative of new trends in computer crimes and increased influence of criminal hackers and electronic bulletin boards.

As noted in **Table 3.7**, the probability of various types of computer crimes is calculated based on prosecutions. Consequently, it is likely that certain categories of crimes which do not result in indictments may be understated. Moreover, the rate of prosecutions is generally low for computer crimes. Between 1984 and 1987, about 2% of 335 cases identified as being "serious computer crimes" were prosecuted. In 1988, prosecutions of serious computer crimes showed a sharp increase; 6% of 485 reported cases were prosecuted. Conversely about 94% of all serious computer crime cases are not prosecuted.

Although the NCCCD estimates the annual cost of computer crime to data processing departments to be about $1 billion, *The Lipman Report*, as previously stated, noted it is possible that the annual cost to the nation could be $200 billion.[75] The Lipman article does note that such estimates vary dramatically. In the banking industry alone, losses are estimated as high as $10 billion in specious electronic funds transfers.[76] Further, according to the Communications Fraud Control Association, the annual loss due to telephone fraud and theft of service is estimated to be about $500 million annually. Overall, however, the Hallcrest research staff was unable to validate any particular estimate of the national, annual cost of computer crimes.

TABLE 3.7
SUMMARY OF RATES OF
COMPUTER CRIMES
(Based on prosecution data)

Type of Computer Crime	Probability of Occurrence: 1986	Probability of Occurrence: 1989
Money Theft	45%	36%
Information Theft	16%	12%
Damage to Software	16%	2%
Malicious Alteration	6%	6%
Deceptive Alteration	6%	2%
Theft of Service	10%	34%
Harassment	0%	2%
Extortion	0%	4%

SOURCE: National Center for Computer Crime Data

THE COMPUTER SECURITY INDUSTRY

The Size of the Market

According to the NCCCD data presented in **Table 3.3**, on **page 63**, by 1991 about 75% (see the estimates for access control) of all computers will be protected by some type of computer security product. By contrast, other market research studies project that by 1993 only about 17% of all computers will be protected by some form of security.[77] The Hallcrest staff reconciled this apparent contradiction with the assumption that the NCCCD data are primarily anchored to governmental and commercial computer users, while the 17% estimate may be viewing all computers in use--governmental, commercial, and private.

The apparent rapid growth of computer security products among commercial computer networks and systems is supported by other data. The NCCCD reported that in 1986 computer security accounted for 8% of security department budgets and 1.4% of data processing department budgets. By 1988, these percentages increased to 12% and 2.3%, respectively.[78] This equates to about a 25% increase each year. Assuming this rate of growth was maintained to 1990, then about 18% of security department budgets is being spent on computer security, as is approximately 3.8% of data processing department budgets. While these rates of annual growth cannot be mathematically sustained to the year 2000,** it is clear that current growth is robust.

The Value of the Market

There is a great deal of variance among market research sources when it comes to computer security equipment and service revenues estimates. The major dilemma in evaluating such estimates is that each major study classifies the components of this segment quite differently. Products regarded as falling within the category of security by one study may be treated as computer industry products by another and as electronic equipment by

---

** The percentage of security department budgets would exceed 100% by 1999, and computer security would account for 45% of data processing budgets by 2000. Therefore, it is evident that annual rates of growth can be expected to sharply decrease over the next few years.

yet another. Many of the reported sources include equipment and services in calculating their estimates that are not thought of as being a part of the security industry. For example, computer backup equipment and software, although playing an essential role in protecting data, would not be regarded by some industry authorities as traditional security products. As another example, many communications security products are not related to computer security, although they can be if the data lines of a computer network are being protected. The Hallcrest research staff was unable to extricate computer security products and services from electronic emanation and interference shielding products and services. Accordingly, the predictions and estimates of various market studies are presented in the following.

Frost and Sullivan

According to a Frost and Sullivan market research study, the sales of computer security software and services will increase from $588 million in 1988 to about $1 billion in 1993.[79] This represents an annual rate of growth of 10.6%. On this basis, the value of this market is approximately $768 million in 1990, and if this rate of growth is sustained, the value of sales and services would reach $2.2 billion by the year 2000.

IRD/NCCCD

A *Washington Post* article reported (sources not identified) that the business of protecting computer data is currently valued at $3 billion.[80] Yet higher estimates have been proposed. According to a report published by International Resource Development, Inc. (IRD), as reported by NCCCD, the value of access control, backup, and communications security equipment sales was $3.7 billion in 1987 and will be $10.2 billion by 1997.[81] This equates to an average annual rate of growth of 10.7%. On the basis of this rate of growth, the market is worth about $4.5 billion in 1990 and would be valued at $12.4 billion by the year 2000. While the IRD estimated rate of growth is virtually the same as the rate proposed by Frost and Sullivan, end-of-decade estimates differ greatly: $2.2 billion versus $12.4 billion.

Leading Edge

According to the 1990 *Leading Edge Report*, the value of computer security sales (adjusted for changes in the GNP) in 1989 was $215 million, by 1992 will be $350 million, and by the year 2000, $1.4 billion.[82] Leading Edge predicts that by the end of the decade computer security products will represent about 4.6% of the security equipment market and will experience an average rate of annual growth (in constant dollars) of approximately 17.2%, increasing from an annual rate of growth of 15.5% in 1989. Of additional interest, Leading Edge estimated that in 1987 approximately 25% of all computing equipment sales were in the computer security category, represented by encryption, call-back, and password protection products.[83] This is a surprisingly high percentage.

Hallcrest

Although the Hallcrest research staff has confidence in its estimates and projections, as previously noted, the staff was unable to derive data to separate computer security from electronic emanation and interference shielding products (identified as EMI/EMR), all of which are not necessarily restricted to computer applications. Nevertheless, Hallcrest estimates that in 1980 the value of computer security equipment sales and service revenues was $48 million. In 1980, this segment accounted for about 1% of all security equipment revenues. The average rate of annual growth was estimated as 17%. Hallcrest also estimated that in 1980 there were approximately 85 original equipment manufacturers (OEMs) and major distributors of computer security products.

Hallcrest estimates that in 1990 this segment earned revenues of $244 million, accounted for 2% of all security equipment revenues, and grew at an average annual rate of 17%. It is estimated that there are now about 250 OEMs and distributors of computer security products. By the year 2000, the Hallcrest staff projects that revenues will increase to $864 million at an average annual rate of growth of 13% and will represent about 3% of the security equipment market, slightly less than the Leading Edge estimate. The number of OEMs and major distributors is expected to increase to 700.

Summary

Estimates of projected computer security segment revenues for 2000 range from $864 million (Hallcrest), to $1.4 billion (Leading Edge), and to $2.2 billion (Frost and Sullivan). The IRD/NCCCD estimate is significantly higher at $12.4 billion, but the variance is likely due to their inclusion of revenues from backup and disaster recovery services and products, which the other studies may not have included. A comparison of estimated rates of annual growth fall closer together. Frost and Sullivan and IRD/NCCCD estimated rates of 10.6% and 10.7%, respectively. Hallcrest falls in the middle with an estimate of 13%, while Leading Edge projects the highest rate of growth at 17%. (Leading Edge estimated a rate of growth of 19%, but when adjusted for constant dollars, the rate decreased to 17%.) In summary, by the year 2000 the value of the computer security market, as traditionally viewed, can be generalized as $1 billion, growing at an average annual rate of 12%.

OTHER GROWING CONCERNS

Counterfeiting and software piracy: A raid of a warehouse in Hong Kong in 1989 resulted in the seizure of more than 100,000 pirated computer programs.[84] It was estimated that the street value of this one seizure was $2.6 million. According to the International Trade Commission, Hong Kong is not, however, among the top 7 countries reported to be the sources of software piracy.[85] Taiwan and Brazil head the list with estimates of $530 million and $528 million, respectively. They are followed by Singapore ($26 million), Mexico ($15 million), Argentina ($5 million), India ($3 million), and Thailand ($2 million). This totals approximately $1.1 billion in costs, with Taiwan and Brazil accounting for about 95% of the total. When lost profits, lost revenues, losses due to infringing sales, and enforcement costs are considered, the annual cost of software piracy is estimated to exceed $11 billion.[86]

This loss estimate is indicative of a serious and perhaps massive problem facing software companies today. It also has many repercussions for all businesses. Pirated software brought into the workplace, either intentionally or unintentionally, can result in data losses due to unreliable computer programs. It can also introduce computer viruses into company computer networks; and the use of pirated commercial software exposes the company to civil lawsuits by software manufacturers and distributors. The major software companies have been aggressive in starting legal proceedings against companies using unauthorized copies of their programs. Many computer security authorities believe that only the tip of the iceberg is being reported and because of international law and copyright protection problems, software piracy may become one of the major computer security issues during the coming decade.

74

Desktop forgery: The advent of desktop publishing, including the ability to manipulate computer graphic images, pixel by pixel, has created a dangerous tool in the hands of forgers and other criminals. Using personal computers, laser printers, publishing software, and scanners, criminals have been able to replicate documents, such as company checks, with amazing accuracy.[87] This is a new threat many corporate security departments know very little about. While manufacturers have cooperated with law enforcement agencies in making certain modifications intended to mitigate the threat of desktop forgery (such as avoiding one-to-one size ratios for color reproduction on most copiers), desktop forgery also has the potential of becoming a monumental problem for law enforcement and private security in the future.

Tempest: "Tempest," formerly a government codeword, refers to the ability to gain intelligent information by analyzing the electromagnetic emanations of most electronic and electrical equipment, including computers. Generally regarded as an exotic form of electronic attack, reserved for the CIA and KGB, the Tempest threat has become inexpensive and easy--by some accounts.[88] Reportedly, for $300 to $3,000, depending on the sophistication desired, it is possible to purchase and assemble commercially available electronic gear that would enable an "eavesdropper" to monitor the CRT displays of a personal computer within several hundred yards. Although some industry experts believe that interest among governmental and commercial organizations in Tempest protection is going to ebb in the near future (and some believe that it peaked during the mid-1980s), the availability of inexpensive technology to eavesdrop on computer systems--if true--has the potential of increasing attention to this unique vulnerability.

COMPUTER SECURITY MANAGEMENT PROBLEMS

Management of computer security may be the greatest individual challenge facing private security managers over the next decade. Many corporate security directors have little personal understanding of computers. While they may be aware of computer security requirements, many have few skills and very limited experience in this field. They tend to rely either on the managers in their own data processing departments or on private outside consultants. **Table 4.4, page 120,** in Chapter 4 of this report presents the findings of a survey that asked proprietary and contractual security managers to list their primary security functions in rank order. Out of 13 functions, proprietary security managers placed information security in 12th place and contractual managers placed it in 10th place. These rankings are indicative of the reluctance of security managers to become involved in computer security, despite the fact that the loss of trade secret data could be as devastating to a company as property losses. In the future, security managers who perceive that computer security is an important aspect of their responsibilities may be adding computer specialists, systems engineers, or other technical specialists to their staffs.

Managers and directors of data processing departments may also be handicapped in meeting the computer security threat. They often have an adequate technical understanding of computer security requirements, but many have a poor understanding of the principles of security management and of physical and electronic security equipment and systems outside of the direct realm of computer security. Moreover, they are often isolated from the corporate security department, frequently by mutual consent. It is not uncommon to find an adversarial relationship between these 2 departments, and sometimes the relationship between the departments is outright hostile. Data processing managers and corporate security managers need one another and, yet, have been traditionally poor at establishing cooperative relationships. These departments are sometimes operated as fiefdoms and are occasionally jealous of one another's overlapping authority.

It is evident that security managers are not well grounded in the computer sciences, but how versed are data processing managers in security? The 1989 report of the National Center for Computer Crime Data included an analysis of how Data Processing Management Association (DPMA) members learned about security.[89] The following was reported:

Self-education	**40%**
Seminars	**25%**
Other	**17%**
No training	**13%**
College extension	**5%**

It is not clear how representative the DPMA is of the entire industry, but the data do suggest that more than 53% of people employed in the computer field either learn on the job or have had no security training. Assuming that seminars represent no more than a 1-day or 2-day session (sessions may be counted in hours, not days), then about 78% of the personnel have had no formal training or education in security. In these regards, were the corollary professional association for security specialists, the American Society for Industrial Security (ASIS), to conduct a comparable study of its membership to determine how many security personnel have had formal training or education in the computer sciences, it is highly likely that parallel statistics would be developed. It is doubtful that all but a small fraction of ASIS members have had such training or education.

THE SECURITY & TERRORISM INTERFACE

Reviewing the literature pertaining to terrorism--grown to a massive collection in recent years--reveals that very little of it contains really meaningful solutions or exceptionally useful prognostication. The literature is often subjective and is replete with case histories and "war stories." The empirical data are largely limited to body counts and incident graphs and chronologies, which may be the best anyone can do given the lack of a universally-accepted definition of terrorism. An assessment of the effects of terrorism on private security over the coming decade in America, therefore, will have these identical limitations. What has already happened can be easily documented, but forecasting what will happen is highly speculative. Moreover, reports of specific international terrorist incidents are highly determined by their context. It is doubtful that there is substantive utility in translating incidents from one context to another or from one region of the world to the United States.

Many factors that are relevant in Northern Ireland, for example, may have little bearing in Lebanon, and even less, if any, relevance in Coeur d'Alene, Idaho.

To date, international terrorism has been virtually statistically insignificant in the United States, as compared with worldwide incident rates.

FIGURE 3.1: TERRORIST INCIDENTS IN THE U.S., 1983-1987
Source: FBI, 1987.

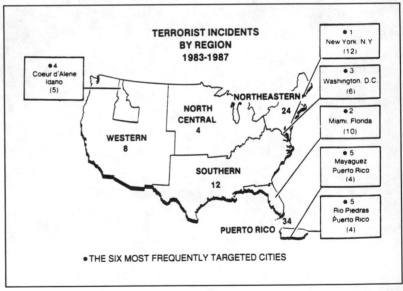

The terrorist incidents that have occurred in North America (.3% of worldwide incidents) have been primarily restricted to Puerto Rico, several major American metropolitan areas, and Canada. **Figure 3.1** illustrates the location of most terrorist incidents in the United States during the period 1983 to 1987. There are fairly limited incident data available that would aid in analyzing the impact of either domestic or international terrorism.

THE "HYPE" FACTOR

Since there is no universal consensus as to how terrorism is to be defined, it is understandable that the emotional foundation of international terrorism has been subtly exploited by a very few to serve their own interests. Alarmist statistics sell security equipment, specialized services, and guards, as well as newspapers and high television ratings. Further, even when "empire-building" is not a major factor, private and public officials may be succumbing to extreme political and reactionary pressures to respond to specific incidents and to quell public outrage and fear fanned by sensationalist worldwide news attention to the incidents. Most officials are likely to consider it "career suicide" not to respond to a notorious incident or to suggest carefully measured responses to the true risks associated with the incidents. It is difficult to avoid the thought that a significant part of the current terrorism scare may be yet another product of the era of "hype."

The question constantly heard is, "What would you have us do, just ignore it?" It is doubtful that anyone would agree that acts of terrorism should be ignored, but most people might agree that the responses should be measured and proportional to the risk. The U.S. Department of State has budgeted $4.4 billion for counterterrorism programs, of which about 75% is reportedly designated for the private sector--more than $3 billion.[90] While this is a windfall for some American companies, has this expenditure been synchronized with an objective assessment of risk? How much of the "business" of counterterrorism is driven by the "hype" factor? It is doubtful that there are any concrete answers, but this chapter attempts to probe the questions.

THE QUESTION OF A MEASURED RESPONSE

The International Conference on Terrorism, sponsored by *Discover Magazine*, reported that U.S. businesses spent about $21 billion in 1986 to protect plants and executives abroad.[91] *** The State Department program was budgeted for $4.4 billion; thus, the combined outlay may potentially total more than $25 billion (although the State Department budget is projected over a number of years).

In 1986, 12 Americans were killed and 100 were wounded in worldwide international terrorist incidents. In 1987, this dropped to 7 Americans killed and 40 wounded. In 1988, 192 were killed and 40 were injured, of which a substantial part is attributed to the casualties suffered as the result of the bombing of Pan Am Flight 103. The following year, 1989, victimization levels dropped to 16 killed and 19 wounded.[92]

On the hypothetical basis of $25 billion in counterterrorism spending overseas, the spending in 1986 is equivalent to $223 million per victim. By 1989, this ratio increases to $714 million. A reasonable argument could be made that there is no other precedent of spending sums so large for mortality and morbidity rates so low. Consider the status of air bags in cars, smoke detectors in homes, research for AIDS, or even government-sponsored programs to end smoking; in many instances relatively little is spent where death and injury rates are extremely high. Can the answer to this paradox be found in the "hype" factor and in the sensational nature of the terrorism phenomenon?

The Hallcrest staff is not trivializing terrorism or placing price tags on victims, but rather the intent is to raise the question of whether America's responses are in proportion to the risks. Terrorist events are intended to be heinous by design. Moral outrage and disgust can be so overwhelming that a dispassionate reaction can hardly be expected, yet eventually an objective assessment must be made.

*** The Hallcrest research staff has no basis to challenge the claim that U.S. business spent $21 billion for security overseas. However, the staff could find no additional collaboration of this figure either. The estimates of private security revenues and expenditures in Chapter 6 of this report intended to exclude overseas revenues and expenditures, but it was not feasible for the staff to extract all overseas sales and spending from the data base. It could not be reliably determined how much overseas spending remained in the data base. The Hallcrest staff estimates that domestic revenues and expenditures for private security were approximately $35 billion in 1986. Consequently, it does not seem credible that overseas spending approached 60% of domestic spending or that total domestic and overseas revenues and expenditures were $56 billion in 1986. The Hallcrest staff assumes, therefore, that the $21 billion figure may include construction costs beyond security equipment, services and architectural hardening, or that the $21 billion estimate may simply be overstated.

The graph in **Figure 3.2** depicts all international terrorist incidents (not just anti-U.S. incidents) for the period of 1968 to 1989. In 1989, there were 528 international terrorist incidents, resulting in 390 deaths and 397 injuries. This represents marked reduction from 1988 when 638 people were killed and 1,125 were wounded.[93] No dramatic effects resulted from the massive sums being spent internationally for counterterrorism; in fact, except for 1988 to 1989, the rate of incidents is climbing each year. How much less could have been spent to achieve the same results!

FIGURE 3.2:   INTERNATIONAL TERRORIST INCIDENTS 1968-1989
SOURCE: *Patterns of Global Terrorism: 1989*, U.S. Department of State

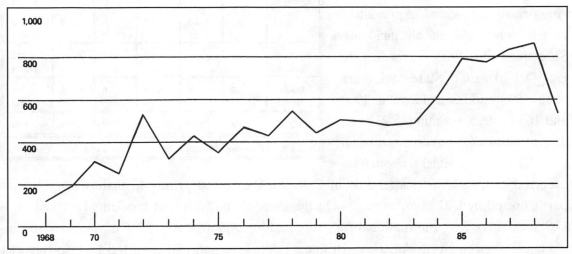

It would be hard to dispute that spending billions of dollars reduces the risks of terrorism for the facilities involved in security-enhancement programs. There is, however, another point of view. Looking to 1989 as a representative year, as noted, there were 35 American victims worldwide. As long as terrorists can find at least 35 unprotected victims outside of highly protected facilities, what effect do counterterrorism programs have in reducing victimization rates? For example, despite the U.S. government's best efforts to get all Americans out of Lebanon, the terrorists had little difficulty kidnapping several of the very few Americans who had decided to remain. It would seem, then, that expenditures on security may displace terrorist incidents, but have minimal effects on reducing incident rates. Terrorist acts are merely displaced to unprotected or less protected facilities.

While international terrorist incidents are increasing each year, the number of incidents in North America appears to be decreasing.**** Table 3.8 identifies worldwide terrorist incidents directed against United States interests. As is evident from this table, during 1981 to 1985, North America accounted for only 2% of all worldwide incidents specifically directed against American interests, and, as previously noted, only 0.3% of all incidents. Subsequent to 1985, according to U.S. Department of State data, there were 193 anti-U.S. incidents in 1988 and 165 in 1989, resulting in 232 and 35 American victims, respectively. Of the 1989 anti-U.S. attacks, about 64%

TABLE 3.8 TERRORIST INCIDENTS AGAINST THE UNITED STATES 1981 - 1985						
Region	1985	1984	1983	1982	1981	TOTAL
Africa	4	8	4	4	3	23 (2.6%)
Asia	8	6	18	13	9	54 (6.2%)
Eastern Europe	0	0	0	3	1	4 (.5%)
Latin America	86	45	58	46	66	301 (34%)
Mid East	16	23	24	8	8	79 (9%)
Western Europe	61	49	95	128	64	397 (45%)
North America	2	2	0	6	8	18 (2%)
TOTAL	177	133	199	208	159	876

SOURCE: Press Conference Fact Sheet, International Conference on Terrorism, 1986.

occurred in Latin America (mostly in Colombia), directed primarily against oil pipelines partly owned by U.S. companies. [94] On the basis of "all" terrorist incidents (not just anti-U.S. incidents), Risk International *[sic]* reported in 1985 that only 0.3% of all terrorist incidents occurred in North America. Business Risks International reported that no terrorist acts occurred in North America in 1988.[95]

On the other hand, and demonstrating the influence on statistics of how terrorism is defined, the FBI identified 26 domestic terrorist incidents in the United States in 1986, 7 in 1987,***** and 7 in 1988.[96] In 1989, State Department sources reported 3 suspected Iranian terrorist incidents in New York City related to the sale of Salman Rushdie's book *The Satanic Verses* and 1 confirmed incident in Canada.[97] During 1988 and 1989 there

---

**** Many data sources only identify "North America" as a statistical region. The numbers of incidents specifically occurring in the United States or in Canada are often not reported.

***** In 1987, all of the 7 terrorist incidents occurred on one day in Puerto Rico. The Guerilla Forces of Liberation, a Puerto Rican independence terrorist group, claimed responsibility.

were no casualties from the reported incidents. It is evident that terrorist incidents are very infrequent in the United States and North America, as compared to worldwide terrorist attacks.

As already noted, in 1988 232 Americans were killed or injured worldwide as a result of international terrorist incidents; in 1989, only 35. From an average tourist's perspective, these are still distressing numbers. It is important to point out, however, that during this period there were probably more than 3 million Americans living and traveling overseas.[98] Thus, in 1988, approximately 1 in every 12,900 Americans overseas was a victim of terrorism. In 1989, the ratio increases to 1 in every 86,000. These figures have more meaning if contrasted to more familiar statistics. By way of comparison (on the basis of 1984 data), 1 out of every 111 persons in the United States will die each year from all causes. About 1 out of 588 people will contract cancer, and 1 out of every 22 males in the United States will be the victim of a violent crime.[99] In comparison, therefore, the risk of becoming a victim of a terrorist attack is exceptionally low for the average American traveling overseas. At home, there is virtually no risk at all.

In summary, there is a basis to conclude that, in general, expenditures to manage the risks of terrorism are out of proportion to the actual threat. Clearly, overseas government facilities and some of the largest multinational corporations have a very high risk and must dedicate considerable resources to counter the threat, but it is not evident that there is high risk for everyone else. It is likely that many responses to terrorist risk are based largely on emotional and political factors or on considerations other than verifiable risk assessments.

DEFINING RISK AND TERRORISM

A brief examination of how terrorism is variously defined, both implicitly and explicitly, and how essential a definition is to interpreting terrorism statistics, may aid in understanding why the literature on terrorism often appears to contain contradictory and inconsistent data.

As a point of reference for this section, it is useful to establish a base definition. The Private Security Advisory Council's Committee on the Prevention of Terroristic Crimes defined terrorism as:[100]

> *Criminal acts and/or threats by individuals or groups designed to achieve political or economic objectives by fear, intimidation, coercion or violence.*

A more detailed definition is utilized by the Federal Bureau of Investigation in its annual publication *Terrorism in the United States*. Its definition of a terrorist incident is the following: [101]

> *A terrorism incident is a violent act or an act dangerous to human life in violation of the criminal laws of the United States or of any state to intimidate or coerce a government, the civilian population, or any segment thereof, in furtherance of political or social objectives.*

Defining Victimization Data and Political Terrorism

A U.S. Department of State publication reported, as one example, that there were 856 international terrorist incidents in 1988, resulting in 658 deaths.[102] By contrast, a Business Risks International report identified 3,734 incidents in 1988 and the death of 7,371 people.[103] This is at variance with the State Department figures by 436% and 1,120%, respectively. These discrepancies reveal the basic lack of uniformity in defining terrorism. An assessment of whether a response is measured is influenced by the definition of terrorism, since the definition determines how risk is quantified. While many authorities and organizations have defined "terrorism" many times over the last 10 years, a practical definition that represents a general consensus has never materialized.

The United States government tends to define terrorist incidents on the basis of political or ideological motivation behind the incident. Often, the incident must be carried out by an identifiable terrorist group, although this criterion can, at times, be quite flexible. Other sources tend to describe "terrifying" violent acts committed by criminals and lunatics, as well as by political or ideological extremists, as "terrorist" incidents, regardless of the orientations of the perpetrators. Neither approach is necessarily wrong; it is a matter of definition only.

A loose definition of terrorism can be extremely utilitarian for some, because the broader the definition, the higher the numbers become. The higher the numbers, the better it is for those few private security, and to some extent, public officials, who may professionally or economically benefit from high public perceptions of risk. Such motivations often account for the introduction of new interpretations of terrorism that satisfy special interests. Consider that the presentation of statistics that include a category of victim or incident that has not been presented by others is a *de facto* definition.

Defining Counterterrorism Equipment

Another extremely problematic aspect of defining terrorism is the difficulty of determining exactly what private security revenue or expenditure can be truly attributed to counterterrorism. Counterterrorism equipment is poorly defined. Bullet-resistant glazing for counterterrorism is the same glazing used to protect against criminals. A walk-through metal detector is used to deter and detect both terrorists and criminals alike. Facility hardening is as effective against bombs placed by a disgruntled employee as it is against a terrorist. If the definition of terrorism is broadened to encompass all "terrifying" violent crimes, then few violent criminal acts would not be included. Consequently, any attempt to determine the value of the counterterrorism private security market, either domestic or international, is probably futile.

Most authorities would likely describe certain products as primarily counterterrorism equipment, such as motorized barriers to protect against vehicle ramming. A handful of specialized activities are largely based on counterterrorism services, such as hostage negotiations and risk assessment newsletters. Even these products and services, however, also have counter-criminal dimensions. The lack of a widely accepted definition of terrorism hampers any serious attempt to quantify the growth and earnings of what is commonly understood as the counterterrorism market. It is highly doubtful that there will be a consensus as to what terrorism is or that this portion of the private security market can be accurately quantified. These failings are all the more frustrating since few would disagree that terrorism has substantially influenced private security revenues and expenditures. The irony is, then, that terrorism has increased spending, but no one can be sure how much!

THE BUSINESS OF COUNTERTERRORISM

Although international terrorism may have many indirect influences on private security, the major direct effects are increased revenues for:

- research and development, particularly in areas related to explosives and metal detection

- the provision of security systems and equipment at airports and for aircraft

- risk analysis and crisis management services

- "bodyguard" businesses, especially for those specializing in executive protection

- traditional security guard services in the United States and, especially, overseas

- specialized counterterrorism equipment, such as dynamic vehicle barriers, explosives and metal detection, bullet-resistant construction, and armored vehicles

- architectural and engineering firms providing services that include facility hardening

It is difficult to determine what portion of the current growth of the private security industry is attributable to international terrorism, but it is possible to interpolate these data from other statistics. The counterterrorism market is believed to be currently growing at a significantly faster rate than the private security sector. Since the private sector is growing at a rate of 7% to 8%, a reasonable estimate of the current annual rate of growth of the counterterrorism segment of the private security industry is about 15% to 20%. Some segments, such as the sale of specialized equipment, may be achieving 30% to 35% growth on a short-term basis. This rate of growth will probably continue for the first few years of the 1990s but may decline to 9%, or less, by the end of the decade as the market becomes saturated and the clients become more sophisticated and elect a more measured response to international terrorism incidents.

The current rate of growth of the counterterrorism market is generally perceived to be robust. However, there is scant evidence to suggest that this portion of the private security industry accounts for more than 1% to 2% of the industry's gross annual revenues and expenditures, amounting to $500 million to $1 billion in domestic spending for counterterrorism. The amount spent and earned overseas is unclear. As noted earlier in this section, one source reported that American business spent more than $21 billion overseas in 1986 for counterterrorism. Conceivably, a large portion of this sum may have included construction costs not directly associated with security enhancements or, at least, not for counterterrorism systems and equipment. The actual figure is probably much lower. There is likely no accurate tally of either worldwide American counterterrorism revenues and expenditures or how much can be genuinely assigned to counterterrorism.

Although there is no firm evidence that terrorism poses a significant threat within the United States (or North America), reactions to the perception of risk will, nevertheless, have a slight, but measurable, effect on private security and public law enforcement in America over the next decade. It is important to note that a great deal of facility hardening overseas and in the United States, particularly in the private security sector, is justified by American companies not only to protect against terrorist acts, but also--and perhaps more so--to protect against all external and violent criminal acts. Urban crime is probably far more threatening to American business, both domestically and internationally, than terrorism, particularly in terms of actual asset loss and risks to employees. Consequently, expenditures to improve security in office buildings may be primarily for protection against criminal acts even though a project may be identified as, or budgeted on the basis of, counterterrorism enhancements. Only those enhancement features directly related to protection against typical terrorist acts, such as bombings, should be properly designated counterterrorism measures. Data that would make this type of analysis possible are rarely available for most construction projects.

Although the value of the counterterrorism market cannot be estimated, it does not appear that "terrorism," as a market niche, will continue to be especially lucrative on an industry-wide basis--assuming for the moment that it currently is. Moreover, the profile of terrorism could change radically over the next 10 years, potentially resulting in a dramatic shrinking of this niche. On a very speculative basis, international political events that could trigger a significant reduction of risk to the United States include the following:

(1) The Soviet Union is entrenching within "Mother Russia."

The ability, if not the willingness, of the Soviet Union to provide continued meaningful support to international terrorist organizations may ebb, perhaps significantly. It is unlikely that Iran, Libya, North Korea and other nations involved in supporting terrorism could pick up the slack. This may be, of course, largely linked to President Gorbachev's political survival. The dramatic changes in the Soviet Union's world posture and the imminent reunification of West and East Germany, resulting in the dissolution of the militant East German State, may also be expected to reduce support of terrorism in Western Europe. Some authorities also credit the closing of Libyan diplomatic missions in Western Europe and an increase in international cooperation, coordination, and intelligence-sharing among West European nations as also significantly curtailing terrorism in Europe.[104] The net result could be a major reduction of terrorist attacks against American interests in Europe, and a concurrent reduction of the risk of these incidents spilling over into the United States.

(2) The problem of a Palestinian homeland finally shows some signs--albeit weak--of being resolved over the coming decade.

This is possible for various reasons, including: (a) The *intifada* [uprising] in the occupied West Bank and Gaza Strip appears to be winning its objectives; (b) Israel may be compelled to compromise since it seems to be losing ground in terms of world opinion and U.S. support; and (c) Palestinian-linked terrorist groups have been fundamentally successful in their tactics and should continue to be. Further, some of these groups are becoming much more sophisticated in manipulating the political dimensions of their plan to achieve long-term objectives.

Should a time come when Palestinians and their allies are no longer sponsoring transnational terrorism, except for a few small splinter groups, transnational terrorism may wind down and the counterterrorism market niche in the United States could collapse. Many organized terrorist organizations would probably revert to generally regional and local influence, losing most of their links to Palestinian groups. Moreover, reduced Soviet support may cause small local groups to wither away. Continued success against the Andean drug cartels could mitigate violence in the South Florida region, further reducing support for counterterrorism markets.

(3) A source of violence imported into the United States has been drug trafficking from South America, particularly from Colombia.

The Colombians have demonstrated progress in challenging the drug lords in their region. If Colombian and the other Andean nations continue to show success against the drug cartels, it is a reasonable expectation that drug-related violence in the Miami region, and in other American cities, could abate significantly.

The State Department now uses the term "narcoterrorism" to describe these criminal events. While narcoterrorism cannot be easily linked to, or described as, international political terrorism, it is difficult for the American public to view drug-related crime in the South Florida region as anything other than terroristic. Consequently, and with the exception of Puerto Rican incidents, progress in curtailing "narcoterrorism" could result in marked reductions on terrorist and terrorist-type events occurring in the United States.

Aside from drug-related incidents, Central and South America continue to experience high rates of insurgency, political revolution, and guerilla wars, resulting in terrorist-type incidents. Serious incidents directed against U.S. companies continue to occur, particularly in Colombia and Peru, but the affects on the continental United States have been largely regional and internecine, focused primarily on Miami, Washington, D.C., and New York City. It is conceivable that progress in eliminating or curtailing drug cartels could reduce the number of incidents directed against American companies in South America.

Other sources of terrorist incidents in Latin America may not be significantly influenced by reductions in drug trafficking. Puerto Rico, for example, has had major terrorist activity tied to Puerto Rican nationalistic movements, and these activities are likely to continue. Cuban nationalistic activities, however, appear to have dissipated in recent years, but there could be a resurgence of nationalistic spirit among Cuban expatriates as Cuba is increasingly isolated among nations espousing Marxism--notably from a reduction of support from the Soviet Union. Anti-Castro elements could be encouraged by any signs of weakness in Havana. It would be probable that, were this to happen, an increase of terrorist incidents could be expected in the Miami area.

In conclusion, the Hallcrest research staff believes that the counterterrorism market in the United States represents a small part of private security annual revenues and expenditures, amounting to less than 2%. (Higher estimates usually include categories of equipment and services unrelated to counterterrorism.) While the overseas market may be much more significant, there are few data to assess its value. Moreover, the staff believes that this market is transitory and should dwindle by the end of this decade, as many political events are occurring that may ultimately have a profound effect on risks from international terrorism.

EFFECTS ON CORPORATE AMERICA

Brian Jenkins, a long-time student of worldwide terrorism, noted in 1986 that the largest and the best-known corporations in the world were the most likely to be targeted; in fact, 20 of the top 25 American firms have been targeted by terrorist groups.[105] Terrorism has had an impact on virtually every American corporation with overseas facilities. While the number of incidents is still small, the largest corporations have taken the threat very seriously.[106] Further, it is likely that terrorism has had a significantly greater influence on proprietary security departments than it has had on contract security services.

What are some of the manifestations of the concern over terrorism by the nation's biggest companies? Some of the largest have gone so far as to develop internal building codes which, among many other objectives, specify in detail how security systems are to be incorporated into new facility designs and into renovation projects. Typical security enhancements include:

- anti-tailgating designs for electronic access control

- X-ray and metal detection screening of visitors

- landscape and architectural features that mitigate vulnerability to motor vehicles crashing into the building

- use of bullet-resistant glazing and shatter-resistant laminates

- extensive closed-circuit television surveillance

The needs of these top corporations have also brought about the creation of a number of highly specialized private security segments, particularly risk analysis newsletters and counterterrorism consulting services. Without support, many of these security companies would probably go out of business.

There have also been revenue-reduction effects resulting from terrorism, such as the avoidance by companies of certain major air carriers with a reputation for being frequently targeted by terrorists. In early 1989, several major American companies advised employees to avoid flying U.S. carriers from Europe and the Middle East for a period of time, in response to a Federal Aviation Administration (FAA) hijacking alert. According to a study conducted by Citicorp Diners Club and *Corporate Travel*, 16% of business travelers had requested that they not be booked on U.S. carriers.[107]

Another manifestation of these counterterrorism trends has been the proliferation of what some term the "ugly fortress" mentality. Most notable of this trend--and most quoted-- was the temporary placement of dump trucks filled with sand around the U.S. Capitol and White House to protect against suicide "ram" attacks by vehicles filled with explosives. The trend toward building new facilities with anti-vehicle attack barriers and specialized roadway designs can be seen elsewhere as well. In this regard, one of Washington's most notable architects, Arthur Cotton Moore, stated: "What I am arguing for is not the abolition of security barriers. Terrorism has been virtually institutionalized, and that requires preventive measures in the architecture of the capital. What I am arguing for instead is appropriate design to complement beautiful places, well-designed objects that also happen to be obstacles to determined truck bombers."[108]

Recognizing that international terrorist groups are not targeting the American firms as much as they are attacking the United States government by proxy, private industry was invited by the U.S. government to participate in finding solutions to the problem. In 1985, the U.S. Department of State, Bureau of Diplomatic Security, created the Overseas Security Advisory Council (OSAC), made up of 25 members. Four members are from government agencies and 21 from the private sector representing many of America's largest multinational companies. The chief objective of this organization is to promote security for Americans and American private sector facilities abroad, largely through information exchange.[109]

91

EFFECTS ON PUBLIC LAW ENFORCEMENT AND GOVERNMENT

International terrorism has had limited effect on most public law enforcement agencies in the United States. Predictions about terrorist acts during the bicentennial celebrations in 1976 utterly failed to materialize, and the great sums given to police departments through federal programs were ultimately regarded by many as being squandered. Support for counterterrorism programs for most police departments has since waned. On the other hand, some major cities, such as New York, Washington, Miami and Los Angeles, have had to make fairly heavy commitments to terrorism programs, largely to counter various nationalistic and independence groups, as well as various left-wing and right-wing radicals. Further, the protection of visiting dignitaries is particularly costly for any police department since it may receive no compensation from federal budgets. This can be a major problem for departments already stretched to their budgeting limits. Beyond these considerations, however, the effects on other state and local law enforcement agencies have been minimal.

International terrorism has significantly influenced most federal law enforcement agencies in terms of the commitment of resources. Federal agencies had been hampered by a lack of appropriate federal laws that could be enforced against terrorists. For a time terrorism and skyjacking were not, of themselves, criminal acts. It was necessary to apply other criminal laws since terrorism had not been legally defined. Eventually, the U.S. Congress passed 2 laws that established a legal structure for prosecuting individuals who attack U.S. citizens abroad: the Comprehensive Crime Control Act of 1984 and the Omnibus Diplomatic Security and Anti-Terrorism Act of 1986.[110] As yet, similar federal legislation to bring domestic terrorist acts under the federal umbrella have not passed, a step urged by many terrorism authorities to allow the FBI to get involved as soon as possible. The legal definition of "terrorism" continues to be the major factor delaying passage of new legislation.

Terrorism has also led to the introduction of relatively new requirements on public law enforcement, as well as on state and local legislation. For example, during the past year there has been a great deal of public concern about the restrictions on the sale of certain firearms, particularly AK-47 semi-automatic assault rifles, which have been used in a number of notorious mass killings. These events are not linked to terrorism, but the effect is comparable in the public mind. During this same period a handful of letter-bomb incidents have occurred which received extensive news coverage. Again, these letter-bombings are not tied to any international terrorist group, but by some definitions some may classify these bombings as domestic terrorism.

Local police departments face some new, potentially troublesome situations that could be linked to international terrorism. A number of isolated incidents have indicated that international terrorist groups have infiltrated America's borders. To date, these incidents have been largely inconsequential. As one example, IRA members were arrested in various American cities attempting to purchase weapons. In another case, a Japanese Red Army operative was arrested on the New Jersey Turnpike in 1988. And, other similar incidents have occurred. Police departments are now forced to pay closer attention to foreign nationals in the United States, fearing that terrorists may be slipping in with legal and illegal immigrants.[111] There has also been concern that some students from nations that sponsor terrorism may be terrorists. In addition, many cities have sizable communities of foreign nationals, both residents and students, such as Iranians. There is concern by some law enforcement officials that these communities may be harboring terrorists and terrorist supporters. Many large police department intelligence units have included such groups as areas of interest.

Another area of some concern to many major police departments has been the alleged linkage between illegal drugs and terrorist groups. For example, it is feared that Los Angeles gangs, which have learned to finance themselves by selling drugs, have allegedly had ties with terrorist groups as suppliers. Security specialists Theodore Shackley, Robert Oatman, and Richard Finney envision such possibilities in their recent book, *You're The Target*, noting that Ramon Milian Rodreguez, an advisor to the Medellin Colombian drug cartel, warned a Senate investigating committee of this possibility.[112] He testified that the major sources of drugs in Colombia were already in partnership with terrorist/guerilla organizations. The linkage to American drug pushers may not be far behind.

LOOKING TO THE YEAR 2000

Many authorities on transnational terrorism have speculated about why terrorism has never really taken root in America. No satisfactory explanations have ever been found. While there have been isolated incidents, the United States is substantively free of terrorism, certainly when compared to many other nations. The FBI identified 25 domestic terrorist incidents in the United States in 1986, 8 in 1987, and 7 in 1988.[113] No international terrorist incidents have occurred in the United States since 1983. At present, there is still no basis to project that terrorism in America will reach levels comparable to those in Western Europe. However, there is no question that the United States is highly vulnerable to terrorist-style attacks.

What terrorists could do is frightening and the effects on both private security and law enforcement could be massive if such attacks occurred. A noted authority on terrorism and high technology, Dr. Alvin Buckelew, wrote a classic article in 1983 in *Security Management* entitled "The Threat of Technoterrorism," which is still of relevant interest today.[114] He writes extensively on the potential for terrorist and other radical groups to acquire and utilize nuclear, biological and radiological weapons. His discussion of the relative ease of manufacturing and utilizing many biological and toxic agents is terrifying. Should any group ever resort to such weapons, the demands on private security and law enforcement would be virtually unimaginable. There have already been a number of extortion attacks on water supplies, and, reportedly, there have been 14 bombings of U.S. nuclear installations between 1975 and 1985, as well as 300 threats--none of which resulted in serious damage or injury.[115] Fortunately, "technoterrorism" remains a threat and not a reality.

Certain special-interest groups have increasingly used more forceful means in asserting their positions. For example, some groups supporting anti-abortion beliefs have already shown a willingness and ability to resort to violence to promote their cause. Their targets are, of course, highly specific. Although the Indian rights groups have been fairly quiet in recent years, their concerns have not diminished. The possibility always exists that if radical leaders appeared in the movement, it could radicalize overnight. White supremacist groups have also been active and occasionally violent, but their numbers are small and their resources are thought to be relatively meager.

Various nationalistic groups have been active in cycles, such as groups promoting Puerto Rican and Cuban independence. The loss of key leadership among Cuban groups in recent years appears to have subdued their activities for the present, and their activities have generally been internecine. Similarly, some foreign nationalistic groups, such as the Armenians, continue to be sporadically active, but their targets are other nationalist groups.

One new group of growing concern to police departments is the animal rights activists. Overseas groups have already resorted to violent actions, including arson. In Norwalk, Connecticut, in November 1988, a bomb was allegedly planted at the headquarters of a company that uses live dogs in surgical training sessions. An animal-rights activist was subsequently arrested and indicted for attempted murder, manufacturing bombs, and possession of explosives. [116] Some violent animal rights events have occurred in the United States, but outright terrorist-type acts have not yet occurred. Many fear that such incidents might occur, however. On the other hand, environmentalist groups seem to have popular support and large numbers, but they have not, in sum, shown any substantive inclination toward violence, merely civil disobedience and militancy. The effects of these 2 groups on private security are evident already. Many companies involved in animal testing, and creating of toxic or nuclear waste, or environmental impact have taken security measures in recent years to protect themselves against the activities of these special-interest groups.

NEW DEFENSES

Few new defenses have been proposed by any sector. The official position of the FBI has been that the most effective measure against terrorism in the United States is the vigorous prosecution of existing criminal laws.[117] To date, the FBI has, indeed, been effective in identifying and prosecuting would-be terrorists.

There have been some technological advances, particularly in detecting explosives, weapons, and metal. Improvements in passenger screening at U.S. airports have been a key goal of the Federal Aviation Administration. Several airports are currently planning to install new equipment for baggage screening, such as thermal neutron activation (TNA) devices. TNA systems are, however, expensive, heavy (there is concern about floor-loading weight), and subject to a high rate of nuisance alarms. At about $1 million per machine, implementation is problematic. It is likely that the cost and weight will come down in the next few years. Moreover, other new technology for baggage and personnel screening is on the horizon.

Some technological advances that could aid in counterterrorism have run head-on into political and economic obstacles, curtailing the likelihood of implementation. For example, many authorities agree that the placement of microtaggants in the manufacturing process of explosive materials could force many terrorists to use less effective and more risky alternatives.[118] The microtaggants would survive an explosion and permit investigators to specifically identify where and when the material was sold. This approach has actually been around for quite a few years, but manufacturers have been reluctant to support the program, reportedly due to increased manufacturing costs. They also properly state that it would be of limited value unless every manufacturer in the world agreed to participate in the program.

SUMMARY

A dispassionate observer of international terrorism would probably conclude that "hype" is, indeed, a factor in the effect of terrorism on the world scene. This observer also would view countermeasures and expenditures as being out of proportion to the actual risk for most persons and companies. Our observer may agree that there is a need to better define terrorism.

While America is highly vulnerable to domestic and international terrorist attacks, such incidents are infrequent in the United States. The dispassionate observer would note that there is little the country can do to substantively mitigate its vulnerability. America will continue to be vulnerable despite our best efforts. Even if the nation were to expend vast sums for counterterrorism, the gain would be minimal, because there would always be unprotected targets.

While terrorist incidents have the potential of increasing at any time, no current evidence suggests that they will. It is conceivable to this observer that domestic terrorist attacks based on political or ideological motivations could increase, but these, too, are likely to remain infrequent.

Clearly, terrorism has had a significant influence on private security (particularly on proprietary security), especially in increased spending to protect overseas facilities and personnel. While there is no doubt that terrorism has been a major influence on protective services, there is presently no basis by which the true dollar value of terrorism can be assessed, either as a cost or as a source of revenues. Counterterrorism probably represents a fairly small portion of security revenues and expenditures--perhaps 2%--and it is likely that it will remain so for the next decade.

ENDNOTES

1. Leonard Silk, "Does Morality Have a Place in the Boardroom?" *Business Month*, October 1989, p. 11.

2. Thomas Murray, "Can Business Schools Teach Ethics?" *Business Month*, April 1987, p. 24.

3. Andy Pasztor and Rick Wartzman, "How A Spy for Boeing and His Pals Gleaned Data on Defense Plans," *The Wall Street Journal*, January 15, 1990, p. A1.

4. "An Ethical Double Standard," *Business Month*, December 1989, p. 7.

5. Silk, p. 11.

6. Ibid.

7. Thomas Murray, p. 25.

8. "An Ethical Double Standard," p. 7.

9. Robert McCrie, *Security Letter*, December 1, 1987, Part I.

10. "Ethics: Business Standards Viewed as Healthy," *Security*, March 1988, p. 12.

11. Orr Kelly, "Corporate Crime: The Untold Story," *U.S. News and World Report*, September 6, 1982, p. 25.

12. Robert Wasserman and Mark Moore, "Values in Policing," *Perspectives in Policing*, No. 8, National Institute of Justice, U.S. Department of Justice, November 1988, p. 1.

13. Paul Edwards (editor in chief), *Encyclopedia of Philosophy*, Volume III (New York: McMillian Company and The Free Press), 1967.

14. "Who Do We Trust," *Gallup Report*, December 1988.

15. "An Ethical Double Standard," p. 7.

16. Ibid.

17. Wasserman and Moore, p. 2.

18.   *Security Letter*, December 1, 1987, p. 1.

19.   Richard Hanselman, "A CEO's Perspective," *Security Management*, December 1981, p. 40.

20.   John Clark and Richard Hollinger, *Theft by Employees in Work Organizations* (Minneapolis: University of Minnesota, 1981).

21.   Kenneth Derr, "Security Management in Transition," *Security Management*, October 1982, p. 31.

22.   Max Thomas, "Classroom Conundrum: Profits + Ethics = ?" *Business Month*, February 1990, p. 6.

23.   Thomas Murray, p. 24.

24.   Allen Murray, "Protecting The Environment," Mobil Corporation, January 1990, p. 4.

25.   Ibid.

26.   McCrie, *Security Letter*, p. 1.

27.   Ibid.

28.   "Business Ethics Get Renewed Push," *The Wall Street Journal*, February 6, 1990, p. 1.

29.   Jack Kelly, "Poll: On-Job Drug Use Is Significant," *USA Today*, December 13, 1989, p. 1.

30.   "Final Report," The White House Conference for a Drug-Free America, June 1988.

31.   National Institute on Drug Abuse (NIDA), "National Household Survey on Drug Abuse: 1988 Population Estimates," p. 17. [Also see: Peter Bensinger, "Drug Testing in the Workplace," *The Annals* {The Private Security Industry: Issues and Tends}, American Academy of Political and Social Science, July 1988, pp. 43-50.]

32.   Michael McQueen and David Shribman, "Battle Against Drugs Is Chief Issue Facing Nation, Americans Say," *The Wall Street Journal*, September 22, 1989, p.1.

33.   Mary Graham, "Controlling drug abuse and crime: A research update," "Drugs and Crime," NIJ Report SNI 202, National Institute of Justice, U.S. Department of Justice, March/April 1987, p. 2. [Note: The source for this data may be a study conducted by the

Research Triangle Institute (RTI), which as early as 1983 reported a $47 billion figure for 1980. It appears that the $47 billion estimate may have been adjusted to $59 billion for 1987 by others reporting the RTI findings. Also see: David Warner, "Firms Urged to Fight Drug Abuse," *The Business Advocate*, U.S. Chamber of Commerce, July 1988, p.1.]

34.   "Final Report," The White House Conference for a Drug-Free America, June 1988.

35.   Donald Bacon, "Business Moves Against Drugs," *Nation's Business*, November 1989, p. 82. An estimate of $114 billion was reported by Warren True, "Drug Testing Arrives," *Oil & Gas Journal*, November 27, 1989, p. 13.

36.   James Cook, "The Paradox of Antidrug Enforcement," *Forbes*, November 13, 1989, p. 105, based on a 1984 House subcommittee report not further identified.

37.   Presented in a speech by Sam Huchins of the U.S. District Attorney's Office to a chapter meeting of the American Society for Industrial Security (ASIS), as reported in "Chapter News," *ASIS Dynamics*, January/February 1990, p. 30.

38.   Mark de Bernardo, "Employers' Role in War on Drugs," *The Drug-Free Workplace*, Institute for a Drug-Free Workplace, Fall 1989, p. 1.

39.   Robert Feldcamp, "Bush Drug Strategy Has Something for Everyone, But Not Nearly Enough," *Narcotics Demand Reduction Digest*, Washington Crime News Service, Vol. 1, No. 4, September, 1989, pp. 1-3.

40.   "NIDA Capsules: Highlights of the 1988 National Household Survey on Drug Abuse," National Institute on Drug Abuse.

41.   "Drugs of Abuse Testing Markets," Report No. A214B, Market Intelligence Research Company, July 1987.

42.   "The Drug Monitoring and Abuse Testing Business," Business Communications Co., Inc., Report C-104, Norwalk, CT., December 1988.

43.   "Security Wrap-Up: Drug Testing, Crime Trends," *Security*, April 1990, p. 9.

44.   "Drug Use Forecasting Update," National Institute of Justice Reports, Office of Justice Programs, U.S. Department of Justice, No. 215, July-August 1989, p. 8.

45.   "Final Report," The White House Conference for a Drug-Free America, June 1988.

46.   Christopher Innes, "Drug Use and Crime," State Prison Inmate Survey--1986, Bureau of Justice Statistics, U.S. Department of Justice, 1986.

47.   J. Thomas McEwen, Barbara Manili, and Edward Conners, "Employee Drug Testing Policies in Police Departments," *Research in Brief*, National Institute of Justice, U.S. Department of Justice, October 1986. [Also see: James Stewart, "Police and Drug Testing: A Look at Some Issues," *The Police Chief*, October 1986, pp. 27-32.]

48.   "Use of Drugs by Sworn Officers," Order No. D-18, San Francisco Police Department General Order Control Code (88-05), March 24, 1988.

49.   Cindy Skrzycki, "Taking a Risk on Rehabilitation," *The Washington Post*, April 6, 1989, p. C1.

50.   Donald Bacon, "Business Moves Against Drugs," *Nation's Business*, November 1989, p. 82.

51.   Jack Kelly, p. 1.

52.   David Warner, "Firms Urged to Fight Drug Abuse," *The Business Advocate*, U.S. Chamber of Commerce, July 1988, p. 1.

53.   Associated Press, "Few workers tested for drugs, study says," *The Seattle Times*, January 11, 1989, Section F (Business).

54.   The 12% figure correlates with a study by Bio-Analytical Technologies, Inc., of 8,000 job applicant tests, reported by "Getting Drugs Out of the Workplace," *Business Month*, November 1989, p. 18.

55.   "Drug Testing At Work," *The Drug-Free Workplace*, Institute for a Drug-Free Workplace, summer 1988, p. 11.

56.   Jack Kelly, p. 1.

57.   "Results of the 1989 Arthur Andersen enterprise survey," Arthur Andersen, November 1989.

58.   Stan Stahl, ed., *Commitment to Security*, National Center for Computer Crime Data, 1989, p. 22.

59.   Catherine Conly and J. Thomas McEwen, "Computer Crime," *NIJ Reports*, No. 218, January/February 1990, pp. 2-7.

60.   "Private Business to Benefit from Security Bulletin Board," *Security*, January 1989, p. 20.

61.   It is estimated that from 1% to 3% of all incidents are related to an "external human threat." See: Carl Jackson, "The Need for Security," *Datapro Reports on Information Security*, Datapro Research Corporation, McGraw-Hill, 1987.

62.   John Burgess, "Computer Virus Sparks a User Scare," *The Washington Post*, September 17, 1989.

63.   Stan Stahl, ed., *Commitment to Security*, National Center for Computer Crime Data, 1989, p. 12, based on data from the Computer and Business Equipment Manufacturers Association.

64.   John McAfee, "Managing the Virus Threat," *Computerworld*, February 13, 1989, p. 89.

65.   Ibid.

66.   John Hogan, "Thwarting the Information Thieves," *IEEE Spectrum*, July 1985, p. 32. [Note: This 11-page article provides an excellent overview of all aspects of electronic spying. Further, Hogan is not persuaded that the computer security threat is serious and provides useful viewpoints.]

67.   "Corporate Espionage Spreads," *American Business*, summer 1984, p. 2.

68.   For additional information about this topic, see: Bill Zalud, "Spy Business," *Security*, January 1989, pp. 52-55.

69.   "One in Four Florida Business Organizations Victims of Computer Crimes, Study Finds," *Corporate Security Digest*, June 19, 1989, p. 1.

70.   Carl Jackson, "The Need for Security," *Datapro Reports on Information Security*, Datapro Research Corporation, McGraw-Hill, 1987. [Note: Virtually the same data are reported in: Stan Stahl, ed., *Commitment to Security*, National Center for Computer Crime Data, 1989.]

71.   Ibid.

72.   Conly and McEwen, p. 3.

73.   "Computer Crime Survey," *Data Processing & Communications Security*, spring 1989, p. 5. The source of *Data Processing and Information Security* data was not reported. Virtually the same data are reported in: Stan Stahl, ed., *Commitment to Security*, National Center for Computer Crime Data (NCCCD), 1989, and in "Safeguarding Against Computer Crime," *The Lipman Report*, November 15, 1988. This latter article noted that the average known computer crime loss was $500,000. It is assumed that both articles used the NCCCD report as the source for their data.

74.   "Computer Crime, Computer Security, Computer Ethics," *Computer Crime Census 1988*, National Center for Computer Crime Data (NCCCD), as reported in: *Commitment to Security*, 1989, p. 28.

75.   "Safeguarding Against Computer Crime," *The Lipman Report*, November 15, 1988.

76.   Jack Bologna, "High-Tech Crime Is Here to Stay," *The White Paper*, National Association of Certified Fraud Examiners, Vol. 3, No. 1, spring 1989, pp. 3-4.

77.   "Computer Data Locks, Keys Market to Reach $1 Billion Annually in U.S. by 1993," *Corporate Security Digest*, August 1, 1988, p. 3.

78.   Stan Stahl, ed., *Commitment to Security*, National Center for Computer Crime Data (NCCCD), 1989, p. 18.

79.   The Frost and Sullivan study was not identified.

80.   John Burgess, "Race to Secure Computers Threatens Free Exchange of Data," *The Washington Post*, March 4, 1989, p. D11.

81.   Stan Stahl, ed., *Commitment to Security*, National Center for Computer Crime Data, 1989, reporting: *Computer Security Markets, #731*, 1987; *Data, Text, and Voice Encryption Worldwide Markets, #754*, 1988, International Resource Development, Inc.

82.   "Security Products and Services," *Leading Edge Reports* (Study LE 7203), March 1990.

83.   Ibid. See also Stan Stahl, ed., *Commitment to Security*, National Center for Computer Crime Data, 1989, p.18.

84.   John Burgess, "Hong Kong Authorities Seize Computer Disks, Books in Raid, *The Washington Post*, November 18, 1989, p. D1.

85.   "Foreign Protection of International Property Rights," International Trade Commission, 1988, as reported by the National Center for Computer Crime Data, p. 33.

86.   "Foreign Protection of International Property Rights," International Trade Commission, 1988, as reported by the National Center for Computer Crime Data, p. 33.

87.   David Churbuck, "Desktop Forgery," *Forbes*, November 27, 1989, pp. 246-253.

88.   See: Ian Murphy, "Who's Listening - Part 1," *Data Processing & Communications Security*, fall 1988, and "Who's Listening - Part 2," winter 1989.

89.   Stan Stahl, ed., *Commitment to Security*, National Center for Computer Crime Data, 1989, p. 15, citing Forcht, "Including Computer Security Topics in College Curriculum."

90.   Joanne Omang, "Businesses That Offer Defense Against Terrorism Are Booming," *The Washington Post*, January 3, 1986, p. A22.

91.   Press Conference Fact Sheet, International Conference on Terrorism, November 20, 1986, Washington, DC

92.   *Patterns of Global Terrorism: 1989*, Department of State Publication 9705, Office of the Secretary of State, Ambassador-at-Large for Counterterrorism, April 1990. [Reports from previous years were also consulted.]

93.   Ibid, p. 2.

94.   Ibid, pp. 2-5.

95.   "A Record Year for Terrorism in 1988," *Security Management*, May 1989, p. 116.

96.   Oliver Revell [Executive Assistant Director - Investigations, Federal Bureau of Investigations], "International Terrorism in the United States, *The Police Chief*, March 1989, pp. 16-22. Also, *Terrorism in the United States 1987*, Counterterrorism Section, Terrorist Research and Analytical Center, Federal Bureau of Investigation, U.S. Department of Justice, December 1987.

97.   *Patterns of Global Terrorism: 1989*, p. 23.

98.   According to the U.S. Department of State, 4,060,803 passports were issued in 1988. This report assumes that about 25% of the passport holders did not actually travel that year. It is likely that the 3 million figure is understated.

99.   John Strauchs, "Living with Violence Abroad," *Security Management*, June 1984, p. 30, citing U.S. Public Health Services statistics, and "Victims of Crime," Bureau of Justice Statistics Bulletin NCJ-79615, November 1981.

100.   William Cunningham and Philip Gross, *Prevention of Terrorism: Security Guidelines for Business and Other Organizations*, (McLean, Virginia: Hallcrest Press) June 1978, p. 3.

101.   *Terrorism in the United States 1987*, Counterterrorism Section, Terrorist Research and Analytical Center, Federal Bureau of Investigation, U.S. Department of Justice, December 1987, p. iv.

102.   *Patterns of Global Terrorism: 1988*, p. 4.

103.   "A Record Year for Terrorism in 1988," *Security Management*, May 1989, p.116.

104. William Corbett, "A Time to Redefine Policy?," *Security Management*, June 1990, p. 40.

105. Theodore Shackley, Robert Oatman and Richard Finney, "With a Little Help From Their Friends," *You're the Target*, New World Publishing, 1989, p. 48, citing Brian Jenkins, "Terrorism and Today's Leaders," *Leaders*, December 1986.

106. See "Multinational Firms Act to Protect Overseas Workers from Terrorism," *The Wall Street Journal*, April 29, 1986, Section 2, p. 1, for more information.

107. Kathy Passero, "Fearing Terrorism, Firms Limit Use of U.S. Carriers," *Corporate Travel*, May 1989.

108. Arthur Cotton Moore, "Yes, We Have to Beef Up Security, But Ugly Barriers Hand Terrorists Their First Victory. There Are Better Ways," *The Washingtonian*, July 1986, p. 87.

109. More information can be obtained by writing: OSAC, Bureau of Diplomatic Security, U.S. Department of State, Washington, D.C. 20520.

110. Revell.

111. For more information see: Matt Moffett, "Fear of Terrorists Directs New Attention to Illegal Immigrants," *The Wall Street Journal*, May 14, 1986, p. 1.

112. Theodore Shackley, Robert Oatman and Richard Finney, "A Look into the Future," *You're the Target*, New World Publishing, 1989, p. 48.

113. Revell, p. 16.

114. Alvin Buckelew, "The Threat of Technoterrorism," *Security Management*, November 1983, pp. 38-46.

115. Thomas O'Toole, "U.S. Tightens Guard on Nuclear Facilities," *The Washington Post*, August 27, 1985, p. A3. Of related interest, the U.S. Department of Energy maintains a security force of about 4,500 persons.

116. "Target: United States," *The Lipman Report*, April 15, 1989.

117. Revell, p. 19.

118. Larry Green, "Combatting Terrorism: Designing the Shield - Part II," *Consulting-Specifying Engineer*, February 1987, p. 65.

PART II

SECURITY RESOURCES

CHAPTER 4
DIMENSIONS OF PROTECTION

The roles, objectives, and components of the 2 major protective resources, private security and public law enforcement, need to be understood if comparisons are to be made between them. Further, it is important to recognize the emphasis and priorities of private security and the police in order to understand variations and similarities. This chapter also notes the increasing role of individuals, neighborhoods, and businesses in crime prevention as co-producers of protection. The concept of "co-production" combines the elements of private security, law enforcement, and citizens in a relationship of interdependence in maintaining order and in preventing crimes.

Most discussions in the literature compare private security and law enforcement on the basis of their sponsorship (private or public), the source of their authority (criminal vs. tort, property, and contract law), and functions or activities (shared or mutually exclusive). A common denominator for comparing law enforcement and private security can be generically described as protective functions or services. A classic security text, *Security Administration* (Post and Kingsbury), suggests 10 generic protective service functions of law enforcement and private security that are performed "in furtherance of some specified protective services goal": prevention, protection, enforcement, detection, investigation, deterrence, emergency services, reporting, inspections, and general service.[1]

Within this context, the crime prevention effort simply becomes one of the many functions that support a specific organizational goal: to protect lives and property. Labeling private security as "private police" (the term used in the earliest study of private security by Rand in 1971) unfairly and incorrectly restricts their scope. Also, the term "private police" invites comparisons from a police perspective rather than from the comprehensive framework of protective functions, including physical, information, and personnel security.

THE POLICE ROLE: CRIME CONTROL

American policing has its roots in private protective initiatives. Early settlements, frontiers, and colonies promoted the ideas of self-help and mutual aid.[2] Each new village and city had its version of citizen watchmen or private "door rattlers" until formal police organizations were created in the mid-1800s by state and local laws in larger cities. The initial mission of the public police was primarily one of order maintenance. As James Wilson noted, the Wickersham Report in 1931 evaluated the public police primarily on their effectiveness in combatting crime.[3] Since that time the police have become identified mainly with a societal mission or role of crime control.

In general, the literature describes the role of law enforcement as the prevention of crime, detection and apprehension of criminals, the protection of life and property, maintenance of public order, the regulation of traffic, and the performance of various auxiliary functions. The most visible activities of policing involve patrolling and investigation. Substantive and procedural criminal law prescribe specific guidelines for activities and procedures of the police. Yet, considerable discretion is exercised by both law enforcement agencies and police officers in the emphasis placed upon, and the disposition of, events.

Some of the earliest research on police activity suggested that between 80 and 90% of citizen demands for police services were non-crime-related.[4] Several studies over the last 20 years have consistently supported those findings. Despite differences in methodology and activity classification schemes, Eric Scott (1981) summarizes the conclusion to be drawn from these studies: "...the preponderance of evidence indicates that demand for, and police response to, noncriminal service requests comprises 80% of patrol officer workload."[5]

The crime-control-oriented components of the police role, then, are incongruent with actual behavior and tasks performed by police officers. Police researchers and practitioners have developed 2 responses to these findings: a professional model of policing and a service model. In the professional model, the importance of the police crime control mission is enhanced by attempting to relieve police officers of those tasks and activities which are not directly crime-related. Task reduction can be accomplished by completely eliminating the task, by using civilian or non-sworn personnel, or by transferring the tasks to other public agencies or social service organizations. No studies were found on the ability of the police to simply cease performing certain functions without a viable alternative mechanism for delivering the service to the public. Civilians have been increasingly used to release higher paid, skilled and trained sworn personnel to perform crime control tasks, but this generally involves only civilians in support functions, not call-response tasks. In the early 1980s, Eric Scott found that the majority of referrals (55%) were made not to external agencies, but to internal police department units or to other law enforcement agencies (23%).[6] It seems, then, that task elimination, "civilianization," and external agency referral does not necessarily reduce the high workload of non-crime-related police activities.

In the service model of policing, law enforcement becomes only 1 of several major missions of the police, and the other missions (e.g., community services and other non-crime-related tasks) become formally recognized, legitimized, and supported at a level commensurate with their importance. Interactions with citizens in these noncriminal activities are postulated to increase the overall level of police and public cooperation, and to produce greater citizen satisfactions with police performance in other noncriminal service tasks. These service activities range from fear reduction and community relations programs to highway safety and youth programs. Also included in the service model are the various approaches to the nebulous concept called "community policing."

Perhaps, this service model involving neighborhood or community policing is both a return to "order maintenance" and an attempt by law enforcement administrators to be closer and more responsive to perceived neighborhood security needs. George Kelling and James Stewart identify certain police roles that are viewed differently by the police and citizens:

- *Police saw their primary responsibility as crime control and solving crimes; citizens wanted police to improve the quality of urban life and create feelings of personal security, as well as to control crime*

- *Police wanted to be independent of political and neighborhood control--they viewed such accountability as tantamount to corruption; citizens wanted police to be accountable to neighborhoods-- inevitably a form of political accountability*

- *Police wanted to structure impersonal relations with citizens and neighborhoods; citizens wanted intimate relations with police*

111

- *Police tactics emphasized automobile preventive patrol and rapid response to calls for service; citizens wanted foot patrol or other tactics that would increase the quantity and improve the quality of police/citizen interaction (as well as rapid response)*

- *Police saw themselves as the thin blue line between order and chaos; citizens often saw themselves as the primary source of control, backed up by police*

- *Police emphasized centralized efficiency; citizens desired decentralized operations and local decision making. An expression of this is participation in meetings; police send community relations or crime prevention personnel outside the decision making chain of command for the neighborhood; citizens prefer personnel empowered to make decisions[7]*

This concern about police being isolated from the community is not new. Superintendent Brian Butcher in a book commemorating 150 years of the Norfolk, England, Constabulary noted:

In opposing the formation of the Norfolk Rural Police in 1839, the Rev. C. Brereton claimed that no place or hamlet was without a recognized guardian of the peace 'to whom any citizen can at all times, within 5 minutes, refer.' A professional force was seen as 'a movable rambling police,' which no one will ever know where to find.[8]

The traditional approach of having the police independent of citizens in neighborhoods, working in a "hands-off" mode, will likely change. Greater co-production of neighborhood (residential, business, etc.) security by citizens, law enforcement, and/or private security will occur as the members of various communities take a larger stake in decision making about their protective options.

The Rand and Private Security Task Force Reports of the 1970s stated that law enforcement primarily serves the public interest by providing a general level of protection for the community at large. Traditionally, the police role has been largely defined according to 3 broad categories: deterrence, suppression, and apprehension, as these terms relate to criminal activity. Responsibility for deterrence or reducing opportunities for crime is increasingly being assumed by private security, individuals, businesses, and citizen groups, sometimes with a coordinating function by the police. Suppression of crime by patrols, investigations, and police crackdown[9] as well as apprehensions have largely remained in the law enforcement domain. Given the growing use of other dimensions of protection, public law enforcement needs to be reexamined as one of several protective choices available for safety and security in the community--as part of a "community protective service network"[10] of public and private protective resources.

CITIZEN CRIME PREVENTION

Citizens and property owners are taking greater responsibility in protecting themselves. No data have thus far indicated that the public undertakes these responsibilities because of reduced confidence in the police. Law enforcement is one of numerous options or "protective choices" available to individuals and entities.[11] In addition to public law enforcement agencies, Post and Kingsbury suggest many "self-help" initiatives that include actions by individuals (locks, alarms, etc.), collective measures (proprietary security programs, community-based crime prevention), and commercial agencies (private security services and products).[12]

Neighborhood Watch, Crime Stoppers,[13] and other citizen-based programs complement police efforts in crime deterrence, suppression, and apprehension. Perhaps law enforcement executives have begun to realize that partnerships with nonpolice groups are necessary for effective crime prevention. A 1989 survey sponsored by the National Crime Prevention Council reported that "chief law enforcement executives acknowledged the limitations of law enforcement and the criminal justice system in preventing crime, and recognize a critical need for 'partnerships' with the citizenry, and other public and private sector agencies and institutions."[14]

Until the early 1970s citizen-initiated crime prevention programs usually were not encouraged by police agencies. Citizen patrols, especially, were discouraged and often viewed as "urban vigilantes."[15] A decade later, the Guardian Angels also encountered police indifference and antagonism as their street patrols comprised of young adults and adolescents were established in major cities. In recent years, however, police have recognized and encouraged greater citizen participation in crime prevention. In addition, through the efforts of the National Crime Prevention Council, the National Crime Prevention Institute, and other organizations, crime prevention programming and training have greatly increased.

The Hallcrest national surveys in the early 1980s found that over 90% of police and sheriffs' departments had established formal crime prevention programs; gradually, the police had reached out to the community to forge partnerships with neighborhood groups. The community both sought and embraced proactive programs such as block and apartment watches, property engraving, home security surveys, and street and building patrols. From the "canyon watches" of San Diego to the "alley watches" of Minneapolis, residents have increasingly taken a stake in the safety of their neighborhoods. Civic-minded volunteers have become active in patrolling their neighborhoods as "supervised offspring" of the police and have also started a renewal of police and sheriffs' auxiliary and reserve units.

Ironically, 1 study concluded that crime prevention programs sponsored by law enforcement agencies may actually increase citizen fears of crime. Nevertheless, the Neighborhood Watch and other community-based crime prevention programs, since their inception, have generally been acknowledged to have a measurable impact on crime. Interestingly, Herbert Jacob and Robert Lineberry, in their 3-decade study of police resources, concluded that citizens should take greater precautions with themselves and their property; but they thought it unlikely that "individual" private actions would overcome the national trends which seem to generate crime.[16] Yet, between 1975 and 1988 the percentage of households touched by crime declined 23%.[17] And in 1982, crime reported to the police had slightly decreased nationally for the first time, according to the FBI Uniform Crime Report program. These decreases were experienced in many major cities, not just smaller communities. Law enforcement administrators began praising Neighborhood Watch and other citizen crime prevention programs for contributing significantly to crime control in their communities.[18]

PRIVATE SECURITY ROLE: ASSET PROTECTION

Crime is one of many hazards that can cause a loss of assets in organizations. The main objective of private security is to protect these assets and to prevent losses. As noted by Norman Bottom and John Kostanoski, in their acronym, **WAECUP**, private security more broadly seeks to control 5 types of threats, of which crime is just one: Waste, Accidents, Errors, Crime, and Unethical Practices.[19] Waste and accidents erode company profits; modern technology has resulted in new potential hazards. Errors include not only production processes which impact product quality and customer satisfaction, but also the transmission and storage of information. Waste, accidents, and errors focus attention on an important aspect of many industrial security programs: the use of security personnel for safety and control (shipping, receiving, inventory) functions. Unethical practices (bribery, industrial espionage, etc.) can affect the corporation not only through adverse civil and criminal judgments, but also through loss of prestige.

Nearly 20 years ago, Thomas Scott and Marlys McPherson claimed that private security activities are "virtually identical in many respects to those carried out by the public police.[20] They suggest that the main differences between public and private "policing" are not the activities performed, but for whom the services are performed and the degree of authority exercised. These distinctions are not always clear, since occasionally private security personnel are given police powers within the limited area or premises in which they are employed. One-fourth of medium and large police departments in the 1981 Hallcrest national survey report giving special deputy or police powers to security personnel.

According to *Security Letter*, fear is another reason for having private security, especially in the business community. Private security operations exist to confront at least 5 fears:

- fear of unacceptable losses
- fear of excessive insurance costs or uninsurability
- fear of harm to executives or personnel
- fear of looking stupid after a loss
- fear of litigation[21]

Security and police tasks are depicted in **Figure 4.1** as a continuum in the Private Security Task Force (PSTF) Report.[22] The PSTF draws a distinction between services provided in 5 areas: 1) *input*--the manner in which the service is obtained (citizen or client); 2) *role or function*--predominant activity or purpose (crime response or crime prevention); 3) *targets*--the beneficiaries or objectives to which the service is directed (general public or specific clients); 4) *delivery system*--the mechanism through which services are provided (government agencies or profit-oriented enterprises); and 5) *output*--the end product of services performed (law enforcement/criminal apprehension or loss reduction/assets protection).

FIGURE 4.1 THE SECURITY CONTINUUM

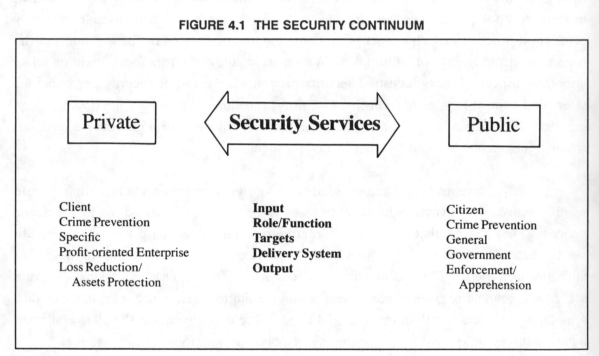

Private	Security Services	Public
Client	**Input**	Citizen
Crime Prevention	**Role/Function**	Crime Prevention
Specific	**Targets**	General
Profit-oriented Enterprise	**Delivery System**	Government
Loss Reduction/	**Output**	Enforcement/
Assets Protection		Apprehension

SHIFT IN TURF

According to several researchers, the growth of modern policing and its expansion from the latter part of the 19th Century through the 1960s and early 1970s resulted from the redistribution of private property protection responsibilities to the public sector.[23] The recent stabilization in law enforcement resources can be attributed in part to a shift back to the private sector of the primary responsibility for protection. This shift suggests a need for realignment of roles and relationships between the public and private sectors.

Colloquially, this phenomenon was expressed as a "turf issue" during the course of the Hallcrest research. Law enforcement agencies have enjoyed a dominant position in providing protective services to their communities but now foresees an erosion of their "turf" to private security. Numerous interviews with both proprietary and contract security managers have confirmed that this fundamental shift has already occurred through technological substitution for labor, and it is now simply being manifested in more highly visible human resources. This position was summarized by a leading police and security educator in an interview with a Hallcrest staff member:

If one were to make a big pie of the protection of the wealth, health, and welfare of a community, law enforcement would be a small part of the pie. Law enforcement which is basically manpower is now seeing a manpower shift to the private sector. A shift of protection resources to the private sector has already happened; cops only see the change in their turf.

This shift in turf seems to have resulted in widespread acceptance of the ability of private security to provide a reasonable level of protection. **Table 4.1** is an illustration of citizen dependence on private security. The table lists the responses of a resident survey regarding the private security protection they receive in the neighborhood of Starrett City, which is part of Brooklyn, in New York City.[24]

TABLE 4.1 RESPONDENTS' OPINIONS OF LIFE WITHOUT PRIVATE SECURITY	
	Percent Agreeing With Statement
Starrett City would not be safe	89.1%
Starrett City would have more crime	87.0%
People would stop shopping in Starrett City	56.5%
I would move from Starrett City	50.8%
More people would be robbed	89.9%
I would not go out at night	73.8%
I would change my way of life	52.5%
Starrett City would be a bad place to live	83.5%

SOURCE: Donovan and Walsh, *An Evaluation of Starrett City Security Services*, Pennsylvania State University, 1986.

Police Functions

In the Hallcrest survey of chiefs of police and sheriffs in all 50 states in 1981, the law enforcement executives were asked to rate on a scale of "highest to lowest" the importance to their agency of 9 functions and activities which are integral parts of the police mission. **Table 4.2** rank orders the frequency of their responses from highest to lowest priority.

These responses are consistent with an orientation to the formal police role of crime control suggested by the literature reviewed. In light of the renewed interest in order maintenance among police researchers and practitioners and its link to criminal activity levels, it is interesting to note that order maintenance is ranked immediately after crime control functions and activities and ahead of crime prevention. When asked how they thought law enforcement would rate these functions and activities, the proprietary and contract security managers surveyed rather accurately perceived the priorities of law enforcement--perhaps because so many security managers come from a law enforcement background.

TABLE 4.2 LAW ENFORCEMENT EXECUTIVE RATINGS OF LAW ENFORCEMENT FUNCTIONS *(Rank Ordered)*
1. protection of lives and property
2. arrest and prosecution of suspects
3. investigation of criminal incidents
4. maintaining public order
5. crime prevention
6. community relations
7. general assistance to the public
8. traffic enforcement
9. traffic control
N = 384
SOURCE: National Survey of Police Chiefs and Sheriffs, Hallcrest Systems, Inc., 1981

Activated burglar alarms are rated a high-priority response by about three-fourths of law enforcement, but small and medium departments rate alarm response a higher priority than large departments. In contrast, only about 40% of proprietary and contract security managers believed that law enforcement in their area is assigning a high response priority for burglar alarms.

Employee theft and shoplifting are low response priorities for law enforcement departments, regardless of department size. About 75% of departments report daily "investigation" of shoplifting crimes, even though they are a low response priority. Employee theft is the crime most frequently investigated by private security, but 85% of the law enforcement agencies report a medium-to-low response priority and infrequent investigation of this crime. Other "crimes against business" are commonly investigated by private security personnel but are seldom investigated by local law enforcement: computer-related crimes, embezzlement, cargo theft, and industrial espionage.

Chiefs and sheriffs were also asked to rate on a scale of highest to lowest the priority of response assigned by their agency to 12 typical calls for service, some of which are private-security-initiated. **Table 4.3** is a rank order of highest to lowest priority responses. A police officer in trouble was rated the "highest priority" response by 99% of law enforcement respondents, while a security guard in trouble was rated by only 60% as a "highest priority." The difference in response priorities for police and security officers in trouble is accurately perceived by private security.

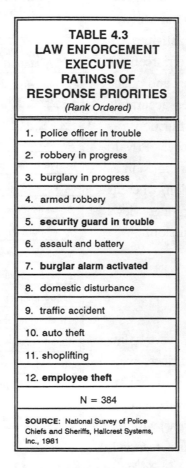

TABLE 4.3
LAW ENFORCEMENT EXECUTIVE RATINGS OF RESPONSE PRIORITIES
(Rank Ordered)

1. police officer in trouble
2. robbery in progress
3. burglary in progress
4. armed robbery
5. **security guard in trouble**
6. assault and battery
7. **burglar alarm activated**
8. domestic disturbance
9. traffic accident
10. auto theft
11. shoplifting
12. **employee theft**

N = 384

SOURCE: National Survey of Police Chiefs and Sheriffs, Hallcrest Systems, Inc., 1981

119

Private Security Functions

Proprietary and contract security managers were asked in the 1981 Hallcrest survey to rate on a scale of highest to lowest the priority of various security functions to their companies or organizations. The functions and activities are similar to those rated by law enforcement. **Table 4.4** displays a rank order of their responses from highest to lowest priority functions.

Proprietary and contract security managers strongly agree on the highest priorities for security functions and activities. The first 5 rank-ordered activities are exactly the same. Both law enforcement executives in the national survey and police officers in the case study sites accurately perceive these 5 top-rated functions as characteristic of private security. Private security clearly views its primary mission as loss (crime, fire, etc.) prevention, whereas law enforcement in its self-ratings views crime control as its primary mission.

Private Security Performance

In the 1981 Hallcrest surveys law enforcement executives and officers were asked to rate the performance of private security. Overall, they gave private security a fair-to-poor rating in most areas, with the highest ratings in reporting crimes, responding to alarms, reasonable use of force, and proper use of weapons. Low ratings were given to private security training, familiarity with legal powers, supervision, and preemployment background checks. However, a significant minority of the law enforcement executives and officers gave "don't know" responses, suggesting infrequent interaction with private security.

TABLE 4.4
SECURITY MANAGER RANKINGS OF PRIVATE SECURITY FUNCTIONS
(Rank Ordered)

PROPRIETARY MANAGERS	CONTRACTUAL MANAGERS
1. protection of lives & property	1. protection of lives & property
2. crime prevention	2. crime prevention
3. loss prevention	3. loss prevention
4. fire prevention	4. fire prevention
5. access control	5. access control
6. crime investigation	6. order maintenance
7. employee identification	7. employee identification
8. order maintenance	8. crime reporting
9. arrest/prosecution	9. arrest/prosecution
10. accident prevention	10. information security
11. crime reporting	11. crime investigation
12. information security	12. accident prevention
13. traffic control	13. traffic control
N = 676	N = 545

SOURCE: National Survey of Private Security Managers, Hallcrest Systems, Inc., 1981

Similar questions were asked of private security personnel. Proprietary security managers rated their own operations as "good," but gave contract security personnel lower rankings in most performance categories. For their part, contract security managers generally gave "poor" ratings to the performance of security firms in their geographical area, with the exception of alarm response. Finally, when the security managers were asked how they were rated by law enforcement, their perception proved to be more critical than the reality, suggesting a negative self-image on the part of contract security and, to a lesser extent, of proprietary security as well.

Hallcrest also probed perceptions of private security's contributions to specific areas of crime prevention and control. The results are shown in **Table 4.5**. Here again, law enforcement executives gave markedly lower ratings than did the private security managers. They agreed, however, on the areas that deserved the highest and lowest ratings. Thus, both the law enforcement executives and the security managers felt that private security was relatively effective in reducing the dollar loss of crime, and relatively ineffective in apprehending larger numbers

TABLE 4.5			
PRIVATE SECURITY CONTRIBUTIONS TO CRIME PREVENTION AND CONTROL			
Ratings by Law Enforcement and Private Security Managers			
	Law Enforcement	Proprietary Security	Contractual Security
overall contribution	2.2	1.5	1.2
reduction in volume of crime	2.4	1.7	1.5
reduction in direct dollar crime loss	2.2	1.6	1.5
number of criminal suspects apprehended	2.6	1.9	2.0
order maintenance	2.4	1.4	1.7
	N = 384	N = 676	N = 545

SCALE: 1 = very effective 2 = somewhat effective 3 = not effective

SOURCE: National Surveys of Police Chiefs and Sheriffs and Proprietary and Contractual Security Managers, Hallcrest Systems, Inc., 1981

of criminals. This ranking is consistent with the preventive orientation of private security, which is more concerned with loss control than with arrest and prosecution for crimes. Consistent, too, is the finding that proprietary security managers gave themselves highest marks for maintaining order.

Interestingly, when the private security managers were asked how their performance in these specific crime prevention and control activities was rated by law enforcement, they

121

correctly perceived that they would receive low ratings. Nevertheless (and in contrast to their perceptions of how law enforcement rated their overall performance), the security managers expected higher marks than they actually received.

The national survey results were reinforced by surveys of police personnel in the case-study sites. The conclusion seems clear: the impact of private security on the overall safety and security of communities has not been fully recognized by law enforcement administrators and operational personnel. Some law enforcement practitioners recognize the dramatic growth of private security but seem to feel that this growth results from a failure of law enforcement and the criminal justice system to do its job. In other words, if law enforcement were given adequate resources, there would be no need for widespread use of private security.

Private security executives, for their part, did not correlate the stabilization in law enforcement resources with public dissatisfaction of police performance, apathy toward the crime problem, or increased use of private protection. Rather, they perceived private security as filling a role that exists regardless of police performance--i.e., protecting property and assets that otherwise would go unprotected. Thus, in the national survey, the "inability of police to affect the crime rate" was ranked 8th among 12 factors presented to contract security managers as influencing client requests for their services.

COMPOSITION OF PRIVATE SECURITY

Definitions of Private Security

What is private security? Unfortunately, there is no generally accepted definition of private security; in fact, there is considerable disagreement. An overview of the positions taken by 2 government-sponsored reports and one text provides insight into the definitional problem.

The Rand Corporation in the earliest research on private security offered the following definition:

The terms private police and private security forces and security personnel are used generically in this report to include all types of private organizations and individuals providing all types of security-related services, including investigation, guard, patrol, lie detection, alarm, and armored transportation.[25]

The Private Security Task Force (PSTF) reviewed this particular definition and took exception to it from several perspectives. First, the PSTF found the Rand definition inadequate because it extended private security to essentially all police and security functions being performed by entities and individuals other than law enforcement agencies. The PSTF recognized that there are a number of quasi-public police such as park and recreation police, housing authorities, and so forth, which were not recognized by the Rand definition. Ironically, the PSTF specifically excluded these types of quasi-police organizations from the recommended standards and goals unless they were paid by private funds.

Further, the PSTF took exception to the definition formulated by the Rand study since it omitted the key elements of the client relationship and the profit nature of private security. Thus, for the purposes of developing standards and goals for private security, the PSTF adopted the following definition:

Private security includes those self-employed individuals and privately funded business entities and organizations providing security-related services to specific clientele for a fee, for the individual or entity that retains or employs them, or for themselves, in order to protect their persons, privates property, or interests from various hazards.[26]

While the PSTF definition is probably the most commonly cited definition for private security, it is not universally accepted. For example, Gion Green in *Introduction to Security* takes exception to the "profit" aspect of the PSTF definition. Green states that airports, hospitals, and schools, to name only 3 types of institutions, frequently employ private security resources without the "profit" orientation. He objects by stating the position that neither the profit nature of the organization being protected nor the source of funds by which personnel are paid are useful distinctions. He provides yet another definition:

...Private security can be defined as those individuals, organizations, and services other than public law enforcement agencies, which are engaged primarily in the prevention of crime, loss, or harm to specific individuals, organizations, or facilities.[27]

The Hallcrest staff finds that all of these definitions seem restricted to private security personnel and to security service businesses. Yet the fastest growing segment of private security is the manufacturing, distribution, and installation of security equipment and technological systems, which seems to be excluded from earlier definitions of private security. The obvious difficulty in establishing a universally accepted definition of private security is indicative of the fragmentation that exists in the private security field.

Proprietary and Contract Security

It is generally accepted that contractual security services and products are provided by a private organization for the protection of assets and personnel belonging to either a business, governmental, community, or individual client. Further, it is generally accepted that proprietary security includes the methods instituted, equipment owned, and personnel employed by an organization for the exclusive protection of its assets and personnel.

There is not general agreement, however, on the advantages of these types of private security arrangements. One often-stated advantage of contractual security is that it is less expensive. Manpower allocations can be more flexible, and contractual security personnel can be more impartial because they are enforcing policies and procedures which they did not establish. For example, if the employing organization excludes their employees from certain parts of the building, it may be easier for a nonemployee (contractual guard) to enforce this type of regulation.

The advantages often cited for proprietary security departments are that (1) they generally have higher quality personnel because of higher pay and fringe benefits; (2) the employing organization has more control over the activities because they are on the firm's payroll; (3) proprietary employees have more loyalty and thus more interest in the organization's goals; and (4) they have higher prestige than contract employees.

Throughout the research effort for this report it was apparent that the traditional issues of contract versus proprietary personnel are becoming less distinct in terms of their utilization. For example, individual and focus group interviews with a wide variety of security managers revealed general agreement that, in the future, security executives will tend to become "brokers" in that they will use contract personnel for certain tasks and rely on proprietary personnel for other tasks.

Specific Protective Measures

It is generally recognized that "protective measures" include 3 basic areas: physical security, information security, and personnel security. Each area is briefly described in the following paragraphs.

Physical Security

The 3 broad categories that comprise physical security are, essentially: (1) controlling and monitoring the access of persons and vehicles, (2) preventing and detecting unauthorized intrusions and (3) safeguarding property (information, buildings, materials, and equipment, etc.). The extent and use of these physical means are largely determined by the potential threats to security and safety and the overall vulnerability of a particular facility. In some cases--for example, banks and nuclear plants--the minimum standards of protection are mandated by a government authority.

Logically, physical security measures begin with protection of the perimeter. Generally recognized measures include physical barriers (fences, gates, walls, and natural barriers), locking systems, security lighting, closed-circuit television (CCTV), intrusion detection sensors, as well as the traditional guards, used either as roving patrols or at guard stations. Another major component of physical security is the widespread use of access control systems. These systems can be as simple as a basic key control system, or as sophisticated as proximity or biometric access control systems. The key issues in choosing the appropriate level of perimeter protection are the vulnerability and criticality of the premises to be protected.

The interior spaces of a facility are typically protected by using alarms, locks, electronic access control, and surveillance systems, either individually or in combination. The trend in recent years has been to integrate the interior space protection procedures with heating, ventilation, air conditioning, and power generating systems at a central monitoring station normally staffed by security personnel.

The key resources in physical security are guards, which are the most visible component of the many available physical security options. Guards have various responsibilities such as patrolling on foot and in vehicles, maintaining fixed security posts, monitoring reception/entrance areas, and overseeing the interior space protection systems.

Information Security

Historically, information security has been largely associated with the handling of classified government information. However, virtually all organizations generate sensitive information which may need to be kept confidential. Information that requires protection commonly includes customer mailing lists, research and development information (as it relates to current or projected products or services), as well as budgets and other financial information critical to the operation of the organization. Theft of critical, proprietary information can have effects just as disastrous to corporate profits as direct loss of physical items through fraud or sabotage.

Other aspects of information security include the disposal of outdated information, off-site storage of records, and the ability to recover computer capabilities in the event of a disaster. Frequently, banks, financial institutions and other business operations have back-up or disaster recovery capability to continue operations.

Clearly, the most prominent issue in information security today is computer security because of the increasing frequency of computer crimes and the vast amounts of information stored in computer systems and transmitted via telecommunication links. A key concern in information security today is that much of the information is stored on computers and can be, in most cases, transferred to floppy disks or sent by a modem and thus removed from an organization relatively easily.

Over the last decade, the insurance industry, led by Lloyd's of London, developed unique coverage for losses involving computer systems and the information contained within the systems. The largest future increases in insurance costs for businesses and organizations will likely be for expanded coverage of the risks involved in maintaining and transmitting information via computers and telecommunication systems.

Personnel Security

Personnel security may include background checks of prospective employees, programs to encourage security awareness among employees, fidelity bonds for certain employees, and protection for key executives. Executive protection is a growing concern for many organizations and may involve additional access and communications controls at the office, residential security measures at the executive's home, special precautions for commuting and travel, and trained chauffeurs and bodyguards. Some states prohibit private guards from carrying concealed weapons--a prohibition which encourages the hiring of off-duty police officers as bodyguards, and which complicates the problem of protecting executives traveling from one state to another. .

MAJOR PRIVATE SECURITY COMPONENTS

For purposes of this research, Hallcrest has divided private security into the following 9 categories:

- Proprietary Security
- Guard and Patrol Services
- Alarm Services
- Private Investigations
- Armored Car Services
- Locksmiths
- Consultants
- Security Equipment Manufacturing and Distributing
- Other

Each of these categories is discussed in detail in Chapter 6, **Security Market Analysis**. This section simply presents a brief overview of these major private security components to illustrate the wide variety of security services, technology, and products used throughout the country.

Proprietary Security Programs

Security programs in business, government, and other organizations are generally organized to protect the assets of the organization and to prevent or control losses. The previous chapters focused on crime, which is only 1 category of potential loss. Equally important are losses resulting from vandalism, accidents, fire, and natural disasters, as well as such intangibles as damage to reputation. For this reason, directors of security frequently report to the top management of the organization. In the 1981 Hallcrest survey of proprietary security managers, 46% of respondents said they reported to a vice president or higher corporate officer. Perhaps an emerging trend will be to place security within the organization's larger "risk management" program, encompassing not only security, but also internal audit, safety, insurance, fire prevention, and perhaps facility management. The legal basis for proprietary security programs in the United States is rooted in the English common-law tradition and right to engage others to protect property, as well as the U.S. constitutional right of persons to defend themselves and their property. Some states have also enacted statutes to delineate specifically the authority of individuals to protect themselves and their property and to hire others to exercise those rights on their behalf.

Guard and Patrol Services

Many people equate the private security industry with guard services. That is, for those who are unfamiliar with the various components of private security, guard services represent the totality of private security. This perception exists because for most people, this is the only element of private security that they will come in contact with; also, guard companies are clearly the most visible component of and largest employer in the contract security industry. Guard services are provided to almost every sector of the American economy. For example, manufacturing, finance, transportation, retailing, health care, and virtually every other organization and industry group contract for guard services. Primary services include:

- prevention and/or detection of unauthorized entry or activity
- prevention and/or detection of fire, theft, and losses
- control and regulation of traffic, either vehicular or pedestrian
- protection of individuals from bodily harm
- enforcement of rules, regulations, and policies related to asset protection

Alarm Services

Alarm service is one of the fastest growing components of private security primarily because of the rising use of residential alarms and rapid technological advances. The movement away from a hard-wire or "telephone-line technology" to a new "wireless technology" has been one of the most significant changes in the security field in the last decade.

Alarm personnel include 4 categories of employees: alarm sales personnel, alarm systems installers/technicians, alarm monitoring personnel, and alarm respondents or "runners." Alarm sales personnel have direct contact with the potential customer in the sale of systems. The alarm installers/technicians are trained to install the various systems as well as to provide maintenance and emergency service. Alarm monitoring personnel at central stations evaluate alarm conditions and notify public safety agencies, subscribers, and/or other alarm company personnel of activated alarm conditions. Alarm runners respond to alarm conditions at the protected site.

Private Investigations

Most people are aware of the private investigator (PI) component of private security because of the number of television shows which have highlighted this type of private security service. However, it must be noted that most real PIs do not see much similarity with their work in these television versions.

Many law firms and insurance companies use investigative services and personnel on a continuous basis. In addition, private investigative services and personnel are commonly retained for:

- background investigations including credit checks on personnel applicants
- internal theft or other employee crimes
- undercover drug investigations
- the location or recovery of stolen property
- the securing of evidence to be used before investigating committees, boards, or in civil or criminal trials

Armored Car Services

Armored car services provide heavily armored vehicles and armed guards to transport currency, coins, securities, precious metals, jewelry, credit cards, and other items of high value. The proliferation of automatic teller machines, the trend toward contracting for the emptying of municipal parking meters, the prevalence of high crime areas, curtailed police escorts for merchants carrying cash, and interest rates which make money more time-sensitive--all have contributed to the market for armored car services. The cost of armored trucks and fidelity insurance is a significant entrance barrier, and the industry is therefore dominated by a few large firms. However, local firms have also carved out their own marketplace, and a few guard companies also provide armored car services.

Not only do armored car companies offer protection to business entities, but they also have been the targets of major criminal attacks. Armored car robberies have involved catastrophic loss. For example, an attack on a Brinks cargo valued at $1.6 million, though foiled, resulted in the deaths of 2 police officers and a guard. Also, the largest thefts in U.S. history--in the past decade, all in New York State--have involved armored car firms: $7.9 million stolen from Wells Fargo (1985), $11 million from Sentry Armored Car (1982), and $10.8 million from Armored Motor Service of America (1990).

Locksmiths

An estimated 70,000 locksmiths install a variety of locking devices for industrial, commercial, and residential customers. In addition, many lock shops sell, install, and repair safes and vaults. Also, some locksmiths sell and install alarm and electronic access control systems, usually in the residential market.

Security Consultant Services

Four generally accepted areas comprise security consultant services: (1) engineering-related, (2) management, (3) executive protection, and (4) computer security. Consultants in each area are usually well-educated people, highly trained to provide the level of service that is expected by their clients.

Engineering-related security consultants typically are involved with the design of security systems and the development of specifications and engineering drawings for both technological and physical security measures. The services normally are based on a survey which determines the need for the protection of assets and which develops the most cost-effective method for implementing security systems. In most cases the consultants/security engineers work closely with architects and the client during the design and installation stages.

Security management consultants conduct security surveys, design security awareness programs, analyze specific loss problems, and structure asset protection programs with associated budget and staffing plans. In some cases, they provide unique services which may require considerable expertise in law, accounting, or business merger and acquisition practices; they may also serve as expert witnesses in litigation cases.

Crisis management and executive protection consultants are involved in planning the protection of key corporate executives and facilities. The executive protection segment of private security has grown quite rapidly, especially because of fear of terrorism and the multinational locations and risk-exposure of many U.S. companies. These consultants develop contingency plans to enable management to respond to crises from external as well as internal sources; the emphasis is on executive kidnapping and extortion attempts.

Computer security consultant services are expanding to meet the growing need to protect trade secrets and computer-based information. Computer security consultants provide services such as auditing of EDP systems, developing security software and data encryption, and conducting risk assessments.

Manufacturers and Distributors

The manufacturing component is a continually expanding sector of private security. Currently about 2,500 companies in the U.S. manufacture and/or distribute security equipment; the Bell Atlantic/ASIS *Security Industry Buyers Guide* for 1990 lists 560 product categories.

Examples of major types of equipment manufacturers included in this technological component of private security are listed below.

- Access control
- Closed-circuit television
- Alarms
- Bomb detection systems
- Metal detection
- Electronic article surveillance devices
- Computer security shielding
- Telephone security
- Security lighting
- Security fencing
- Safes and vaults
- Security locks

Other

More than 20 miscellaneous segments of the private security industry, separate from the major components mentioned above, can be identified. These segments include businesses that specialize in such areas as:

- Guard dogs
- Drug testing
- Forensic analysis
- Security insurance underwriting
- Security market research
- Security publishing
- Security storage
- Security training
- Shopping (honesty) services
- Honesty testing
- Uniform rental/sales

As mentioned earlier, a market analysis of each of the 9 components of private security along with revenues/expenditures, numbers of companies, employment, and other trends are presented in Chapter 6.

END NOTES

1.   Richard Post and Arthur Kingsbury, *Security Administration: An Introduction* (Springfield, IL: Charles Thomas, 1977), p. 473.

2.   Milton Lipson, "Private Security: A Retrospective," *The Annals*, The American Academy of Political and Social Science, Sage Publications, July 1988, p. 14.

3.   James Wilson, *Varieties of Police Behavior* (Cambridge, MA: Harvard University Press, 1968).

4.   Douglas Gourley, "Police-Public Relations," *The Annals*, American Academy of Political and Social Sciences, 1954: p. 291; Charlotte Epstein, *Intergroup Relations for Police Officers* (Baltimore, MD: Williams and Wilkins, 1962).

5.   Eric Scott, *Calls for Service: Citizen Demand and Initial Police Response* (Bloomington, IN: Workshop in Political Theory and Policy Analysis, Indiana University, 1981), p. 6.

6.   Eric Scott, *Police Referral in Metropolitan Areas* (Bloomington, IN: Workshop in Political Theory and Policy Analysis, Indiana University, 1981), p. 29.

7.   George Kelling and James Stewart, "Neighborhoods and Police: The Maintenance of Civil Authority," *Perspectives on Policing*, National Institute of Justice, May 1989, p. 7-8.

8.   Brian Butcher, *A Movable Rambling Police*, Norfolk, England, Police Constabulary, 1989, p. 111.

9.   For an interesting article on crackdowns by the police, see Lawrence Sherman, "Police Crackdowns," *NIJ Reports*, March/April 1990, pp. 2-6.

10.   Post and Kingsbury, (1977: 893)

11.   Ibid.

12.   Ibid, p. 7.

13.   For a summary evaluation report, see Dennis Rosenbaum, Arthur Lurigio, and Paul Lavrakas, "Crime Stoppers - A National Evaluation," *Research in Brief*, National Institute of Justice, September 1986.

14.   National Crime Prevention Council, "Crime Prevention Beliefs, Policies, and Practices of Chief Law Enforcement Executives: Results of a National Survey," February 1989.

15.   Gary Marx and Dane Archer, "The Urban Vigilante," *Psychology Today*, January 1973, p. 45.

16.   Herbert Jacob and Robert Lineberry, *Governmental Responses to Crime: Executive Summary* (Evanston, IL: Center for Urban Affairs and Policy Research, Northwestern University, 1982).

17.   *Households Touched By Crime, 1988*, by the Bureau of Justice Statistics, U.S. Department of Justice, June 1989.

18.   For an assessment of Neighborhood Crime Prevention Programs and their impact, see Judith Feins, *Partnerships for Neighborhood Crime Prevention*, National Institute of Justice, 1983. Also, for a series of excellent articles on situational crime prevention, see *Journal of Security Administration*, December 1988.

19.   Norman Bottom, Jr. and John Kostanoski, "An Informational Theory of Security," *Journal of Security Administration*, Vol. 4 No.1, spring 1981, p. 1.

20.   Thomas Scott and Marlys McPherson, "The Development of the Private Sector of the Criminal Justice System," *Law and Society Review*, Vol. 6 No. 2, 1971, pp. 273-274.

21.   *Security Letter*, November 1, 1983, Vol. XIII, No. 21.

22.   National Advisory Committee on Criminal Justice Standards and Goals, *Report of the Task Force on Private Security* (Washington, D.C.: U.S. Government Printing Office, 1976), p. 7.

23.   For an excellent review of public/private sector shifts in protective responsibility, see Clifford Shearing and Philip Stenning, "Modern Private Security: Its Growth and Implications," in Michael Tonry and Norval Morris, ed., *Crime and Justice: An Annual Review of Research*, Vol. 3 (Chicago, IL: University of Chicago Press, 1981); see also James Calder, "The Security-Criminal Justice Connection: Toward the Elimination of Separate-But-Equal Status," *Journal of Security Administration*, Vol. 3 No. 2, fall 1980.

24.   Edwin Donovan and William Walsh, *An Evaluation of Starrett City Security Services*, (a research project conducted by The Pennsylvania State University with a grant from Starrett Realty Corporation, Brooklyn, New York), April 1986, p. 62. This evaluation is perhaps the first empirical study of neighborhood private security and serves as a useful model for other applied researchers.

25.   James Kakalik, and Sorrel Wildhorn, *Private Police in the United States: Findings and Recommendations* (Washington, D.C.: U.S. Government Printing Office, 1971), Vol. I, p. 3, R-869-/DOJ.

26.   *Private Security: Report of the Task Force on Private Security*, (Washington, D.C.: U.S. Government Printing Office, 1976), p. 4.

27.   Gion Green, *Introduction to Security*, 3rd Edition, (Stoncham, MA: Butterworth Publishers, Inc., 1981), p. 25.

CHAPTER 5
SECURITY PERSONNEL ISSUES

This chapter focuses on several personnel aspects of the private security field. Specifically addressed are changes in personnel characteristics, education and training, compensation, and standards for and regulation of private security. These issues largely affect the quality of private security services. Also, some comparisons between private security and public law enforcement personnel are made in several areas. Because most published information about security practitioners pertains to security guards, the following section primarily profiles the characteristics of security guards and outlines the changes noted over the past 2 decades.

PERSONNEL CHARACTERISTICS

The well-worn, negative stereotype of the aged night watchman still exists among segments of the public and the law enforcement community. When the 1971 Rand Corporation study described the "typical private guard," it became the prevailing stereotype not only for security guards but also for many other security workers over the next 10 to 15 years:

> *The typical private guard is an aging white male who is poorly educated and poorly paid ... he has the following characteristics. His average age is between 40-55; he has little education beyond the ninth grade; he has had a few years of experience in private security; he earns a marginal wage ... many are unskilled; some have retired from a low-level civil service or military career ...*[1]

The Rand researchers further reported: "The fact is the average security guard in this country is underscreened, undertrained, undersupervised, and underpaid."[2]

Beginning with the Rand Corporation study and continuing to the present time, there has been limited research on the types of personnel entering private security. In some cases--for example, St. Louis, Missouri, and a section of New York City--some specific data are available. However, most of the published material on the personnel characteristics of private security comes from perceptions, assumptions, and other nonscientific approaches to the issue.

St. Louis, Missouri, offers an interesting opportunity to examine, from a longitudinal perspective, basic demographic information regarding private security employees for 3 benchmark years (1959, 1975, and 1989) during a 30-year period. Through the cooperation of the St. Louis Metropolitan Police Department, the Hallcrest researchers have compiled data on the personal backgrounds of all security personnel licensed by the St. Louis Police for the benchmark years. **Table 5.1** depicts the number of St. Louis security personnel for each benchmark year along with personal background profiles.

The changes over the 30-year period are rather significant. For example, during this time the continuing increase of licensed private security personnel is dramatic, especially in a city with declining population and a police department with fewer officers than 15 or 30 years before.

TABLE 5.1 CHARACTERISTICS OF PRIVATE SECURITY PERSONNEL ST. LOUIS, MISSOURI (1959-1989)			
Total Licensed Security Personnel	*1959 n=819*	*1975 n=2,977*	*1989 n=4,322*
Profile Data	%	%	%
Sex			
Male	100	93	86
Female	0	7	14
Race			
Caucasian	90	50	49
Black	10	50	51
Other	0	0	0
Age			
Average (in yrs.)	52	42	N/A
24 and under		13	14
25-34		21	38
35-44		22	22
45-54		22	11
55-64		16	10
65-74		5	4
75 and over		0.2	1
Height (average)	N/A	5'8"	N/A
Weight (average)	N/A	181	N/A
Education (average)	9	11	See Note
Marital Status (%)			
Married	74	50	50
Single	19	43	50
Divorced	7	7	

Totals may not add to 100% due to rounding

Note: Averages not available, but data are greater than 12 years; 1535 equal to 12 years: 2201; less than 12 years: 586

Other trends over this 30-year period include:

- The number of women in private security has doubled every 15 years.

- Percentages for Black and Caucasian security employees remained constant at about 50% over the past 15 years. Note, however, that the increase in Black security personnel is striking compared to 1959, when only 10% of total security workers were minorities.

- The average age of private security employees is lower, with the majority under the age of 35 by 1989, compared to the average age of 42 in 1975 and 52 in 1959.

- Educational achievement has increased from an average of 9 years in 1959 to 11 years in 1975; by 1989 more than 85% of security personnel had 12 or more years of formal education.

TABLE 5.2 STARRETT PERSONNEL CHARACTERISTICS		
	Starrett (n=54)	NYCPD (n=141)
Age (average)	39	36
Sex		
Male	90.7%	93.6%
Female	9.3%	6.4%
Race		
White	50.0%	78.0%
Black	35.2%	11.3%
Hispanic	14.8%	7.1%
Refused to state	--	3.6%
Education	High School Graduate	Some College
Average Years Employment	5 years	12 years

A similar collection and analysis of private security demographic data was reported by William Walsh in the first issue of *Security Journal*.[3] Dr. Walsh and his colleague, Edwin Donovan, conducted a comprehensive evaluation of private security operations in Starrett City, a 20,000-resident neighborhood in the borough of Brooklyn in New York City. As part of the study, they surveyed the personal backgrounds of Starrett City's proprietary security officers and of New York City police officers in the precinct surrounding Starrett City. **Table 5.2** presents the profiles of these 2 groups.[4] The major findings relevant to private security personnel are similar to the St. Louis study.

- Educational attainment of high school graduation or higher was realized by 83% of the security officers in Starrett City.

- The Starrett City security force was split evenly between minorities and Caucasians.

The average age of 39 was close to or slightly above the St. Louis average. However, the Starrett City security force is proprietary while the majority of the security personnel in the St. Louis study are contractual. Contractual personnel are usually younger than the more career-oriented proprietary security guards.

While most attention has been focused upon security guard characteristics in this and earlier studies, a composite of the average security manager is useful. In an attempt to profile security decision makers in businesses throughout the country, a *Security* magazine survey in 1987 revealed the following composite:

> *The average security manager was a 45-year-old male, earning $42,000 a year, married, a Republican, and with a bachelor's degree or better.*[5]

Interestingly, this average salary for security managers roughly approximates the annual salary range of $39,530 to $45,150 for police chiefs and sheriffs in jurisdictions between 25,000 and 50,000 in population.[6]

To facilitate comparisons of private security and law enforcement personnel along the same dimensions, one example of police personnel profiling is included. Research on the demographic profile of more than 3,000 public law enforcement officers has been done at the University of Illinois Police Training Institute. The most recent study findings by Gene Westergren are contained in **Table 5.3**.

TABLE 5.3 POLICE RECRUIT PROFILE		1986	1987	1988	Average
Age		26.2 yrs.	26.4 yrs.	26.4 yrs.	26.4 yrs.
Sex					
	Male	94.2%	92.8%	88.8%	92.05%
	Female	5.8%	7.2%	11.2%	8.0%
Race					
	White	94.7%	89.7%	96.3%	93.3%
	Black	5.3%	10.3%	3.75%	6.7%
Education		13.8 yrs.	13.5 yrs.	13.6 yrs.	13.6 yrs.

Based on the available research (supplemented by Hallcrest's literature reviews and interviews), it seems that the long-standing, rather negative stereotype of the private security guard is being replaced. The positive demographic trends over the past 20 years now indicate that the contemporary private security guard is better educated and younger. Also, security organizations currently employ more women and minorities than before.

By contrast, law enforcement officers seem to be somewhat younger than private security guard personnel. Public law enforcement probably employs fewer minorities and women than private security. Law enforcement officers' educational attainment at entry is slightly higher than for private security personnel.

Although the Hallcrest staff disagree, some of the literature indicates that technological changes will likely reduce the number of private security personnel in the next century. Cost is the significant factor--in that personnel costs are clearly the most expensive component of the security operations in most companies. As the cost for people resources increases and the cost for technology decreases, there will, according to some projections, be a shift toward technology replacing personnel.[7] However, at least 1 writer has an interesting observation on the subject: "Guards in some companies will continue to exist, even if they can be replaced by technology, because the chairman of the board does not want to be greeted by a robot."[8]

PERSONNEL SCREENING

The Hallcrest national surveys of contractual and corporate security managers in the early 1980s revealed that both groups used similar techniques for screening prospective employees. Contract security managers reported application review and interviewing (94%), reference checks (80%), criminal history checks (73%), background investigations (59%), and fingerprint checks (58%). Less frequent were polygraph exams, psychological tests, and honesty testing. Proprietary security managers generally followed the same procedures, though they were less likely to make criminal history checks (66%) or fingerprint checks (39%). The field and focus group interviews conducted during 1989-90 disclosed no dramatic changes in security screening practices except that fewer polygraph exams are administered as a result of restrictive federal legislation.

141

In the above-mentioned national surveys, virtually all security managers and law enforcement executives favored mandatory criminal history checks for security personnel. The need for such background checks is illustrated by the situation in California, where about 15,000 applications for security licenses (nearly 20% of the total) are rejected each year because checks reveal criminal convictions, despite the fact that applicants are advised that such a records check is part of the licensing process. Clearly, without such criminal record searches thousands of previously convicted criminals could obtain employment in private security. In states with no licensing agency and no access to criminal history record depositories, it is extremely difficult to validate applicant information concerning prior arrests and convictions. The dilemma is how to balance civil liberty concerns with the need to protect society from abuses by private security personnel. Until all security employers are granted access to criminal history records for purposes of screening applicants, the potential for abuse will remain high because of the uncertainties inherent in the selection process.

ATTRITION

Contract guard security managers surveyed by Hallcrest in 1981 reported an average annual personnel turnover rate of 121%, with a high of 300%. Field and focus group interviews in 1989 disclosed a similar turnover pattern. Although attrition data are not available for proprietary security personnel, field interviews lead the Hallcrest staff to conclude that the annual turnover rate is at least 75% less than for contract guard security personnel. Most contract private security agencies are reluctant to release figures regarding turnover since high numbers would have a negative connotation.

Nearly 15 years ago, the Private Security Task Force reported a concept related to security personnel turnover that has been generally accepted as the "vicious circle." The vicious circle is created by factors which are typically regarded as "norms" within the security guard industry:

- little or no training
- low salaries
- marginal personnel
- little/no promotional opportunities
- ineffective performance

It appears that a cause-effect relationship exists among all of these factors, and they tend to result in high turnover, especially at the low-salary positions.

Many private security executives are defensive on this matter and often use the excuse that "the client will not foot the bill" to justify their inability to retain employees. A counterpoint is found in a study conducted by the Private Security Task Force; it revealed that in the greater Philadelphia area, 72% of the respondents (industrial, commercial, and financial businesses) indicated their willingness to spend more for security if the qualifications of personnel and/or quality of security services were improved.[9]

Until significant advances are made in the areas of training, salary, promotional opportunities, and personnel supervision, the high attrition rate will continue, undermining efforts to upgrade private security.

ARMED PERSONNEL

The Rand study 20 years ago found that 50% of both contract and proprietary guards carried a firearm at least 25% of the time. The 1981 Hallcrest surveys of contract security managers revealed that fewer than 10% of their personnel were armed. The Hallcrest surveys also found that proprietary security guards carry arms slightly more frequently than contract guards. The evidence provided by these data, the literature review, and field interviews indicates a dramatic decrease in the carrying of firearms by security guards in the past 2 decades.

One inescapable fact found during the earlier Hallcrest study is that firearms tend to be used when they are carried. For proprietary security and alarm personnel, the percentages were nearly the same for those who reported ever having carried a gun on any security assignment and those who reported using a firearm on a security assignment. In addition, it appears that those who carry firearms feel that their jobs require them, since about the same proportion of security employees reported carrying and needing a firearm.

The 1981 Hallcrest national surveys and the 1989 field interviews disclosed that firearms training for armed security personnel probably does not exceed 8 hours on the average. This finding does not necessarily indicate a lack of firearms instruction, since many security personnel have received prior firearms training by the military or by law enforcement. Two disturbing aspects concerning firearms training were revealed:

- A large part of firearms training concentrates on the mechanical aspects of firing a gun and on weapons safety, rather than on situations which could be encountered in actual assignments.

- About 40% of armed contract security personnel seem to be "self-taught" in the use of firearms. While sports or recreational weapons training may be technically excellent, it is hardly relevant to the situations potentially encountered by security personnel.

The Private Security Task Force (PSTF) called for 24 hours of firearms training (or evidence of competence) prior to assignment, including 3 hours devoted to legal and policy restraints on firearms use. This requirement seems entirely reasonable, yet fewer than 10 states meet the PSTF standard. In the absence of state requirements, the security industry apparently has not taken the initiative to provide adequate levels of firearms training.

With few exceptions, the 1989-90 field and focus group interviews with security practitioners revealed agreement that the trend toward unarmed security personnel will continue in the future. By the year 2000, the Hallcrest staff project that not more than 5% of private security operational personnel will be armed.

TRAINING AND EDUCATION

Operational Training

For at least 20 years, lack of training has been a matter of great concern not only to people employed in private security but also to public law enforcement officials and to the clients of private security organizations. The importance placed on training by private security practitioners was evident in a survey of participants at the International Security

Conference (ISC-East) in August, 1989. On the question, "What, in your opinion, is the biggest challenge facing private security?" the most frequent response was "lack of security training." To place this response in perspective, **Table 5.4** reflects a summary of the total responses to this significant question.

Richter Moore, who studies how guard training relates to liability cases recently noted, "Only when security companies or companies with their own security guards find liability verdicts exceed the cost of training will they be concerned with training."[10] For contract guard security firms, preassignment training is almost always an overhead expense, so it is to the company's advantage to pass on as much training as possible to the client's job site. Proprietary security, on the other hand, provides more training for its personnel; this is 1 of the advantages often cited for maintaining a proprietary security force.

TABLE 5.4 CHALLENGES FACING PRIVATE SECURITY	
Challenges	**Percentage**
Lack of security training	26%
Lack of product standards, connectability	18%
Low pay for security staff	14%
Lack of top corporate management support	10%
Insurance costs	8%
Government rules and regulations	6%
Low budgets	5%
Poor public image	4%
Privatization	4%
Acquisitions, mergers, buyouts in security	2%
Privacy concerns	2%

Note: Does not include 100% because of rounding.
SOURCE: *Security*, 1989

The Private Security Task Force recommended that operational security personnel complete at least 8 hours of formal preassignment training. The 4-part preassignment guard training recommended by the PSTF included the following:

- general orientation (role of security, appearance, report writing, etc.)   2 hours
- legal powers and limitations   2 hours
- handling emergencies (bomb threats, fires, explosions, etc.)   2 hours
- general duties (patrol and fire prevention)   2 hours

This preassignment training was to be followed within 3 months of assignment by a basic training course of at least 32 hours, with no more than 16 hours consisting of on-the-job training.

Hallcrest staff found several home-study courses, including audio and video cassette programs for entry-level security guards, that encompass most of the PSTF preassignment course, plus additional materials. These programs can usually be purchased as a complete package, and the associated costs should not pose a barrier even for a small security firm. Indeed, 1 program was produced in cooperation with an insurance underwriter, with guaranteed reduced premiums for security firms using the program. In addition, many films and cassettes used in law enforcement training are also suitable for security personnel, covering such topics as first aid, self-defense, conflict resolution, and handling disturbed or hostile individuals.

Although government studies have called for increased training requirements for private security personnel, there is still no accepted national standard, and each state is responsible for establishing its own standards. In a few cases, local regulations specify minimum security training; but as a general rule, the training requirements, if any, are established by state standards.

Table 5.5, assembled by Richter Moore and Norman Spain, lists the status of state-mandated security training.[11] **Table 5.5** notes 23 states that require some form of security training, but only 14 states require any training for unarmed guards. The amount of training varies between 4 and 40 hours depending on whether the guard is armed or unarmed.

TABLE 5.5 STATE-IMPOSED TRAINING REQUIREMENTS											
Alabama	N	Illinois	Y	Montana	Y	Rhode Island	**
Alaska	Y	Indiana	N	Nebraska	N	South Carolina	Y
Arizona	Y	Iowa	*	Nevada	*	South Dakota	N
Arkansas	Y	Kansas	*	New Hampshire	*	Tennessee	N
California	Y	Kentucky	N	New Jersey	N	Texas	Y
Colorado	N	Louisiana	Y	New Mexico	N	Utah	Y
Connecticut	*	Maine	N	New York	N	Vermont	*
Delaware	N	Maryland	N	North Carolina	*	Virginia	Y
D. C.	N	Massachusetts	N	North Dakota	N	Washington	N
Florida	*	Michigan	Y	Ohio	N	West Virginia	**
Georgia	Y	Minnesota	N	Oklahoma	N	Wisconsin	Y
Hawaii	N	Mississippi	N	Oregon	N	Wyoming	N
Idaho	N	Missouri	N	Pennsylvania	*		

Y=Yes N=No *If firearms are carried **Not in private security statute

Source: Richter Moore and Norman Spain, *Security*, July 1989

Exemplary training and certification programs have been developed by the International Association for Hospital Security and the International Foundation for Protection Officers. Also, well-developed training programs exist as a result of federal security requirements for some defense and transportation industries, nuclear power facilities, and foreign embassies.

Given the availability of these and security company training resources, what is the extent of their use? Based on its surveys and interviews, Hallcrest estimates that the typical uniformed guard receives 4 to 6 hours of preassignment training. Many, however, receive only on-the-job training. The training levels for proprietary guards are higher than for contract guards. According to the Hallcrest surveys in the early 1980s, proprietary security employees received 3 times as much preassignment training and 5 times as much on-the-job training, compared to contract employees. The frequently taught subjects for operational security employees are fire protection and prevention, report writing, legal powers, building safety, patrol, and investigation procedures. The training methods most often used seem to be manuals, lectures, films, and slides.

The alarm industry has structured one of the most noteworthy training initiatives in recent years. The National Burglar and Fire Alarm Association (NBFAA) has developed a National Training School for Alarm Professionals through the coordination of its chapters throughout the United States. As of 1989, 6,000 technicians had been trained in alarm system installation and service techniques. A unique aspect of this particular program is that it requires continuing education requirements to insure up-to-date knowledge of the industry.

There are 4 major components of the program. The first component is a beginning course, presented over a 10-week period, which prepares prospective employees to meet hiring requirements for entry-level positions in the alarm industry. The second component, the Level I Alarm Technician Course, is geared to people who have been employed in the alarm industry for a minimum of 3 months. The Level I course contains 20 hours of instruction--largely overview--on the theory, installation, and maintenance of alarm systems. The third component, the Level II Alarm Technician Course, provides further instruction for individuals who have successfully completed the Level I program. Level II subjects are studied in modules that provide in-depth training. The Continuing Education Program, the fourth component, requires the technicians to earn a minimum of 12 continuing education units (CEUs) per year to maintain certification. The CEUs may be earned by attending a wide variety of programs sponsored by chapters, manufacturers/distributors, or dealers, or by providing proof of course work from a trade school, junior college, or university.

The subjects and modules in each of the 3 programs are listed below to illustrate the depth and breadth of this training effort.

ENTRY LEVEL CANDIDATE	LEVEL I ALARM TECHNICIAN	LEVEL II ALARM TECHNICIAN
Introduction to the Alarm Industry	Electronics for the Alarm Professional	Electronics
Basic Electricity	Control Devices for Burglary Protection	Control Panels
Security Systems	Alarm Transmission and Communications	Fire Systems
Detection Devices	Perimeter, Interior, and Specialty Detection Devices	Job Planning and Wiring Techniques
Control Panels	Job Planning and Wiring Techniques	Communications
Reaction Devices	U.L. and the Alarm Industry	Space Detection
Tools	Fire Alarm Equipment and Systems	Perimeter Detection
Building and Trade Skills	Closed-Circuit Television/Video Systems	Access Control
Security Systems Design	Job Safety	U.L. and Control Industry Standards
Installation	Industry Definitions and Terminology	
Closed-Circuit Television		

Higher Education

Clearly, some improvements in operational security training have occurred over the past 15 years. However, growth in security academic programs is far more significant than minor advancements in entry-level security training.

Table 5.6 lists the numbers and types of academic programs in security for 2 benchmark years--1976 and 1990. During the intervening 14 years, a dramatic rise in the number of security-oriented certificate and degree programs is evident. In 1976, certificate and degree programs numbered 33, and by 1990 the total had increased to 164.

Several factors have led to this significant increase. First, private security is an emerging discipline and is following the traditional path of offering initial courses, and then developing a minor and, finally, a degree program. Second, after the Law Enforcement Education Program (LEEP) was phased out in the early 1980s, the academic community responded by focusing on private security courses rather than the traditional police administration courses heavily favored by law enforcement officers. Third, the academic community is reacting to the national trend toward rapid employment growth in private security.

TABLE 5.6 HIGHER EDUCATION IN PRIVATE SECURITY [Number of Programs Nationwide]		
	1977[1]	1990[2,3]
Some courses in private security	77	Not Reported
Certificate	6	49
Associate Degree	22	55
Baccalaureate Degree	5	46
Masters Degree	0	14

SOURCES: 1. Report of the Task Force on Private Security, 1976, pp. 370-377.
2. Security Letter Sourcebook 1990-1991, pp. 305-310.
3. Journal of Security Administration, December 1989, pp. 85-96.

STANDARDS AND REGULATION

The first national study of private security (1972)[12] expressed the need for standards and regulation, and so has each succeeding study group--Private Security Advisory Council (PSAC),[13] Private Security Task Force (PSTF),[14] and *The Hallcrest Report*.[15] Allegations of poor personnel selection practices, little or no training, inadequate supervision, excessive turnover, abuses of authority, and increasing false alarms have surrounded the field of private security for at least 2 decades.[16] Despite the expressed and obvious need, standards or controls for this industry have been slow to develop. Some standards exist, but little attention has been paid to them.

Both the PSAC and the PSTF, whose members were recognized leaders in private security and law enforcement, indicated that establishing standards would help upgrade the quality of private security (contract and proprietary) and prevent abuses and unethical business practices, thereby making a larger contribution to crime prevention. The private security industry, they concluded, was too complex and too broad for emphasis on standards in a single area, so the PSTF suggested development of comprehensive standards in the following areas:

- Selection of Personnel
- Training
- Conduct and Ethics
- Alarm Systems
- Environmental Security
- Law Enforcement Agencies
- Consumers of Security Services
- Higher Education and Research
- Governmental Regulation

The PSTF hoped that its report would be a catalyst in the development of standards by the security field itself:

> *It is recognized that the report is limited in scope. Therefore, continuous analysis of the private security industry and its components is strongly encouraged. However, this report offers a starting point to provide positive direction toward the greater use of private security services in the major effort of crime prevention and crime reduction in this country.*[17]

In the 14 years since the release of that report, probably not more than 10 of the standards recommended have been universally implemented by the contract security industry, proprietary security, and law enforcement. The Hallcrest research staff conducted a detailed review of the 83 standards and goals for private security. Most of these standards are still reasonable and relevant; their acceptance and implementation would unquestionably improve the quality of private security.

Despite the sporadic attempts by some state and national security industry associations to encourage standards, the industry has not taken the lead in promoting, discussing, or adopting standards. In fact, in September 1981, The American Society for Industrial Security (ASIS) abolished its Standards and Codes Committee. Some believed, perhaps, that standards might create liability or restraint-of-trade dangers. However, the Hallcrest staff suggest that wisely developed and implemented standards might help curb the "litigation explosion" that so frequently centers on inadequate or improper security.

Few changes have occurred in the past 15 years in the number of states that license and regulate security. Moreover, relatively few efforts have been made to incorporate the model guard statute (developed by the PSAC) changes into existing licensing legislation.

Some states have amended or revised existing provisions to provide stricter or more comprehensive regulation. The few attempts that have been made by the security industry to enact more effective licensing and regulation or to implement the model guard statute (1976) have not been presented with a unified industry voice.

Most of the government's interest in standards is traceable to the agencies currently regulating private security. Interaction between the contract security industry and these regulatory agencies and the legislatures has been largely reactionary, to prevent inclusion of provisions that they perceive as being too restrictive or imposing an unnecessary financial burden on security companies. Many smaller security firms view standards and regulation as a means to promote increased market share for larger firms that are better able to meet the requirements. Widespread, proactive efforts to enact responsible legislation have not been forthcoming from the security industry, nor have there been similar efforts to adopt comprehensive industry standards in lieu of governmental regulation. In the absence of uniform standards within the security industry, licensing and regulation remains the only tool to assure minimally acceptable private security services. Some observers feel that the leadership for meaningful security legislation must come from public law enforcement rather than from the private security industry. The rationale is that private security has a vested interest and cannot be objective. Also, in most states, public law enforcement has a better organized lobbying system.

Self-Regulation and Standard Setting

The private security industry--with help from liability insurance companies and lawsuits-- has demonstrated that it can impose a reactionary form of standards. The disarming of large numbers of security personnel over the past 15 to 20 years by the contract security industry (to an estimated 10% or less of all security personnel) might be construed as a self-imposed industry standard to deemphasize the need for the use of firearms. Another self-imposed standard is the alarm industry's increased use of improved technology and client training, rather than punitive ordinances, in false alarm abatement programs.

The experience of the British Security Industry Association (BSIA) has demonstrated that industry-imposed standards can be developed at the national level (reportedly encompassing 90% of Britain's security industry business volume) and can help to upgrade private security.[18] For several major components of security services, the BSIA has adopted standards pertaining to personnel screening procedures, wage levels, supervision, training, liability insurance, and physical facilities. As Anthony Purbrick (1990) points out, "If the best of both systems [United Kingdom and United States] could be combined, the result could be high quality control in the industry and top service for clients."[19]

Since 1983 consensus standard setting and an accreditation program for law enforcement agencies have been operated by the Commission on Accreditation for Law Enforcement Agencies (CALEA).[20] Some 900 standards in 9 topical areas (organization and management, personnel, operations, technical services, etc.) were developed by 4 major law enforcement associations-- International Association of Chiefs of Police, National Sheriffs' Association, National Organization of Black Law Enforcement Executives, and the Police Executive Research Forum. While less than 10% of the nation's law enforcement agencies have started or completed the accreditation process, it serves as a useful model since this process, in essence, largely represents self-regulation. Perhaps some form of accreditation could be developed for private security. Achievement of accreditation not only may improve management and service delivery in both proprietary and contract security, but also may have sales appeal for "accredited" security companies and for consumers who associate quality service only with accredited organizations.

TABLE 5.7 STATE REGULATION OF PRIVATE SECURITY FIRMS*	
	No. of States
Guard and Patrol	
Licensing of Businesses	39
Registration	25[1]
Private Investigators	37
Alarm	25
Armored Car	9[2]

[1] plus District of Columbia [2] does not include Public Utility Commissions or Interstate Commerce Commission

Sources:

1. "Security Data Bank," *Security*, June 1990, p.55.

2. *Security Letter Source Book*, 1990-1991, Section II.II.6, Robert McCrie, Editor, Butterworths, Stoneham, MA, March 1990.

3. "Regulations Vary by State," *Security Distributing and Marketing*, September 1989, p.82.

4. Truett Ricks, Gill Tillett, Clifford Van Meter, *Principles of Security*, (Second Edition), Anderson Publishing Co., 1988, pp. 168-171.

5. "Regulation of the Private Security Industry," National Institute of Justice, U.S. Department of Justice, (unpublished), January 1981.

Government Regulation and Licensing

Approximately 75% of the states regulate some aspect of private security and its employees. In addition (or sometimes in place of state regulation), municipal or county governments often have ordinances regulating private security. Because laws pertaining to security licensing have changed often, it is nearly impossible to delineate the regulatory requirements of local and state governments. However, **Table 5.7** provides an overview of state regulatory activity.[21] In addition to security business and personnel regulation, an estimated 2,000 local governments have enacted alarm ordinances.

Hallcrest's current research uncovered no notable changes in the government's approach to security regulation in recent years. Although states have enacted a variety of amendments, the regulatory process remains essentially as the PSTF found it 15 years ago, "some good, some of limited value, and most lacking uniformity and comprehensiveness."[22] The major findings of Hallcrest's national surveys of security, law enforcement, and regulatory officials in the early 1980s were largely confirmed through the 1989 reconnaissance interviews and literature review. These findings include the following:

- State regulation is most often provided by the state police or department of public safety (15 states), the department of commerce or an existing occupational licensing agency (7 states), or the department of state (5 states). Of these mechanisms, regulation by a law enforcement agency appears to be least popular. Three of the state law enforcement agencies said they should not be involved with regulating the security industry, and security firms generally oppose the practice, given the prevalence of moonlighting in private security by police officers. Security executives, for their part, prefer security industry representation on state regulatory boards (15 states).

- The vast majority of security managers favored state licensing and regulation and strongly opposed local licensing of private security. Similarly, about two-thirds of the licensing agencies felt that local ordinances duplicated or even conflicted with state regulation and imposed an unnecessary burden upon security companies. Law enforcement executives, however, favor the use of city or county ordinances, including those that would give them the power to suspend or revoke the license of security firms and employees.

- Some security managers felt that regulatory boards comprised solely of industry representatives could limit competition by enacting provisions that only certain firms could meet. Other managers felt that underrepresentation by the security industry has led to unfair or counterproductive controls, such as emphasizing police training in the curriculum for security guards while overlooking subjects more important for security personnel.

- Differing licensing requirements can pose problems for a guard firm serving a regional or national client, for private investigators pursuing cases into an adjoining state, and for armored car firms transporting shipments across state lines.

- In general, state legislative provisions are not stringent:

  - Liability insurance is required by 11 states, and liability and bonding insurance by 5 states. The amount of surety generally ranges from $2,000 to $10,000.

  - Mandatory training requirements for armed personnel are imposed by 23 states, with 14 having training requirements for unarmed personnel. Only 4 of these require as much as 24 hours of preassignment training, as recommended by the Private Security Task Force. One of the most stringent is Texas, with a required 30-hour basic training course, and Texas law is credited with taking 20,000 weapons out of the hands of untrained personnel.

  - In some states, both armed and unarmed personnel can hold security positions for up to 6 weeks while awaiting licensing approval.

Across all surveyed groups--law enforcement, proprietary and contract security, major national and regional security companies--there was a consensus that state licensing and regulation has not been effective in assuring quality security personnel or sound business practices.[23] Nevertheless, these groups still express a need for government regulation. Despite complaints of stringency by contract security and of laxity by law enforcement and proprietary security in provisions of existing legislation, over 80% of those surveyed agreed that a state regulatory statute is needed. In addition, the same percentage of respondents agreed that there should be mandatory criminal background checks and specified levels of training for both proprietary and contractual security personnel.

COMPENSATION

Guards

For at least the past 20 years, most contract security guards have been hired at or slightly above the minimum wage rate. These low wages have led to high turnover and to employment of minimally qualified workers. Consistently, the salaries of "in-house" or proprietary security personnel have been higher than those of contract guard personnel. This cost differential results in more frequent corporate use of the potentially less expensive contract security rather than an in-house security guard force. On the other hand, compensation of security managers and executives in both contract and corporate security has increased significantly over the past 15 years.[24]

Ten years ago, about 50% of contract guards earned between $3.35 and $4.00 per hour, while the average wage for in-house/proprietary guards was about $6.50 per hour.[25] Estimates pertaining to guard income in 1989-90 vary considerably. One source estimates an average wage of about $6 per hour for contract guards,[26] while another survey puts the average rate at $8.95 per hour.[27] Using the most comprehensive security industry compensation survey available, conducted by Abbott, Langer and Associates, and adjusted for inflation, the Hallcrest research staff estimate a mean wage of $7.70 per hour for unarmed security guards in 1990. The average income of a police officer ($24,000) is about 50% higher than the annual compensation of the average security guard.[28]

Alarm Wages

Noting variances of 30%, an alarm industry wage survey found that junior central station operators earn about $5.10 per hour, senior central station operators average $8.26, junior installers average $7.71 per hour, and senior installers/technicians average slightly above $12 per hour.[29] Alarm salespeople have average annual incomes ranging from about $23,000 to $38,000.[30] The annual incomes of managers of alarm firms vary significantly, but at least 60% earn more than $40,000, and 1 in 5 alarm company managers/owners has an income exceeding $90,000 per year.[31]

Proprietary Security Managers

To develop comparative security management compensation data in the early 1980s, Hallcrest analyzed 3 national surveys. From this analysis, the staff reported income of over $40,000 as the median base salary in 1981 for proprietary security directors with responsibility for national and international operations. Further, $30,000 to $35,000 was the median base salary for security managers responsible for a corporate division/subsidiary, and local facility security managers earned a median salary of $30,000.[32] While contract security managers in Hallcrest's 1981 national survey reported a median salary of about $4,000 less than proprietary security managers at local facilities, most contract managers receive incentive compensation such as profit-sharing, bonuses, etc.[33]

The Abbott, Langer, and Associates compensation survey of the security field in 1989 found the mean annual salary of corporate security directors/managers with policy-making authority to be $52,291.[34] Yet, this figure is significantly lower than the finding of the nationally known compensation consulting firm of Towers, Perrin, Forster, and Crosby (TPF&C).[35] Their national survey presented average base salaries for a number of executive positions by corporate size (sales) and by industry. **Table 5.8** summarizes the TPF&C average salaries for the "top security executive." It is noteworthy that total compensation for the top security executive is often 20% or more above base salary to account for bonuses and other incentives.

TABLE 5.8 AVERAGE BASE SALARY OF TOP CORPORATE SECURITY EXECUTIVES 1989	
By Company sales	
Over $6 Billion	$77,695
$3 to $6 Billion	$78,270
$1 to $3 Billion	$76,129
$500 Million to $1 Billion	$68,706
By Selected Industry	
Aerospace/Electronics	$92,878
Chemicals	$79,092
Consumer Products	$81,125
Energy	$69,939
Pharmaceuticals	$81,884
Source: Towers, Perrin, Forster & Crosby, Inc. (1989)	

Contract Security Management

Adjustments (5% per annum) were made to the base salaries obtained from local contract security owners and managers in our 1981 survey, and the staff estimates an average annual base salary range of $45,000 to $50,000 by 1990. The annual compensation of corporate executives of major privately held security equipment and service companies is largely unknown, although it frequently exceeds $100,000 annually. The 1989 compensation for the top executives of publicly held private security companies ranged from $100,000 to more than $600,000.[36]

SUMMARY

Unfortunately, the circle of relatively low pay and benefits leading to high turnover will likely continue throughout the 1990s for contract security guards. Many owners and managers of contract security firms insist that clients are unwilling to pay higher rates; some clients argue that they would pay higher wages for higher caliber personnel. Nevertheless, to win competitive contracts in government and industry frequently requires wages for security guards that are near federal minimums.

Salaries for the top corporate security executives in the 1990s will likely stay on par with those of managers of other corporate support functions. Hallcrest further anticipates throughout the 1990s that overall actual compensation and rates of salary increases for both corporate and contract security executives will be greater than for federal, state, or local law enforcement executives.

END NOTES

1.   James Kakalik and Sorrel Wildhorn, *The Private Police Industry: Its Nature and Extent*, Vol. 11, The Rand Corporation, 1972, pp. 133, 135, 137. Also see the following Canadian study of contract security employees: Clifford Shearing, Margaret Farnell, and Phillip Stenning, *Contract Security in Ontario*, University of Toronto, 1980.

2.   Ibid, p. 106.

3.   William Walsh, "Private/Public Police Stereotypes: A Different Perspective," *Security Journal*, Vol. 1, 1989, pp. 21-27. For a more complete review of security personnel and performance issues, see Edwin Donovan and William White, *An Evaluation of Starrett City Security Services*, The Pennsylvania State University, April 1986.

4.   Ibid, p. 23.

5.   Kerry Lydon, "Who Makes Security Decisions for US Business?" *Security*, September 1987.

6.   *Profile of State and Local Law Enforcement Agencies, 1987*, Bureau of Justice Statistics, p. 3.

7.   See, for example, Randolph Brock, "The Guard in the Year 2000," *Security in the Year 2000*, Louis Tyska, editor, (ETC Publications, 1987), p. 265.

8.   Ibid, p. 267.

9.   *Private Security: Report of the Task Force on Private Security* (Washington, D.C.: U.S. Government Printing Office, 1976), pp. 12-13.

10.   Rebecca Russell, "Officer Training: Identify Your Options," *Security*, May 1990, p. 49.

11.   Richter Moore and Norman Spain, "No Joke: Training Cuts Liability," *Security*, July 1989, p. 31.

12.   James Kakalik and Sorrel Wildhorn, *The Private Police Industry: Its Nature and Extent, Vol. II*, The Rand Corporation, 1971.

13.   Private Security Advisory Council to the Law Enforcement Assistance Administration, U.S. Department of Justice, (1972-1977), a federal advisory group comprised of a Council (20 members) and 6 committees (about 10 members on each). The PSAC produced the following reports: *A Report on a Model Hold-Up and Burglar Alarm Business Licensing and Regulatory Statute*; *A Report on the Regulation of Private Security Guard Services* (including a model private security licensing and regulatory statute); *Terroristic Crimes: An Annotated Bibliography*; *Potential Secondary Impacts of the Crime Prevention Through Environmental Design Concept*; *Private Security Codes of Ethics for Security Management and Security Employees*; *Prevention of Terroristic Crimes: Security Guidelines for Business, Industry and Other Organizations*; *Law Enforcement and Private Security Sources and Areas of Conflict and Strategies for Conflict Resolution*; *Scope of Legal Authority of Private Security Personnel*; *Model Security Guard Training Curricula*; *Standards for Armored Car and Armed Courier Services*; *Guidelines for the Establishment of State and Local Private Security Advisory Councils*.

14.   *Report of the Task Force on Private Security* (PSTF), National Advisory Committee on Criminal Justice Standards and Goals, 1976.

15.   William Cunningham and Todd Taylor, *The Hallcrest Report: Private Security and Police In America*, 1985.

16.   Normally, several articles highlighting security industry personnel problems appear annually in national publications. See, for example, Art Levine, "Watch Those Watchdogs," *U.S. News and World Report*, July 11, 1988, pp. 36-38.

17.   Private Security Task Force Report, p. 17.

18.   A review of United Kingdom security industry self-policing by the British Security Industry Association is presented by Anthony Purbrick, "A Tale of Two Countries," *Security Management*, January 1990, pp. 77-81.

19.   Ibid, p. 80.

20.   For a list of the standards and accreditation process, see *Standards For Law Enforcement Agencies*, Commission on Accreditation for Law Enforcement Agencies, Inc. (CALEA), (Fairfax, VA), January 1990 edition. Also, see *Accreditation Program Overview*, CALEA.

21.   For another analysis of state regulation, see R. H. Moore, "Licensing and The Regulation of Private Security," *Journal of Security Administration*, Vol. 10, No. 1, June 1987, pp. 10-28.

22.   Private Security Task Force Report, p. 278.

23.   Cunningham and Taylor, pp. 297, 310, and 324.

24.   For comparisons of operational and managerial compensation of security personnel, see the following: "Annual Wage Surveys," *Bureau of Labor Statistics*, 1975 to 1989; "Survey of American Society for Industrial Security (ASIS) Members -1975," *Report of the Task Force on Private Security*, National Advisory Council on Criminal Justice Standards and Goals, Law Enforcement Assistance Administration, 1976, p. 69; William Cunningham and Todd Taylor, *The Hallcrest Report: Private Security and Police In America*, 1985 (Chancellor Press: McLean, VA), pp. 99-102; *Compensation in the Security/Loss Prevention Field*, Abbott, Langer, and Associates, Editions 1 through 6.

25.   Cunningham and Taylor, p. 99.

26.   "Managing Today's Guards," [ASIS] *Dynamics*, November-December 1989, p. 4.

27.   Rebecca Russell, "Changing Times For Contract Officer Pay," *Security*, February 1990, p. 37.

28.   *Report of the National Advisory Commission on Law Enforcement*, General Accounting Office, February 1990. Also, see *Profile of State and Local Law Enforcement Agencies*, 1987, Bureau of Justice Statistics, March 1989.

29.   "Security's Paycheck: An Inside Look," *Security Distributing Marketing*, September 1988, pp. 45-48.

30.   Ibid.

31.   Ibid.

32.   Cunningham and Taylor, p. 102.

33.   See *Security Letter*, November 16, 1987; June 15, 1988; and June 1, 1989. Also used were data from Abbott, Langer, and Associates Compensation Survey, Edition 5, and *The Hallcrest Report: Private Security and Police In America* (1985).

34.   *Compensation in The Security/Loss Prevention Field*, Edition 5, 1988, p. 11.

35.   Stuart Weiss, "Locked Out," *Business Month*, October 1989, pp. 44-49.

36.   *Security Letter*, Part II, June 1, 1989.

PART III

MARKET ANALYSIS

CHAPTER 6
SECURITY MARKET ANALYSIS

INTRODUCTION

For more than 2 decades, private security has experienced robust growth in employment, numbers and types of security businesses, and in revenues and expenditures for security products and services. Private security is more than twice the size of federal, state, and local law enforcement combined. It has assumed ever-increasing responsibilities for corporate and personal protection against crime and other losses. This chapter profiles the private security industry over the past decade, estimates its composition today, and projects what it might look like by the year 2000.

Little has changed in statistical and analytical information about the private security industry since the publication of the original *Hallcrest Report* in 1985. There is still too little information available about the security industry that is well-documented or based on rigorous empirical research. Some data are unreliable or dubious. The major obstacles the Hallcrest research staff had to overcome, therefore, were to select information that was reliable, to validate the information to be used, and to determine how the data could be reasonably projected to the year 2000. The public law enforcement data were more available than private security statistical information, but they, too, were not without problems, especially for law enforcement employment trends.

The Hallcrest projections presented in this chapter include some original data analyses, but the 1990 research effort is largely grounded on secondary and tertiary sources, as well as continuations and extensions of analyses and compilations developed during the 1985 study. The Hallcrest projections and analyses are largely the result of distillation and synthesis processes of other existing data. This chapter does, however, contain original research and information compilations that have either not been previously provided by other market research sources or are at a higher level of detail. The Hallcrest research staff used several new analytic techniques that mitigate the risk of faulty data, such as the development of a modest computer model to calculate and test the data.

In summary, the Hallcrest projections are an attempt to present data that

- meet various unique logic tests,
- are corroborated by reliable sources, or
- are within a believable "cluster range" made up of several reliable sources.

SOURCES

The private security industry information presented in this chapter was largely derived from the sources listed below:

- market research reports prepared by for-profit organizations

- security industry trade journals, newsletters, and books and studies conducted by professional and trade associations

- insights and opinions from security industry leaders

- extrapolations and projections from security and law enforcement studies, including *The Hallcrest Report* (1985)

- government publications pertaining to labor and commerce statistics

Market Research Studies

Except for Bureau of Census data and certain selected studies, market research sources may be limited in terms of definitive research. Some sources may be biased; some commercial market research studies may promote certain industry segments, and clients may be unwilling to pay the high prices for such studies if the forecasts are too gloomy. In addition, market research studies often do not cite or document their sources, authors, or analysts or how the data were derived or treated. Despite these drawbacks, however, they can be a valuable source of data and analyses. Several of the major market research studies influenced the development of the Hallcrest private security market study. One of the most extensive listings of market research resources that include the security industry in their studies is presented in *Security Letter Source Book 1990-1991*, which lists 28 sources.[1] Another valuable resource is the *Guide to Security Industry Market Studies: 1986 to June 1989*, a 60-page bibliography published by the American Society for Industrial Security (ASIS).[2]

Professional and Trade Associations and Journals

As with market research studies, surveys conducted by trade journals and associations are also designed to appeal to their subscribers and members--although probably to a much lesser extent. *Security Letter Source Book 1990-1991* lists 118 professional and trade associations. Of the 118, at least 40 associations are directly involved in the security industry, and 25 to 30 have some form of security-related interests.[3] Professional and trade associations and journals are far more likely to report negative industry trends than many other market research information sources, since many subscribers and association members may use such information in strategic business planning. It seems, however, that the more specialized the security periodical or trade association is, the higher it projects the rates of growth of its own industry segment.

Industry Leaders

Industry leaders' insights and opinions--as either individuals or companies--can be an important source of information. Clearly, they too are biased by their own motivations and are limited by their individual experiences. Few industry leaders, for example, have a comprehensive understanding of those elements of the industry that are far below them in size, such as "mom and pop" guard companies and alarm operations in America's small towns and cities. All in all, however, industry leaders can be reliable and realistic when it comes to those industry segments that they have mastered.

Independent Studies

Extrapolations and projections based on existing government-funded studies and independent research projects, such as *The Hallcrest Report* (1985), are also not perfect. The amount of funding, as one example, can limit the scope and detail of the research effort. Another drawback of any research project is unintentional bias. The researcher's own, inadvertent goal-directed bias is a factor that must be considered. The nature of research survey sampling produces yet another source of bias. Since survey data are a sampling of the industry, the accuracy of the survey is limited by the accuracy of the sample. On the other hand, independent studies generally have few, if any, vested interests to serve and tend to be less biased.

Government Data

Government sources of data, particularly national census and commerce data, are possibly as objective as they can be, given that the scope of such government statistical analyses is extremely broad. However, the sweeping nature of government statistics can also be a drawback. Since the authors of government studies and publications are outside the security industry, they are not especially adept at properly classifying, grouping, or interpreting the information they have collected. Their broad treatment of specific industries often results in either missing and excluding key information or including inappropriate data.

VARIANCE AMONG SOURCES

Of particular concern--and an indication of the overall unreliability of many statistics pertaining to the private security industry--is the significant variance among the major sources of market information. To illustrate this key consideration in evaluating such data, **Table 6.1** lists the gross annual revenues for the alarm industry reported by 7 major sources for the period 1987 to 1989.

The variance between the highest and lowest estimates is about 800%. The data presented in this chapter are based on a conscientious effort to seek a conservative and balanced estimate derived from corroboration wherever possible or from a reconciliation of variances. Neither the highest nor the lowest estimates were generally adopted by the current Hallcrest study. The term "alarm industry" is sufficiently vague to cause potential disparity due to differences in nomenclature, classification, and grouping. "Alarm industry" could conceivably entail, by some definitions, national central stations, local central stations, installing companies, dealers, distributors, and even guard companies that also derive a portion of their annual revenues from alarm services and from the sale and installation of equipment. By some interpretations, even certain manufacturers could be included, as well as fire alarm systems sales and services.

TABLE 6.1 COMPARISON OF VARIOUS ESTIMATES FOR ALARM INDUSTRY ANNUAL REVENUES	
$1,065,000,000	1988
$1,320,000,000	1989
$1,953,000,000	1988
$2,217,610,000	1987
$5,630,000,000	1989
$6,864,000,000	1989
$8,000,000,000	1988

The first 4 estimates presented in **Table 6.1** range from $1 billion to $2.2 billion. Normally, this would be an initial indication of possible confirmation because of the relatively tight grouping of data from different sources. Upon close analysis, however, it was determined that these estimates may have been extremely narrow in their classification and grouping of the alarm industry. The $2.2 billion figure was developed by the U.S. Bureau of the Census. The bureau has generally understated private security earnings in the past due to its very narrow classification scheme. Moreover, the calculation of annual payroll estimates for the alarm industry, based on what were believed to be reliable employment estimates, failed to balance with the first range of revenue estimates. Namely, if the employment data are accurate, revenues in the $1 billion to $2.2 billion would not cover payroll, let alone other overhead costs of the industry. These estimates would have resulted in most alarm companies operating at a loss.

The $6.8 billion to $8 billion estimates are believed to have included some fire alarm equipment and services and may have included some manufacturers and distributors primarily involved in alarm product sales. These estimates were judged to be too high and would have resulted in unrealistic industry revenues and profits. The $5.6 billion figure was close but also failed to bring other alarm industry data into balance. Based on these various analyses, the Hallcrest staff estimates the gross annual revenues of the alarm industry in 1990 to be approximately $4.5 billion with a current annual rate of growth of approximately 12%. The true probable error of this estimate is unknown, but assuming for the sake of the argument that it is about 20%, this 1990 Hallcrest study could have projected gross revenues of the alarm industry to range from about $3.6 billion to $5.4 billion dollars. The $4.5 billion estimate, however, was the only one that brought all alarm segment data into statistical and mathematical balance.

DATA TREATMENT

As each segment of the industry is reviewed in this chapter, some assessment of the reliability of the data is usually provided. Whenever it is particularly pertinent, a brief description of the key criteria of each segment is also discussed. In the case of the alarm industry, the 1990 Hallcrest criteria include an effort to exclude fire equipment and services and to restrict the estimates to private security companies primarily involved in monitoring, installing, and servicing security alarm systems.

When considering the data presented in this chapter, the reader should consider that a particular number is not absolute but rather is in the center of a theoretical range. Moreover, comparisons between the Hallcrest study and other market analyses for a specific segment of the industry may be imprecise since the elements that comprise each segment are likely to vary from study to study. For example, some market research studies may include fire equipment within the category "alarm companies," while others, including this report, do not. Both sources, however, would use the title "alarm companies." This report defines each industry segment and describes which segment components are considered.

Despite these many qualifications and caveats, it is believed that the data presented in this chapter are substantially realistic and generally conservative. Some unique analyses were conducted to cull out entirely unrealistic statistics. For example, when information was collected that reported gross revenues, number of employees, and number of companies, calculations were made to determine revenues per company, revenues per employee, and the ratio of payroll to gross revenues. While these analyses do not necessarily confirm the reliability of the data, they do quickly point to data that are flawed. For example, as a result of these calculations, if it is found that a particular set of data results in annual payroll being much higher than annual gross revenues for a particular segment of the industry--as was the case on several occasions--it is evident that either the gross revenues reported or the numbers of employees reported are in significant error.

METHODOLOGY

Although some aspects of research methodology have already been discussed, it is important to summarize the key analytic approaches taken for this study. The principal methodological issues were: (1) What criteria should be used to select data to be reported? (2) How should the data be treated to derive projections to other years, with a major focus toward the year 2000?

Data Selection Criteria

To determine whether certain data should be used in this report, they were examined according to the following criteria:

1. Was their information corroborated by a reliable source?
2. Did the data fall within an acceptable cluster range?
3. Did the data "pass" certain "logic tests"?
4. Were the data reasonable, as determined by industry experts?

The most important criterion was whether the data were corroborated by an independent reliable source. It was influential, for example, if 3 or more independent market research studies reported statistics in approximately the same range. This did occur in some industry segments, such as gross annual revenues for armored car companies and for alarm companies. Apparent corroboration is not enough, however. It was essential to confirm, whenever possible, that the market research studies did not derive their information from the same source, which appeared to be the case in some instances. The analysis of nomenclature and classification schemes of major sources was also significant to ensure that each market study was considering the same statistical population. The mere fact that a statistical bit of information was reported by a major national newspaper was not, of itself, persuasive to the authors of this study.

Another important test--a variant of the criterion described above--was whether data fell within an acceptable "cluster range." Often, there were wide variances among sources of statistical information. Since it was not feasible to calculate standard deviations (or similar statistical treatments) in view of the small number of sources, occasionally it was necessary to informally establish a reasonable range for some sets of data. Once that was determined, the data were averaged to develop a single figure that could fairly represent the entire cluster range. If there was a choice between 2 figures, this study leaned toward the more conservative figure if convincing reasons could not be found to select the higher number.

The third major criterion was to apply certain "logic tests." For example, as previously noted, various ratios were developed to represent the reasonable percentage of gross annual revenues that could be attributed to direct labor costs. For some segments, such as security consulting, such ratios are reasonably well established. Compensation ranges were also derived for all industry segments. Consequently, it was often apparent that revenues were out of balance with estimates of employment numbers, since the likely labor costs could be calculated. This analysis, in turn, led to the selection of some industry revenue or employment estimates over others since a careful effort was made to select data that balanced properly.

Similar analyses were conducted by computing percentages of totals for various data, compounded rates of average annual growth, total payrolls, average revenues per company, average revenues produced by each employee, and the average number of employees per company. Many of these calculations are not reported in this report since their primary purpose was to test whether other associated data for each industry segment were in balance and reasonable. For example, if a set of data resulted in a huge average revenue per employee figure, it was suspected either that the number of companies estimated for the industry segment was much too low or that revenues collected by the entire segment were much too high. Either or both would be adjusted on the bases of other sources until the relationship was in balance.

The final test was fairly subjective--albeit an important one. The authors of this report asked one another, and on occasion experts in the industry, whether the derived data sounded reasonable. If anyone believed they did not, the data were reinvestigated until everyone was satisfied. Although it has now become somewhat cliche, it could be said that the authors used a modified Delphi Technique for the analysis of the security industry.

Sources

Two of the major sources for this research were *The Hallcrest Report* (1985) and the proprietary files of Hallcrest Systems, Inc. (McLean, VA) and Systech Group, Inc. (Reston, VA). The earlier Hallcrest study was, in turn, derived from most of the major seminal sources of statistics pertaining to the private security and law enforcement sectors. The current effort reviewed all of the previous works and attempted to refine and to expand the research previously conducted.

Commercial market research studies were another key source. This study evaluated data from 13 major market research organizations and sources, as well as relevant information from several other sources. The major security industry reports and compilations reviewed or considered were from the organizations listed below:

Abbott, Langer & Associates (Crete, Illinois)
American Society for Industrial Security (Arlington, Virginia)
Bell Atlantic (Bethesda, Maryland)
Datapro Research (Delran, New Jersey)
The Freedonia Group (Cleveland, Ohio)
Frost & Sullivan (New York, New York)
J. P. Freeman and Company (Newtown, Connecticut)
Joseph Schneider Associates (Cambridge, Massachusetts)
Leading Edge Reports (Cleveland, Ohio; formerly Predicasts)
Support Services Group (San Clemente, California)
Security Letter (New York, New York)
Security (Des Plaines, Illinois; formerly *Security World*)
Stat Resources (Brookline, Massachusetts)

It was decided not to footnote or cite data from specific market research studies primarily because the information was not directly taken from any source. Rather, many of the sources listed above were instrumental in synthesizing or corroborating the data in the tables presented in later sections of this chapter.

Other important sources of information included 19 security association and trade journals and newsletters, published books related to the industry, numerous national magazines and newspapers, and a variety of governmental publications and data bases. Governmental sources were vital for some data, particularly the Bureau of Justice Statistics, the Bureau of Labor Statistics, and the Bureau of the Census. The Hallcrest research staff also conducted more than 100 field interviews to round out the data base.

Projections

The methods used to derive reasonable projections from 1990 and for the year 2000 were primarily variations of traditional trendline extensions, taking into account whenever possible consensus attitudes about acceleration or deceleration of various industry segments. Business failures were also taken into account in establishing trend lines. *The Hallcrest Report* (1985) estimated that approximately 20% of private security businesses failed annually.[4] A more current estimate is not available, but it is likely that the failure rate in 1990 is not less than 20%.

Some projections were major, such as to the year 2000, but others were required to bring data into a common year, such as to convert ostensibly reliable 1978 data to 1980 or to bring 1982 data back to 1980. Growth was projected on established trend lines on the basis of increasing or decreasing compounded average annual rates of growth. While this particular technique is not always accurate for a projection of 1 or 2 years, it is generally effective for long-term extensions.

A computer model was developed on commercial data base software to process the data, to automatically conduct the calculations and balance tests, and to process the trend-line projections. While data entry errors are possible (although 2 data bases were established as a check against entry errors), it is unlikely that significant mathematical errors were made by the program. Some minor distortion occurred due to rounding off.

OVERVIEW OF KEY MARKET INDICATORS
AND EMPLOYMENT

This chapter presents an overview of the entire private security industry and its major elements for the period 1980 to 2000. The key elements for the security industry are the security service sector, proprietary security, and the product sector. These major elements are summarized by the following data sets: gross annual revenues or expenditures, average annual rates of growth for revenues or expenditures, percentages of total revenues or expenditures for each category, number of companies or public agencies in each segment, percentage of company totals, number of employees, and percentage of employment totals for each category. Numbers of original equipment manufacturers (OEMs) and distributors are provided for the private security industry. Average annual rates of growth are also estimated for the numbers of companies and employees at each milestone year after 1980 for each industry segment. This report establishes 1980, 1990, and 2000 as milestone years.

The Hallcrest staff forecasts a slower rate of growth for the private security industry than most other market research sources and the U.S. Departments of Commerce and Labor. The Hallcrest research staff predicts that the average annual rate of growth for revenues/expenditures for the entire private security industry, including the manufacturing and proprietary security sectors, to the year 2000 will be about 7%. This is, nevertheless, about 3 times the national estimates for the average annual rate of growth of the gross national product (GNP).

Despite Hallcrest's more conservative estimates, the sales and revenues for the entire private security industry should continue to be robust in terms of overall averages, outracing most other service revenue categories. Within the industry, it is probable that services and sales may be sluggish in some segments, such as armored car, locksmith, and fencing, largely as the result of maturation or market saturation. The rate of change in expenditures by the proprietary security sector (for example, security departments within private companies) is likely to continue to experience a slowdown in average rates of annual growth, even though there will be cumulative growth in terms of absolute dollars spent. The proprietary sector saw the beginning of a slight deceleration as early as the mid-1980s, as some companies

173

reduced the size of their security departments and a few eliminated them, favoring contracting out and using other departments to take over some duties.

The average annual rate of growth in private security employment is forecast to be 2.3%, which is slightly slower than the 2.6% predicted by the Bureau of Labor Statistics (BLS), but which is still much higher than the 1.2% annual rate predicted for the entire U.S. work force by the BLS. Although the rates of growth for revenues and employment for the current year are slightly higher than the Hallcrest research staff forecasts for the coming decade, the staff anticipates a gradual slowdown over the next 10 years due to a maturing of the industry, market saturation by some industry segments, and continued consolidation of the industry due to mergers, acquisitions, and business failures.

Tables 6.2 to 6.4 summarize Hallcrest estimates and projections of private security revenues/expenditures, numbers of companies, and numbers of employees for the period 1980 to 2000. Both contract and proprietary sectors are considered in these tables. Further, Table 6.2 lists only the service portion of annual revenues for the manufacturing segment; revenues from the sale of equipment are presented later in this report and in Figure 6.1 on page 177.

Table 6.2, on the following page, indicates that the private security industry will experience an average annual rate of growth for revenues and expenditures of 7% over the next decade, probably starting the decade at 10% and slowing to 4% or 5% by the year 2000. The Hallcrest research staff projects that the contract service and manufacturing sector will slow from a decade average of 11% in 1990 to a 10-year average of 9% by 2000. Of more significance, the staff estimates that the proprietary sector's expenditures will drop from an average annual rate of growth of 8% in 1990 to 2% in 2000, slightly less than the rate of growth of the GNP, due to increasing contracting of security services.

When reviewing Table 6.3, which indicates the growth of contract and manufacturing security companies and proprietary security departments, it is important to note that "companies" and not "establishments" are indicated. Some industry tabulations, such as those based on counting yellow page listings, count enterprises, namely all of the branch offices of the same parent company.

TABLE 6.2 HALLCREST ESTIMATES AND PROJECTIONS PRIVATE SECURITY GROSS ANNUAL REVENUES/EXPENDITURES 1980 TO 2000						
Year	Contract Service and Manufacturing Sales Revenues	Average Annual Growth Rate	Proprietary Security Organization Operating Costs	Average Annual Growth Rate	Total Revenues and Expenditures	Total Average Annual Growth Rate
1980	Service: $8,780,000,000 Sales: $4,578,000,000 Total: $13,358,000,000	N/A N/A N/A	$ 6,250,000,000	N/A	$19,250,000,000	N/A
1990	Service: $26,254,000,000 Sales: $11,700,000,000 Total: $37,954,000,000	12% 10% 11%	$13,600,000,000	8%	$51,600,000,000	10%
2000	Service: $63,429,000,000 Sales: $23,723,000,000 Total: $87,152,000,000	9% 7% 9%	$16,000,000,000	2%	$103,000,000,000	7%

Although a few security companies, such as Pinkerton's, can trace their origins to the Civil War period in America, most authorities would concede that private security did not become a nationwide industry until the late 1940s. Thus, the 1990s will represent the sixth decade of private security industry growth. The private security industry is maturing, and as a result, there should be a gradual slowdown, especially in the growth of new companies. There will be fewer start-ups, and the statistical effect of new companies that may be started will be offset by consolidation of the industry due to acquisitions, mergers, and business failures. Most new start-ups will be in the contract service and manufacturing sectors, averaging a 2-to-1 ratio over the proprietary security sector.

TABLE 6.3 PRIVATE SECURITY INDUSTRY HALLCREST PROJECTION OF NUMBER OF COMPANIES (TO THE YEAR 2000)						
Year	Contract Service and Manufacturing Companies	Average Annual Growth Rate	Proprietary Security Organizations	Average Annual Growth Rate	Total Companies	Total Average Annual Growth Rate
1980	29,600	N/A	40,000	N/A	69,600	N/A
1990	57,000	6.8%	50,000	2.3%	107,000	4.4%
2000	92,300	4.9%	60,000	1.8%	152,300	3.6%

Table 6.4 tabulates the numbers of employees working in the private security industry. The Hallcrest research staff predicts that employment in proprietary security will experience a substantial reduction over the next 10 years; annual growth will average out to be negative by the end of the decade. Employment in the contract service and manufacturing sector will continue to be robust, averaging 3 times the rate of growth of the total national work force (1.2%). Overall, however, the private security industry's employment growth rate will be only about twice that of the national work force due to the drop in proprietary security employment. The contract service and manufacturing sectors will continue to see an annual employment rate that is approximately 3 times that of the proprietary sector.

TABLE 6.4 PRIVATE SECURITY INDUSTRY HALLCREST PROJECTION OF NUMBER OF EMPLOYEES (TO THE YEAR 2000)						
Year	Contract Service and Manufacturing Employees	Average Annual Growth Rate	Proprietary Security Organization Employees	Average Annual Growth Rate	Total Private Security Employment	Total Average Annual Growth Rate
1980	556,000	N/A	420,000	N/A	976,000	N/A
1990	965,000	6%	528,000	2%	1,493,000	4%
2000	1,473,000	4%	410,000	-2%	1,883,000	2%

From an entirely speculative point of view, in the event that law enforcement agencies in the United States were to begin to contract out certain duties to the private security sector in a truly major sense (see **Chapter 7**), average rates of growth of revenues and employment could dramatically increase well beyond the rates shown in these tables. There are few, if any, comparable events that would likely have a similar effect on the proprietary sector. An entirely unforeseen explosion in national crime rates or the often-prophesied advent of true international terrorism in America could conceivably have the same influence, but these eventualities are extremely improbable on the basis of any currently available analyses.

Figure 6.1 shows the private security industry in a slightly different way. First, the figure illustrates the revenues and expenditures for private security for each milestone year of the period of 1980 to the year 2000. Second, the manufacturing segment's revenues include both service revenues and equipment sales revenues. The figure shows the major components of the private security industry in terms of revenues and expenditures for 2 decades. Clearly, the manufacturing segment has the greatest total revenues, followed by the proprietary and guard segments. Following in rank order are the alarm segment, "other," locksmiths, private investigators, armored car companies, and consultants/engineers.

FIGURE 6.1

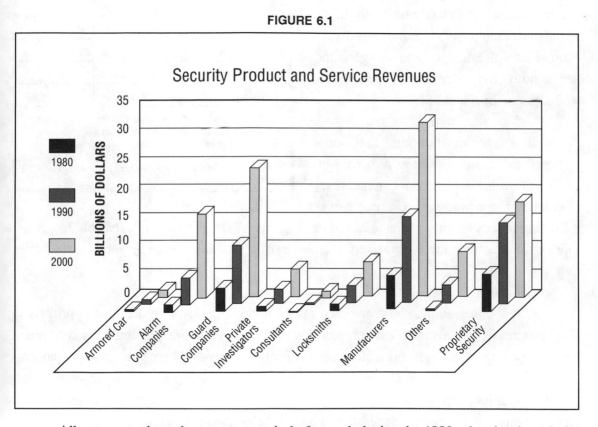

All segments show the greatest period of growth during the 1990s, despite the relative slowdown in growth by some segments, such as proprietary, armored car, and locksmiths. While it is not apparent from this figure, more detailed tabulations presented later in this chapter will indicate that the fastest-growing segments (average annual revenue growth rate to the year 2000) are consultants/engineers (12%), alarm companies (12%), and security manufacturers (12%).

Table 6.5 illustrates average annual revenues/expenditures and employment on a "per company" basis. While the figures for the manufacturing segment are not surprising, the armored car statistics are startling. The explanation, however, is not complicated. About 70 armored car companies share the revenues of the entire segment. Moreover, while the armored car segment is not the oldest (guard companies are the oldest), it is likely to be the most mature segment, having experienced substantial consolidation due to mergers and acquisitions of armored car companies, as well as some business failures.

It is also worth noting that some armored car companies have also entered the guard business. The gross annual revenues shown for armored car companies include revenues for other than armored car services. Presently, it is not feasible to extract those revenues for a more accurate picture of earnings derived from armored car services only.

TABLE 6.5 HALLCREST ESTIMATE OF AVERAGE ANNUAL REVENUES PER COMPANY AND AVERAGE EMPLOYMENT PER COMPANY - 1990		
Industry Segment	Average Annual Revenues Per Company	Average Employment Per Company
Armored Car	$10,714,000	214
Alarm	$354,000	9
Guard	$980,000	52
Private Investigator	$160,000	5
Consultant/Engineer	$412,500	4
Locksmith	$242,000	6
Manufacturing	$5,710,000	35
Other	$750,000	20
Proprietary	$272,000*	11*

NOTE: See **page 217** and **Table 6.26** for a discussion of the effect the largest companies have on the statistical averages of all companies in each industry segment.

* Average annual operating costs; security department employees

A few observations about armored car company employment are also appropriate. The chief reason the armored car company average of 214 persons per company is so much higher than any other segments is that there virtually are no small armored car companies--relatively speaking. Conversely, in the guard segment, the fact that there are many small guard companies brings that segment's average employment per company down substantially. Related to this point, the reader is directed to **Table 6.27** on **page 218** which discusses the influence the largest companies in industry segments have on the statistical averages for their respective segments. For example, if the top 40 guard companies are eliminated from consideration, the average number of employees per company drops from 52 persons to 27. Other significant aspects of **Table 6.5** are that the average private investigation firm has gross revenues of $160,000 per year and employs 5 persons. Further, the typical consulting or security engineering firm has annual revenues of about $412,000 and has 4 employees. In these industry segments it is unlikely that there are sufficiently large companies to substantially distort these averages.

Although it is discussed in greater detail later in this chapter, a few brief comments about the proprietary segment averages are in order. Hallcrest estimates that in 1990 the average corporate security department (they are, in point of fact, not all designated as departments by their companies) has an annual operating budget of $272,000 and employs approximately 11 persons. Although many industry authorities would support the employment estimate, some specialists on corporate security departments would argue with the operating cost estimate, believing it to be about double that estimated by the Hallcrest research staff. The research staff members are convinced, however, that higher estimates are due to substantial underreporting by very small company security staffs.

It is certain that very large corporations in America have annual security department operating costs in the millions of dollars and employ hundreds of persons. Conversely, were one to arbitrarily eliminate the 500 largest companies in the United States from consideration, then--based on very speculative estimates--the resulting average operating budget for security elements within the remaining companies may be far below $200,000 per year and may support 5, or fewer, persons. This would probably describe thousands of small businesses that--one could hypothesize--employ several off-duty, moonlighting police officers or traditional night watchmen and that have virtually no electronic security systems, or, at most, 1 or 2 closed-circuit television cameras or glass-foil window alarms. Moreover, there is no question that there are thousands of small businesses in America that employ no security personnel and have no security operating budget whatsoever. It is doubtful, therefore, that anyone has a clear picture of the truly average security department.

Security Compared With Other Service Industries

The Bureau of Labor Statistics (BLS) recently published *Outlook 2000*, which attempts to predict the shape of the economy and occupations to the year 2000.[5] Although the BLS predicts slower growth for U.S. industries, it is noteworthy that within the service sector (**Table 6.6**), security operations and maintenance ranks in the top 8 service industries in terms of growth rates for 1990. For the period of 1988 to 2000, **Table 6.7,** also from the

BLS, ranks "detective and protective services" among the top 20 fastest-growing service industries, growing at an estimated average annual rate of 2.6%, only slightly higher than Hallcrest's prediction of 2.3%.

Since the BLS projects a very high rate of growth for security services, it is of related interest that *The Hallcrest Report* (1985) recounted Lester Thurow's comment in his book *The Zero-Sum Society* (1982) that private security guards constrain rather than stimulate the national economy.[6] He stated:

While less than 30% of the additional man-hours added to the economy from 1965 to 1972 had been in services, 47% of all man-hours added to the private economy after 1972 were in services. Since service productivity is 40% below the national average, every worker moving into services represented a sharp cut in average productivity...The essence of the problem can be seen in the 300,000 security guards added to our economy since 1972. Since security guards protect old goods and do not produce new goods, they add nothing to output, but they increase man-hours of work.

As noted in *The Hallcrest Report* (1985), many security managers would successfully argue that goods lost to theft, fire, and other forms of loss affect the profitability of a company and thus the economy. The lost goods are not automatically replaced with the purchase of new goods. In the case of manufacturing and industrial uses of security personnel, the protection of raw materials, precious metals, production machinery, and proprietary information all have a direct bearing on the ability of the company to produce new goods at a profit.

TABLE 6.6 THE SERVICE SECTOR IN 1990 Growth Rates for Selected Industries Predicted for 1990	
INDUSTRY	**PERCENT CHANGE**
Space Commerce	20.0%
Electronic Information Services	20.0%
Computer Software	18.0%
Computer Professional Services	17.6%
Data Processing	16.0%
Management Consulting & Public Relations	15.0%
Operations and Maintenance	
Airlines	15.0%
SECURITY	**15.0%**
Buildings	10.0%
Electric Power	07.5%
Prerecorded Music	14.0%
Health and Medical Services	10.4%
Cable Television	10.0%
Home Entertainment	10.0%
Hotels and Motels	08.5%
Electric Power	07.5%
Equipment Testing	07.5%
Food Retailing	07.5%
Airlines	07.0%
Trucking	06.5%
SOURCE: *U.S. Industrial Outlook*	

180

SERVICE SECTOR

The major segments of the service and manufacturing sector include 7 major categories of companies: armored car, alarm, contract guard and patrol, private investigation, consulting and/or engineering, locksmithing, and manufacturing and distributing. Information pertaining to the manufacturing and distributing segment is presented in 2 parts, equipment or product revenues and service revenues. This section addresses service industry revenues and does not include equipment revenues. Revenues derived from services provided resulting from the sale of equipment are included. Information about revenues derived from the sale of security equipment and materials is presented separately further in this chapter. The eighth category in this study is "other," used to subsume the remaining service segments not represented within the other service categories. There are approximately 26 miscellaneous services included within "other."

TABLE 6.7 EMPLOYMENT CHANGE IN SELECTED INDUSTRIES: 1988-2000	
INDUSTRY*	**Annual rate of change 1988-2000**
Fastest growing:	
Computer and data processing services	4.9 %
Outpatient facilities and health services	4.7 %
Personnel supply services	4.1 %
Water and sanitation including combined services	3.9 %
Residential care	3.8 %
Office of health practitioners	3.5 %
Arrangement of passenger transportation	3.4 %
Research, management, and consulting services	3.2 %
Individual and miscellaneous social services	3.2 %
Personal services	3.2 %
Nursing and personal care facilities	3.1 %
Credit reporting and business services	3.1 %
Miscellaneous publishing	3.1 %
Security and commodity brokers and exchanges	3.0 %
Advertising	2.8 %
Legal services	2.8 %
Automotive rentals, without drivers	2.7 %
Accounting, auditing, and services	2.7 %
Miscellaneous transportation services	2.7 %
DETECTIVE AND PROTECTIVE SERVICES	**2.6% ****

SOURCE: Valerie Personick, "Industry Output and Employment: A Slower Trend for the Nineties," Monthly Labor Review, Bureau of Labor Statistics, U.S. Department of Labor, Vol. 112, No. 11, November 1989, p.31.
  * Ranking is based on industries with employment levels of more than 50,000 in 1988.
  ** Hallcrest projection for rate of growth is 2.3%

There is considerable overlap among some of the major segments addressed by this study, as well as among the numerous miscellaneous categories covered by "other." Many of the segments provide services associated with other segments in addition to their own. Many guard companies, for example, provide investigative and consulting services, and some are involved in alarm systems sales and services as well. An increasing number of armored car companies provide traditional guard services. Locksmiths and private investigation companies, on the other hand, primarily restrict their services to their own segment, with the exception that some private investigative firms do offer security consulting services. For the reader to fully understand the tables and figures presented further in this chapter, a brief description of the major service and manufacturing segments is presented below.

Armored Car

This report restricts this category to armored car companies and excludes couriers. Couriers were included in *The Hallcrest Report* (1985) but are deleted from this category for the current report because they are virtually indistinguishable from express delivery and messenger services. Armored car companies have a critical fiduciary relationship with their clients in assuming significant liabilities for shipments of valuables while in their care. The high capitalization involved in armored trucks, as well as the costly and difficult-to-obtain fidelity insurance have been significant barriers to entry into the armored car industry. The industry has clearly been dominated by a relatively small number of national firms. As **Table 6.5** on **page 178** indicated, armored car companies have average annual revenues per company of about $11 million, far higher than any other service industry segment. As noted earlier in this chapter, about 70 armored car companies share the revenues of the entire segment. Moreover, the armored car segment is likely to be the most mature segment in the service sector, having experienced substantial consolidation over the years, primarily due to mergers and acquisitions of armored car companies. It is generally believed that the armored car segment has not only matured as a business, but also saturated its market in terms of "old business." New accounts would primarily come from new businesses rather than from established companies. For these reasons trendline projections for this segment predict very slow growth and a decrease in the number of operating companies as the result of consolidation from acquisitions and, possibly, from business failures.

The Hallcrest staff estimates that in 1990 armored car companies will have annual revenues of about $750 million (up from $350 million in 1980) at an average annual rate of growth for the preceding decade of 8%. The research staff projects revenues will rise to $1.3 billion at a slower average annual rate of 5% by the year 2000. The greatest slowdown should occur during the last half of the next 10 years. It is also worth noting that some armored car companies have also entered the guard business. The gross annual revenues shown for armored car companies include revenues for other than armored car services.

There were about 120 armored car companies in 1980. By 1990, this number fell to 70, primarily due to acquisitions and mergers. The Hallcrest research staff believes that the number of armored car companies will decrease to about 60 over the next 10 years. If any unforeseen changes occur, there may be yet fewer companies in 2000.

Over the 3 milestone years, employment will rise only slightly. In 1980 there were approximately 12,000 employees in this segment. By 1990 employment rose to 15,000 and should peak at 16,500 by the end of the decade. The average annual rate of growth in employment in the armored car segment is estimated to be about 1% (roughly the same as for the national work force), down from 3% for the previous 10-year period. In the year 2000, the average armored car company will have revenues of $18 million and will employ almost 250 persons.

Alarm Companies

The alarm company category is intended to describe companies that primarily derive income from the sale, installation, monitoring, maintenance, and repair of security alarm systems. Commercial alarm firms, national and local, are a major element of this service industry segment, deriving most of their income from annual recurring revenues for monitoring services and from the sale and installation of new systems. Local installing alarm companies and dealers are other major components of this segment. It is also worth noting that many alarm companies derive substantial income from the sale, installation, and monitoring of fire and life-safety systems. These revenues have not been extracted from the data.

Alarm company revenues totaled $1.3 billion in 1980, increasing rapidly to $4.5 billion in 1990 at an annual rate of 13%, and are projected at $14 billion by 2000, at the same rate of growth. Alarm companies' average annual rate of growth, as well as that of consultants and manufacturers, is the highest rate of all segments of the service industry. The number of alarm companies operating in America will increase from about 13,000 in 1990 to an estimated 24,000 in the year 2000, tied only with manufacturers as the fastest-growing segment in terms of new company start-ups, at an annual rate of 7%.

The rate of employment in the alarm company segment will be about 6 times the national employment rate of growth. There are currently about 120,000 persons employed by alarm companies. Over the next 10 years employment will increase to a quarter of a million. Although somewhat speculative, in the event that the cost of residential security systems were to decrease dramatically in the next few years (a distinct possibility), the gross annual revenues and employment levels for the alarm segment could conceivably increase well beyond the projections of this report. Otherwise, however, the Hallcrest research staff expects alarm company earnings and employment to peak during the mid-1990s and to start a gradual slowdown by the end of the decade.

Contract Guards

The contract guard and patrol segment was split from private investigative services for this report. They had been combined for *The Hallcrest Report* (1985), as they are in most other market analysis reports. A comparison of the 2 Hallcrest reports would reveal that some information is in apparent variance. The separation of guard and investigative services caused some of the variance. Another reason for the differences is that it now appears that gross annual revenues and employment levels for 1980 were slightly understated in the 1985 report. The employment statistics for the guard industry are generally more available and more reliable than the data for gross annual revenues. Although the Hallcrest research staff believes that the BLS and Census data for employment in the guard industry are generally low, the Hallcrest estimates are only slightly higher and are within 1 standard deviation. The Hallcrest estimates and projections for the milestone years of 1980, 1990, and 2000 were, therefore, anchored on employment data.

The gross annual revenues for the guard and patrol industry are estimated to have been $3.8 billion in 1980. By 1990 the revenues increased to $9.8 billion at an average annual rate of 10%. By 2000, Hallcrest projects that revenues will increase to about $21 billion at an annual rate of 8%--a slight slowdown.

When reviewing gross annual revenue estimates, it should be noted that guard companies, particularly the largest companies, are usually involved in many revenue-producing activities in addition to guard and patrol services. The services offered include security consulting, investigations, bodyguard and executive protection details, equipment sales, installation of systems, employment screening, shopping (honesty testing) services, and for-profit operation of prisons and fire departments. There is presently insufficient information available to sort out the proportion of guard company revenues derived from traditional guard services. While this may be possible to do for the major guard companies, it is not feasible for the entire industry.

The number of guard companies operating in the United States increased from 7,500 in 1980 to 10,000 in 1990 and will likely rise to 15,000 by the year 2000. The current annual rate of growth of new guard companies--the largest employers in the security service industry--is approximately 3%. Contract guard employment is already larger than proprietary guard employment; in 1980 they were about equal. Presently, there are about 520,000 contract guards as compared to 528,000 proprietary security personnel, of which an estimated 393,000 are proprietary guards. Hallcrest predicts that contract guards will be more than double the number of proprietary guards by the year 2000. At the end of the decade, there will be 750,000 contract guards, compared to 410,000 proprietary security personnel of which about 280,000 will be guards. The average annual rate of growth for employment in the contract guard industry was about 5% during the 1980s, and should decline slightly to about 4% during the 1990s.

Private Investigators

"Private investigators," a new category for *The Hallcrest Report* (1990), is intended to represent only those firms that primarily provide private investigative services. Traditionally, investigators have been reported in combination with guard services since many, and probably most, guard companies provide some form of investigative service.

In 1982, a national mailing list firm estimated that there were 5,500 detective agencies and 4,000 guard firms. On the basis of this information, about 60% of guard and investigative firms were private investigative concerns. It was recognized, however, that mailing list and yellow pages counts often resulted in inflated figures because branch offices were often counted as separate entities and because many guard companies listed themselves in both categories. On the basis of various corrections, the 1985 Hallcrest study speculated that there were 2,500 firms primarily engaged in private investigative services and 8,500 guard companies.[7] The Hallcrest data seemed to indicate that less than 25% of guard and investigative companies were primarily private investigation firms. With the aid of more accurate data, especially state licensing and registration information, the Hallcrest staff now believes that the 1985 private investigation firm estimates were low and that the guard company estimates were too high.

In 1989, approximately 67,000 private investigators were registered with state regulatory commissions in 37 states. Generally, these people were not also registered as security guards. The 13 states that do not register private investigators would increase the estimate. Some sources estimated total private investigation employment in 1989 to be as high as 98,000.[8] Moreover, there are likely private investigators who have not registered with their state governments. On the other hand, some of the most populous states, such as California (which alone accounts for 5,000 private investigators), were in the counted states where it is known that private security employment is 4 to 5 times higher than national averages. Therefore, it was not practical to increase the 67,000 estimate proportionally on the basis of the 13 uncounted states since they may not represent the same per state ratio of investigators as the 37 counted states. It was also noted that there is a high annual attrition of private investigators, some of whom are eventually hired by guard companies. Consequently, this report maintained a very conservative estimate of 70,000 private investigators for 1990.

Given that the private investigation industry is believed to be fairly stable, a conservative annual rate of growth in employment is estimated as 4.5%. Although some sources had placed that rate as high as 20% on a short-term basis, Hallcrest elected to use 4.5% as a long-term trend rate because most of the data were fairly suspect. *Security* reported that the average private investigation firm grossed about $85,000 annually in 1989 and employed 2.5 investigators, and that there were approximately 26,000 firms.[9] Although the Hallcrest research team believed that the 26,000 figure was double what it should be (since the addition of guard and private investigation companies would have brought the total of both categories well beyond reasonable levels), the revenue and employment data developed by *Security* were helpful in refining estimates for this category.

As a consequence of these analyses, the Hallcrest staff estimates that there are about 15,000 private investigation companies in 1990. On the basis of licensing data, it is estimated that about 70,000 full-time private investigators are employed by these firms. Using the above-noted 4.5% employment growth rate and a 12% company growth rate--both rates applied retroactively--Hallcrest now estimates that in 1980 there were approximately 5,000 private investigation firms employing at least 45,000 persons. Hallcrest projects that by the year 2000 there will be 23,000 private investigation firms employing about 90,000 investigators.

Payroll estimates were utilized to calculate reasonable annual revenues for this segment of the industry. The gross annual revenues for private investigation firms in 1980 are estimated to have been $850 million. By 1990, the revenues had increased at an annual rate of 11% to $2.4 billion. By 2000, the annual rate of growth for revenues should decrease to 7%, totalling about $4.6 billion for private investigation services.

Consultants/Security Engineers

The category of security consultants is intended to classify those security firms and employees deriving their primary income from consultation fees. This is another industry segment that has received very limited analysis and sketchy reporting. The International Association of Professional Security Consultants (IAPSC) reports a mailing list of more than 600 persons. A 1972 government-published *Directory of Security Consultants* listed 6,622 persons employed by 128 firms.[10] Upon review, however, it was noted that guard companies, academic institutions, associations, security book authors, and publishers were included in the listing.   Additional information was obtained from a 1988 report prepared by Freedonia Group, which estimated that the security consultant segment would receive gross annual revenues of $625 million in 1991 and would grow at an average annual rate of 13%.[11] *The Hallcrest Report* (1985) contained additional information about the consulting segment useful in deriving reasonable estimates.

On the basis of these often conflicting sources of information, the Hallcrest staff used employment and payroll estimates to balance consulting firm employment, number of companies, and gross annual revenues. This report estimates that in 1980 the consulting segment collected approximately $80 million in gross annual revenues and that there were about 270 firms employing 1,200 persons. By 1990, revenues grew at a rate of 15% to $330 million, the highest rate of growth of all service categories with the exception of "other."

The number of firms increased to 800 and employment rose to 2,900 persons. Hallcrest projects that by the end of the next decade, revenues will be about $1 billion, growing at an annual rate of 12%. As proprietary security departments gradually decrease in size, it is believed that more and more work will be contracted out to consultants. In the year 2000 there may be 1,400 consulting firms, employing 6,200 persons.

Over the next 10 years the consulting and security engineering segment may be 1 of the fastest-growing categories, tied for first place with alarm companies and security manufacturers. The steepest rate of growth may well be during the second half of the coming decade. The average annual growth of new companies may be about 6% over the next 10 years. This segment may experience one of the highest rates of increase in employment among all service segments--about 8%.

Security engineering appears to be a significant emerging element within the consulting segment. Many new major construction projects and national-level architectural firms are routinely adding security engineering firms to the design team. Hallcrest predicts exceptionally high growth rates for the security engineering element of the consultant category. While there are no statistics collected about this element, it is doubtful that there are currently more than 25 specialized security engineering firms in the nation or that they collectively employ more than 300 persons. Considering all of American industry, namely security engineers working for architectural, engineering, and construction firms as well as for federal and military agencies, it is possible that there may be as many as 1,500 security engineers. It is not a state-registered engineering practice; most security engineers tend to have begun work as electrical engineers and obtained their specialized training on the job.

Locksmiths

Locksmiths have not been tabulated by most private security industry studies and were not fully considered by *The Hallcrest Report* (1985). It is evident that locksmiths primarily serve a security function. However, they generally operate outside of conventional security circles, with their own trade associations and journals. It is, perhaps, for these reasons that locksmiths have been ignored by virtually all security studies. In addition to the sale and installation of locks and locking devices, such as safes, many lock shops sell security alarm equipment. The Hallcrest research staff thought it was important to begin considering this service industry segment in order to have an accurate profile of the entire industry. The addition of locksmiths to the study, to include revisions of earlier Hallcrest data, caused significant shifts in industry estimates of annual revenues, employment, and the number of private security companies.

Based on locksmith trade association and journal data, the Hallcrest staff estimates that in 1980 locksmiths grossed at least $1.1 billion and that there were 6,000 operating lock shops employing about 45,000 persons. Revenues for this segment grew at an average annual rate of 10%, and by 1990 annual revenues increased to $2.9 billion, the number of firms increased to 12,000, and employment rose to almost 70,000 persons. Hallcrest projects that at the end of the coming decade gross revenues will climb to $5.7 billion at an average annual rate of 7%. There will be 17,000 lock shops, employing 88,000 persons.

Manufacturers and Distributors

While security equipment manufacturers have always been a key element of private security industry studies, the focus has usually been on equipment and product revenues. This report attempts to broaden the analysis by estimating the size of employment among manufacturers, as well as the portions of the industry's gross annual revenues that may be attributed to service revenues by manufacturers. Many manufacturers derive meaningful income from the installation, maintenance, and repair of security equipment and systems in addition to revenues from the sales of shipments of equipment. This category also includes distributors, who may be considered intermediaries between manufacturers and installing companies and local dealers. Ideally, distributors should be separated from manufacturing service revenues since they primarily collected revenues from marking up equipment sales. For this study, it was not feasible to extract distributor statistics from the project data base. Inquiries into traditional markups by both manufacturers and distributors were made, however, and these markups were useful in assessing and calculating statistics for the entire category.

It is estimated that in 1980 manufacturers and distributors collected $1 billion in service-related revenues and about $4.6 billion in equipment sales. This segment grew at an average annual rate of 10% from 1980 to 1990 for both sales and service revenues. Currently, the Hallcrest research staff estimates that this segment had gross annual service revenues of $2.6 billion and equipment revenues of $11.7 billion in 1990. The staff projects that manufacturer and distributor service revenue growth will be about 12% over the next 10 years; sales revenues will grow at a rate of 7%. Combined revenues will grow at an average annual rate of 8%. By 2000, service revenues should be almost $8 billion, and the value of shipments will approach $24 billion. The growth of new manufacturing and distributing companies will be strong during the next decade, averaging almost 7% per year. Employment will increase more slowly at 4%, but still about 3 times faster than the national employment average for the decade.

Other

There are at least 26 service segments in the service and manufacturing sector separate from the major 7 noted above. These service areas are listed below. Several of the services are general business services; they are included on the list only because some companies providing these services specialize primarily, or exclusively, in the security industry.

- Couriers (security)
- Credit/check approval
- Data conversion
- Disaster recovery
- Document destruction
- Dogs, guard
- Drug testing
- Eavesdropping detection
- Executive/VIP protection
- Expert witness
- Forensic analysis
- Hostage negotiations
- Identification badges
- Insurance underwriting
- Market research
- Penetration testing
- Personnel recruitment (security)
- Property marking/analysis
- Property repossession
- Publishing
- Risk information service
- Security storage
- Security training
- Shopping (honesty) services
- Truth/honesty verification
- Uniform rental

The Hallcrest research staff is not aware of any comprehensive breakdowns for most of these miscellaneous service segments. In total, however, the "other" category is a significant portion of the private security industry. For this reason it was decided that the category could not be arbitrarily deleted from the industry profile. On the basis of estimates by numerous sources, in addition to the interviews conducted by the Hallcrest staff, reasonable totals were estimated for revenues and employment for the entire private security industry. The estimates for the "other" category were, consequently, developed on the basis of what could not otherwise be accounted for, as well as calculations related to balancing the numbers of employees for this category with possible aggregate gross annual revenues. The estimates for this category are speculative.

Clearly, some elements of this miscellaneous category are experiencing a boom period of growth. With the virtual abolition of commercial polygraph testing, alternate means of honesty forecasting (commonly dubbed "paper and pencil" honesty testing) are experiencing record-breaking growth. More than 50 such firms are listed in major security service directories. Another rapidly growing segment consists of those firms involved in drug testing and drug awareness training services. While some elements of these firms may only be indirectly linked to security services, many of the service contracts are being managed through corporate security departments.

The Hallcrest staff estimates that the gross revenues for this category were $300 million in 1980, are $3 billion in 1990, and will be $7.5 billion by 2000. The rate of growth of gross annual revenues from 1980 to 1990 is roughly estimated as being 26% per year--an astonishing rate, if valid. The number of firms in this category is believed to have been approximately 1,000 in 1980, increasing to 4,000 by 1990, and is expected to reach 7,000 over the next 10 years. The annual rate of growth of new companies entering this miscellaneous category was 15% until 1990, but is expected to slow to 6% by the year 2000. Employment followed the same pattern. The number of employees was 13,000, 80,000, and 140,000 for this period. It is thought, however, that the high annual rates of growth for the 1980 to 1990 period are probably due to underestimating base figures and that true rates of growth, while very strong, probably did not actually exceed 15% for revenues and 12% for start-up companies.

SERVICE REVENUES 1980 TO 2000

Tables **6.8**, **6.9**, and **6.10** provide a more detailed tabulation of estimates and projections of gross annual revenues and expenditures for the service and manufacturing segments of the private security industry from 1980 to the year 2000. **Table 6.8** provides revenue data for 1980. The preceding sections of this chapter summarized the individual profiles of the service segments. **Table 6.9** provides the same information for 1990 but additionally presents a comparison among service areas in terms of annual revenues and the percent of the total revenues for the service sector each segment collected. This and subsequent tables also permit the reader to rank the service segments, in terms of both revenues and average annual rates of growth. **Table 6.10** presents estimates of average annual rates of growth since 1980, as well as changes in service revenue market share.

TABLE 6.8		
SECURITY SERVICE AND MANUFACTURING SECTOR - 1980		
Hallcrest Estimates of Gross Annual Service Revenues		
Segment	*Annual Revenues*	*Percent of Market Share*
Armored Car	$350,000,000	4%
Alarm Companies	$1,300,000,000	15%
Contract Guards	$3,800,000,000	43%
Private Investigators	$850,000,000	10%
Consultants/Engineers	$80,000,000	1%
Locksmiths	$1,100,000,000	13%
Manufacturers and Distributors*	$1,000,000,000	11%
Other	$300,000,000	3%
TOTAL	**$8,780,000,000**	

* Only service revenues represented; sales (shipment) revenues presented later in this chapter.

Year 2000 projections are tabulated in **Table 6.10**. Changes in the average rate of annual growth for revenues from 1980 to 1990 and from 1990 to 2000 are indicated. Slowdowns are predicted for all service segments with the exception of manufacturing service revenues, which are anticipated to increase by 2%. Changes in service industry market shares for the periods of 1980 to 1990 and 1980 to 2000 are also identified. These changes suggest that by the end of the next decade alarm companies, consulting firms, and manufacturers should gain market share, while the remaining areas are expected to lose ground. The greatest percentage decrease in security service industry market share will occur for the guard segment. This is misleading, since guard services will continue to see strong growth in revenues; the drop in market share only reflects strong growth by other segments, notably alarm companies and manufacturers. The guard segment will have a 34% service sector market share in 2000, followed by alarm companies with a 22% share. The guard industry's loss of 3% of market share in the coming decade is regarded as comparatively minor.

192

TABLE 6.9
SECURITY SERVICE AND MANUFACTURING SECTOR - 1990
Hallcrest Estimates of Gross Annual Service Revenues

Segment	Annual Revenues	Average Annual Rate of Growth (since 1980)	Market Share	Change in Market Share (since 1980)
Armored Car	$750,000,000	8%	3%	-1%
Alarm Companies	$4,500,000,000	13%	17%	+2%
Contract Guards	$9,800,000,000	10%	37%	-6%
Private Investigators	$2,400,000,000	11%	9%	-1%
Consultants/Engineers	$330,000,000	15%	1%	0%
Locksmiths	$2,900,000,000	10%	11%	-2%
Manufacturers and Distributors*	$2,574,000,000	10%	10%	-1%
Other	$3,000,000,000	26%	11%	+8%
TOTAL	**$26,254,000,000**	12%		

* Only service revenues represented; sales (shipment) revenues are presented later in this chapter. Proprietary security data is not provided in this table.

Another interesting way to view private security revenue and expenditure data is in a pie chart, as depicted in **Figure 6.2**. This illustration also presents a very different industry profile than shown in the tables, because it also includes the proprietary security sector, which is not tabulated in the previous tables. Another variance from the tables is that the manufacturing sector depicts both service revenues and equipment revenues, whereas the table only tabulated service earnings. On these bases, the largest component of the private security industry in 1990 in terms of revenues/expenditures is the manufacturing segment, representing about 28% of all revenues.

TABLE 6.10
SECURITY SERVICE AND MANUFACTURING SECTOR - 2000
Hallcrest Projections of Gross Annual Service Revenues

Segment	Annual Revenues	Average Annual Rate of Growth (since 1990)	Change in Rate of Growth (since 1990)	Market Share	Change in Market Share (since 1990)	Change in Market Share (since 1980)
Armored Car	$1,250,000,000	5%	-3%	2%	-2%	-1%
Alarm Companies	$14,000,000,000	12%	-1%	22%	+5%	+7%
Contract Guards	$21,500,000,000	8%	-2%	34%	-3%	-9%
Private Investigators	$4,600,000,000	7%	-4%	7%	-2%	-3%
Consultants/Engineers	$1,050,000,000	12%	-3%	2%	+1%	+1%
Locksmiths	$5,700,000,000	7%	-3%	9%	-2%	-4%
Manufacturers and Distributors	$7,829,000,000	12%	+2%	12%	+2%	-1%
Other	$7,500,000,000	10%	-16%	12%	+1%	+9%
TOTAL	**$63,429,000,000**	9%	-3%			

FIGURE 6.2

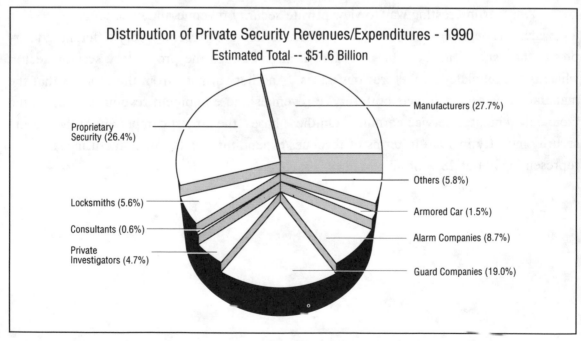

Distribution of Private Security Revenues/Expenditures - 1990
Estimated Total -- $51.6 Billion

Manufacturers (27.7%)

Proprietary Security (26.4%)

Others (5.8%)

Locksmiths (5.6%)

Armored Car (1.5%)

Consultants (0.6%)

Alarm Companies (8.7%)

Private Investigators (4.7%)

Guard Companies (19.0%)

194

The proprietary sector is close with 26%, followed by guards at 19%. Consequently, these 3 components amount to almost three-quarters of all revenues and expenditures in 1990. For a related view, refer to **Figure 6.1** on **page 177**, which depicts the private security industry in bar-graph form for the entire 1980 to 2000 period.

NUMBERS OF PRIVATE SECURITY COMPANIES
1980 - 2000

Table 6.11 depicts the growth of private security companies from 1980 to the year 2000. The most significant information represented by this table is that the majority of new company growth (percent of total) over the coming decade will be in the alarm, private investigator, and locksmith segments. On the basis of rates of annual growth of new companies the alarm and manufacturing segments will both experience the highest rate, 7%. The alarm and manufacturing segments will have the highest rates in terms of average annual rates of new company growth.

Segment	Companies in 1980	Percent of Total 1980	Companies in 1990	Percent of Total 1990	Average Annual Rate of Growth 1980 to 1990	Companies in 2000	Percent of Total 2000	Average Annual Rate of Growth 1990 to 2000
Armored Car	120	0.4%	70	0.1%	-5%	60	0.1%	0%
Alarm Companies	8,500	29%	12,700	22%	+4%	24,000	26%	+7%
Contract Guards	7,500	25%	10,000	18%	+3%	15,000	16%	+4%
Private Investigators	5,000	17%	15,000	26%	+12%	23,000	25%	+4%
Consultants/ Engineers	270	1%	800	1%	+12%	1,400	2%	+6%
Locksmiths	6,000	20%	12,000	11%	+7%	17,000	18%	+4%
Manufacturers and Distributors	1,200	4%	2,500	10%	+8%	4,800	5%	+7%
Other	1,000	3%	4,000	11%	+15%	7,000	8%	+6%
TOTAL	29,590		57,070		+7%	92,270		+5%

TABLE 6.11
SECURITY SERVICE AND MANUFACTURING SECTOR
Hallcrest Projections of Number of Companies to 2000

PRIVATE SECURITY EMPLOYMENT

Table 6.12 presents the composition of private security employment in 1990, including proprietary security employment to depict the employment profile of the entire industry. It is evident that the proprietary sector continues to be one of the major employers of security personnel, representing more than 35% of all private security employees. In 1990 contract security guards are virtually tied at 35%. Thus, these 2 segments account for almost three-quarters of all employment. Most other segments range from 5% to 8% of the total of all employees, except for armored car company employees and consultants at 1% and 0.2%, respectively. The Hallcrest staff believes that the proprietary sector will rapidly begin to lose ground in terms of employment by the end of the coming decade. Hallcrest estimates that by 2000 proprietary employment will account for only 20%. Guard companies will maintain their 35% share, and most employment gains will be made by the remaining segments, but particularly by alarm companies, manufacturers, and services represented by the "other" category.

TABLE 6.12 SECURITY SERVICE AND MANUFACTURING SECTOR HALLCREST ESTIMATES OF PRIVATE SECURITY EMPLOYMENT - 1990		
Segment	Employees in 1990	Percent of Total
Armored Car	15,000	1.0%
Alarm Companies	120,000	8.0%
Contract Guards	520,000	34.8%
Private Investigators	70,000	4.7%
Consultants/Engineers	2,900	0.2%
Locksmiths	69,600	4.7%
Manufacturers and Distributors	88,300	5.9%
Other	79,500	5.3%
Proprietary Security	528,000	35.4%
TOTAL	**1,493,300**	**100%**

Table 6.13, on the following page, presents employment data without the heavy influence of the proprietary sector. On this basis, about 54% of all private security employees work for guard companies. Alarm companies are the next largest employer, accounting for 12% of employment. As of 1990, there are about 4 times as many guard company employees as alarm company personnel. By the year 2000, the difference narrows and the ratio is only 3 times. With the exception of the "other" segement, the highest rates of annual growth for employment in 1990 are for security consultants and engineers at 9% and alarm company employment at 8%. The Hallcrest staff expects these segments to continue robust growth at the same approximate rates until the end of the decade. As a minor related note, the growth of employment for the "other" category is depicted as 19%

in 1990. This is largely discounted since the high rate is probably more due to under-reporting in 1980 than to actual growth at that rate. The Hallcrest staff does believe that the miscellaneous service segments represented by this category are experiencing an overall high rate of employment expansion, but the staff doubts that it is as high as 19%. This is regarded as merely a statistical anomaly.

			TABLE 6.13 SECURITY SERVICE AND MANUFACTURING SECTOR Hallcrest Projections of Number of Employees to 2000					
Segment	Employees In 1980	Percent of Total 1980	Employees In 1990	Percent of Total 1990	Average Annual Rate of Growth 1980 to 1990	Employees In 2000	Percent of Total 2000	Average Annual Rate of Growth 1990 to 2000
Armored Car	11,500	2%	15,000	2%	3%	16,500	1%	1%
Alarm Companies	55,000	10%	120,000	12%	8%	250,000	17%	8%
Contract Guards	330,000	59%	520,000	54%	5%	750,000	51%	4%
Private Investigators	45,000	8%	70,000	7%	4%	90,000	6%	2%
Consultants/ Engineers	1,200	0.2%	2,900	0.3%	9%	6,200	0.4%	8%
Locksmiths	45,000	8%	69,600	7%	4%	88,000	6%	2%
Manufacturers and Distributors	55,000	10%	88,300	9%	5%	132,000	9%	4%
Other	13,500	2%	79,500	8%	19%	140,000	10%	6%
TOTAL	556,200		965,300		6%	1,472,700		4%

197

HOW AMERICA USES SECURITY SERVICES

Table 6.14 lists in rank order the distribution of expenditures for private security services and equipment among various segments of American commerce and industry. The industrial and manufacturing sector is the largest purchaser of security services and equipment. Hallcrest estimates that this sector is spending up to $13.4 billion annually, which amounts to more than one-quarter of total revenues collected by private security in 1990.

This table was derived from a 1981 *Security World* survey that estimated the distribution of revenues for 1980 across consumer groups. Since the total revenues estimated by *Security World* were virtually identical to the current Hallcrest estimate for 1980, the Hallcrest staff adjusted the table for 1990. The same percentages were maintained for 1990, but the total was increased to the Hallcrest 1990 estimate of $51.5 billion. The research staff then made minor adjustments of the percentages to reflect perceived trends over the past 10 years.

TABLE 6.14 HALLCREST ESTIMATE DISTRIBUTION OF PRIVATE SECURITY SERVICES AMONG CONSUMER GROUPS - 1990		
Service Area	Expenditures	Percent of Total
Transportation	$500,000,000	1%
Distribution/Warehousing	$2,000,000,000	4%
Utilities/Communications	$2,200,000,000	4%
Hotel/Motel/Resort	$2,500,000,000	5%
Educational Institutions	$2,800,000,000	5%
Health Care Facilities	$2,800,000,000	5%
Financial Institutions	$4,200,000,000	8%
Retail	$9,500,000,000	18%
Government	$10,000,000,000	19%
Industrial/Manufacturing*	$13,400,000,000	26%
Other	$1,800,000,000	3%
TOTAL	**$51,500,000,000**	

SOURCE: " Key Market Coverage," *Security World*, 1981.
* Adjusted from $5.9 billion originally reported, to $5.5 billion to conform with current Hallcrest estimates.

VALUE OF SECURITY SHIPMENTS

The categories in this section are intended to reflect the value of shipments or sales of the described equipment and materials, as well as the total of all ancillary products and materials. For example, the closed-circuit television (CCTV) category would include not only CCTV cameras, monitors, lenses, housings, mounts, and controls, but also coaxial cable, fiber-optic cable, fittings, and any other associated equipment and materials. Following is a brief description of each category:

Access Control

This category includes all types of electronic access control products: electronic card reader systems, biometric systems, badge and identification products, and photographic and digital-storage CCTV identification systems. It also considers mechanical turnstiles, optical turnstiles, and vehicle control systems.

Closed-Circuit Television

As noted, all CCTV products and related products are covered here. Photographic surveillance cameras are not included; these products would fall into the "other" category.

Alarms

This category counts all alarms and alarm components. These include intrusion detection equipment, control panels and control consoles, annunciation devices, control devices, power supplies, duress alarms, point protection alarms, and similar and related products. Associated conduit, wiring, and fittings would also be considered.

Bomb Detection and X-Ray

All forms of bomb detection and X-ray systems are in this category. Included are ion vapor characterization equipment, thermal neutron activation scanners, fixed and portable X-ray equipment, and many other related systems using differing technologies.

Metal Detection

The majority of the products in this category are walk-through metal detectors and hand-held metal detection devices. Also included are letter bomb detectors, which represent a different technology but still involve either metal detection or pattern detection.

Electronic Article Surveillance

Without going into technical descriptions of various methods used to protect articles against theft, this category primarily totals the sales of all systems intended to prevent shoplifting.

Computer Security and Shielding

Included here are all forms of computer security equipment and software. This category also covers equipment and materials designed either to minimize electromagnetic radiation or to reduce the effect of electromagnetic interference. Shielding materials commonly referred to as Tempest equipment (which some market research reports designate as a separate equipment category) are also covered.

Telephone Security

All types of equipment, materials, and encryption hardware and software for telephone, telephone data line, and facsimile machine protection are considered.

Security Lighting

It is difficult to separate the amount of lighting products primarily serving security purposes--sometimes termed "protective lighting." Only rough estimates are made for the value of security lighting shipments.

Security Fencing

In 1980 and for all subsequent milestone years, the largest revenues within the equipment sector were collected by the security fencing segment. Although market share for security fencing drops from 52% to 25% over the 20-year period to 2000, it is expected to remain dominant. This statistic may be misleading because the Hallcrest research staff has not determined what portion of security fence shipments can be regarded as serving primarily security needs, as opposed to decorative or nonsecurity containment purposes, such as for livestock and animal barriers.

Safes, Vaults, and Secure Storage

Aside from safes and vaults, this category also includes security file cabinets, money boxes, classified waste containers, and similar equipment designed to provide secure storage.

Security Locks

This category comprises all types of locking products, both mechanical and electronic. It includes security cylinders, door locks, padlocks, wheel locks, combination locks, and many other types of mechanical locking devices. It also covers electric deadbolts, electric strikes, and electromagnetic locks.

Other

The Bell Atlantic/ASIS *Security Industry Buyers Guide* for 1990 identifies 560 product categories. It is beyond the scope of this chapter to list these categories, but it is evident that there are far more types of products in the security industry than are represented by the 12 categories listed above. The Hallcrest staff estimates that the miscellaneous category, "other," earned about 21% of all sales revenues in 1990. The staff projects that this will increase to 23% by the year 2000. In the aggregate, the "other" category not only has substantial collective earnings, but also is expected to maintain a comparatively high rate of annual growth throughout the 1990s.

Equipment Categories Not Covered

Various security equipment market studies predict high sales volumes for automotive vehicle alarms and garage door openers. *Leading Edge Reports* (1990) predicts that by the year 2000 annual vehicle alarm sales will be $6.2 billion and garage door openers will earn $2.2 billion.[12] The Hallcrest research staff did not include these categories in its analyses of security equipment sales. The staff agrees that these equipment segments should experience brisk growth over the coming decade. It is likely, however, that electronic vehicle alarms are, in large measure, already included in alarm system revenue estimates and forecasts. With regard to garage door openers, the staff concluded that this category of equipment sales was only marginally related to security industry equipment sales. The bulk of garage door opener sales are likely to occur in American industry segments (such as hardware and department stores and the home building industry) that are not traditionally regarded as being within the security industry. Another category of equipment that is not clearly identified in any of the data tables in this report is "over-the-counter" security alarms, also termed "do-it-yourself" security alarms. This category is primarily related to residential security alarms. The scope of this study did not allow for a separation of residential security systems revenues and expenditures from other applications. It is assumed that these revenues and expenditures are already subsumed in various equipment segments.

Value of Shipments - 1980

Table 6.15 tabulates equipment sales for 1980. As expected, security fencing led sales by a wide margin, accounting for 52% of all revenues. The value of shipments for locks and "other" was also high, representing a market share of about 13% each. Security lighting and alarms both had market shares of about 8%. Sales among the remaining categories were fairly uniformly distributed. The total value of shipments for security equipment in 1980 is estimated to have been $4.6 billion.

TABLE 6.15 HALLCREST ESTIMATES OF GROSS ANNUAL EQUIPMENT SALES REVENUES - 1980		
Category	Annual Revenues (Shipments)	Market Share
Access Control	$19,000,000	0.4%
Closed-Circuit Television	$61,000,000	1.3%
Alarms	$358,000,000	7.8%
Bomb Detection & X-Ray	$26,000,000	0.6%
Metal Detection	$12,000,000	0.3%
Electronic Article Surveillance	$31,000,000	0.7%
Computer Security & Shielding	$40,000,000	0.9%
Telephone Security	$10,000,000	0.2%
Security Lighting	$358,000,000	7.8%
Security Fencing	$2,359,000,000	51.5%
Safes, Vaults & Secure Storage	$105,000,000	2.3%
Locks	$574,000,000	12.5%
Other	$625,000,000	13.7%
TOTAL	**$4,578,000,000**	

Value of Shipments - 1990

Table 6.16 presents Hallcrest's estimates for the value of shipments of security equipment in 1990. In addition to the data tabulated for 1990 shipments, this table also calculates the average annual rate of growth since 1980, as well as the change in security equipment market share.

TABLE 6.16				
HALLCREST ESTIMATES OF GROSS ANNUAL EQUIPMENT SALES REVENUES - 1990				
Category*	Annual Revenues (Shipments**)	Average Annual Rate of Growth	Market Share	Change in Market Share from 1980
Access Control	$500,000,000	39%	4%	+4%
Closed-Circuit Television	$260,000,000	16%	2%	+1%
Alarms	$780,000,000	8%	7%	-1%
Bomb Detection & X-Ray	$70,000,000	10%	1%	0%
Metal Detection	$30,000,000	10%	0.3%	0%
Electronic Article Surveillance	$300,000,000	25%	3%	+2%
Computer Security; Shielding	$200,000,000	17%	2%	+1%
Telephone Security	$50,000,000	17%	0.4%	+0.2%
Security Lighting	$790,000,000	8%	7%	-1%
Security Fencing	$4,000,000,000	5%	34%	-17%
Safes, Vaults & Secure Storage	$420,000,000	15%	4%	+2%
Locks	$1,800,000,000	12%	15%	+2%
Other	$2,500,000,000	15%	21%	+7%
TOTAL	**$11,700,000,000**	15%		

* Includes all ancillary products and materials. ** U.S. sales (shipments) only.

Access control equipment and systems maintained an astonishing annual growth rate of 39%. It is probable that low estimates in 1980 contributed to determining this rate, but the Hallcrest staff believes that the access control segment experienced a boom period, certainly higher than 25% per year. Electronic article surveillance has enjoyed a high rate of growth at 25%. The other leaders for this 10-year period are computer security and shielding, telephone security, closed-circuit television, and safes and vaults, in that order. Alarm sales are estimated to have grown at 8% per year. While this is about 3 times the

GNP growth rate, the comparatively low rate for alarm equipment cannot be explained. The research staff anticipated a much higher annual growth rate for alarms; error in the data base is a possible explanation. Hallcrest estimates that the value of shipments for security equipment in 1990 is about $11.7 billion. As expected, access control equipment and electronic article surveillance systems had the greatest gains in security equipment market share. The market share leaders, however, continue to be security fencing and locks.

Despite high revenues, security fencing lost ground, dropping from 52% to 34% in market share. This is probably a reflection that the security fencing industry may be approaching market saturation. The fencing segment has the lowest rate of annual growth. The remaining categories fall into a market share range of 0.3% to 7%. Similarly, with the exception of 2 categories, change in market share for all other categories ranged from -1% to 4%. **Figure 6.3** depicts the percentage of total revenue ($11.7 billion as equipment revenue and $2.6 billion as service revenues for manufacturers) for each segment of security equipment. The dominance of fencing, locks, and the "other" category is self-evident, accounting for almost three-quarters of the equipment/materials market.

FIGURE 6.3

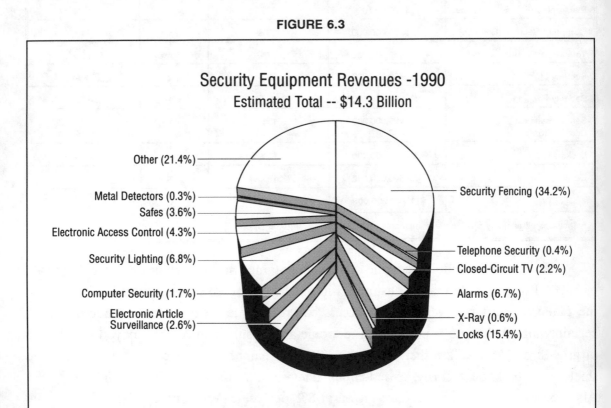

Security Equipment Revenues -1990
Estimated Total -- $14.3 Billion

Other (21.4%)
Metal Detectors (0.3%)
Safes (3.6%)
Electronic Access Control (4.3%)
Security Lighting (6.8%)
Computer Security (1.7%)
Electronic Article Surveillance (2.6%)

Security Fencing (34.2%)
Telephone Security (0.4%)
Closed-Circuit TV (2.2%)
Alarms (6.7%)
X-Ray (0.6%)
Locks (15.4%)

Year 2000 data for security equipment sales are presented in **Table 6.17**. The Hallcrest research staff projects that the annual value of security equipment shipments will be approximately $24 billion by the end of the decade. Hallcrest predicts that the highest rates of annual revenue growth will be for electronic article surveillance (14%), access control (13%), and computer security and shielding equipment and materials (13%). The slowest rates of growth will be in the categories of security fencing (4%), telephone security (5%), and safes and vaults (6%).

Category*	Annual Revenues (Shipments**)	Average Annual Rate of Growth	Change in Annual Rate of Growth from 1990	Market Share	Change in Market Share from 1990	Change in Market Share from 1980
Access Control	$1,700,000,000	13%	-26%	7%	+3%	+7%
Closed-Circuit Television	$755,000,000	11%	-5%	3%	+1%	+2%
Alarms	$1,650,000,000	8%	0%	7%	0%	-1%
Bomb Detection & X-Ray	$190,000,000	11%	+1%	1%	0%	0%
Metal Detection	$84,000,000	11%	+1%	0.4%	0%	0%
Electronic Article Surveillance	$1,100,000,000	14%	-11%	5%	+2%	+4%
Computer Security; Shielding	$650,000,000	13%	-4%	3%	+1%	+2%
Telephone Security	$85,000,000	5%	-12%	0.4%	0%	0%
Security Lighting	$1,737,000,000	8%	0%	7%	0%	-1%
Security Fencing	$6,000,000,000	4%	-1%	25%	-9%	-27%
Safes, Vaults & Secure Storage	$731,000,000	6%	-9%	3%	-1%	+1%
Locks	$3,541,000,000	7%	-5%	15%	0%	+2%
Other	$5,500,000,000	8%	-7%	23%	+2%	+9%
TOTAL	**$23,723,000,000**	**7%**	**-3%**			

TABLE 6.17
HALLCREST ESTIMATES OF GROSS ANNUAL EQUIPMENT SALES REVENUES - 2000

* Includes all ancillary products and materials.   ** U.S. sales (shipments) only.

The greatest change in the annual growth rate is for access control equipment (-26%), but this is primarily the result of an adjustment to the remarkable rate of growth of this equipment segment during the 1980s. Slowdowns occurred for the same reason for telephone security (-12%) and for electronic article surveillance (-11%). In general, all categories are expected to show a decrease in growth rates, with the exceptions of bomb detection/X-ray and metal detection equipment, which will increase their rate of growth by 1%. Security lighting growth will remain unchanged. Security fencing (25%), "other" (23%), and locks (15%) will continue to dominate security equipment market share, but, whereas these categories had 78% of the market in 1980, by 2000 their dominance will drop to 63%. For the period 1980 to 2000, the greatest gains in market share will be by "other" (9%), access control (7%), and electronic article surveillance (4%).

ORIGINAL EQUIPMENT MANUFACTURERS
AND DISTRIBUTORS

The Hallcrest research staff is not aware of any other major market research study that has attempted to quantify original equipment manufacturers (OEMs) and distributors. In that this is a fledgling effort, comments and criticism are encouraged so that the estimates presented in **Table 6.18** may be enhanced over time. The estimates and projections for the milestone years of 1980, 1990, and 2000 are primarily based on counting various listings of equipment manufacturers and suppliers. The key listings include, but are not limited to, *The 1990-1991 Security Letter Source Book*, the 1990 Bell Atlantic/ASIS *Security Industry Buyers Guide*, the "1990 Directory of Products and Services" published by *Security*, and the "Buyers Guide" published by *Security Distributing & Marketing* (SDM).

Another important source is the technical files of Systech Group, Inc., in Reston, VA. Systech Group maintains computerized and hard copy files on approximately 1,200 manufacturers and suppliers, estimated to represent about 40% of all manufacturers and distributors. This assessment was helpful in Hallcrest's estimate that in 1990 there are at least 2,500 companies in this category. It was an early goal to count only OEMs and not distributors, but it was quickly evident that this was not feasible. Some companies are regarded as OEMs by many members of the security industry but, in fact, are distributors and only place their own label on the equipment they are selling. Thus, "relabeling" practices[*] and the use of American distributors by foreign manufacturers make it difficult to separate OEMs from major distributors. High turnover rates among companies due to business failures, and acquisitions add to the difficulties of identifying all manufacturers in the industry.

	1980		1990			2000		
Category	OEM/D	Percent of Total	OEM/D	Percent of Total	Annual Growth Rate	OEM/D	Percent of Total	Annual Growth Rate
Access Control	80	7%	175	7%	8%	400	8%	9%
Closed-Circuit Television	50	4%	80	3%	5%	150	3%	6%
Alarms	90	8%	350	14%	15%	700	15%	7%
Bomb Detection/ X-Ray	25	2%	50	2%	7%	100	2%	7%
Metal Detection	15	1%	25	1%	5%	40	1%	5%
Electronic Article Surveillance	15	1%	30	1%	7%	55	1%	6%
Computer Security; Shielding	85	7%	250	10%	11%	700	15%	11%
Telephone Security	25	2%	50	2%	7%	70	1%	3%
Security Lighting	70	6%	150	6%	8%	220	5%	4%
Security Fencing	110	9%	175	7%	5%	255	5%	4%
Safes, Vaults	50	4%	100	4%	7%	140	3%	3%
Locks	120	10%	300	12%	10%	470	10%	5%
Other	450	38%	765	31%	5%	1,500	31%	7%
TOTAL	**1,185**		**2,500**		**8%**	**4,800**		**7%**

TABLE 6.18
HALLCREST ESTIMATES AND PROJECTIONS OF
NUMBER OF ORIGINAL EQUIPMENT MANUFACTURERS AND DISTRIBUTORS

---

[*] Some manufacturers and distributors replace the original manufacturer's label with their own by special agreement. This practice is prevalent in the security equipment industry. Although most equipment categories follow this practice to some degree, it is especially common for some overseas manufacturers to allow relabeling to enhance sales in the United States. Further, since major manufacturers produce equipment in several categories, some duplicate counting exists in this table.

Hallcrest estimates that in 1980 there were about 1,200 OEMs and distributors. By 1990, this number increased to 2,500, and it is expected to grow to 4,800 by the year 2000. In that the "other" category reflects up to 560 products, it is understandable that this category has the greatest number of companies. Excluding the "other" segment, in 1990 the highest numbers of companies were in the categories for alarms (350), locks (300), computer security/shielding (250), access control (175), security fencing (175), and security lighting (150). The fewest companies were in the categories for metal detection (25) and electronic article surveillance (30).

The projections to the year 2000 were based on Hallcrest's calculations of overall average annual rate of growth of new companies in each category. This was tempered, however, by an analysis of each equipment segment in terms of annual revenue rates of growth. The rank ordering of the number of companies remains largely unchanged at the end of the decade, except that the computer security/shielding category moves to first place, and access control moves up to third place. The security locks category stays in second place. The categories with the lowest number of companies, metal detection and electronic article surveillance, are unchanged. By 2000, the equipment categories with the highest annual rates of growth of new OEMs and distributors are computer security/shielding (11%), access control (9%), alarms (7%), and bomb detection/X-ray (7%). The slowest rates of annual growth are projected by Hallcrest to be the categories of telephone security (3%), safes and vaults (3%), security lighting (4%), and security fencing (4%). Although sales revenues for security fencing and safes and vaults will continue to be high, these industry segments have solidified, and it will be difficult for new companies to break into the market.

ELECTRONIC SECURITY PRODUCTS AND SERVICES

A number of security market research authorities and reports identify electronic security equipment and service revenues as a separate category. The data tabulated in **Table 6.19** were derived by adding all service revenues and equipment sales related to electronic equipment. They are presented to permit comparisons of Hallcrest estimates and projections with others.

TABLE 6.19 HALLCREST ESTIMATES AND PROJECTIONS FOR ELECTRONIC SECURITY PRODUCTS AND SERVICES ANNUAL REVENUES 1980 - 2000		
Year	Annual Revenues	Average Annual Rate of Growth
1980	$557,000,000	N/A
1990	$2,190,000,000	15%
2000	$6,214,000,000	11%

208

Hallcrest estimates that from 1980 to 1990 the private security industry experienced an average annual rate of growth of revenues of about 10%. The rate of growth for electronic security revenues is estimated to be 15% for the same period. Similarly, it is projected that revenues/expenditures for the entire private security industry will grow at an average annual rate of 7% over the next 10 years, but that the electronic security sector will have a substantially higher rate, 11%.

PROPRIETARY SECURITY

This section of the chapter introduces a brief overview of a major sector of the private security industry, the proprietary sector, which currently represents about 26% of all revenues and expenditures. Even though this sector is expected to decrease to 16% by the end of the decade, it will continue to be a vitally important part of the industry.

Table 6.20 covers the period 1980 to 2000 and tabulates annual operating costs for the proprietary security sector, average annual growth of costs, total numbers of security departments operating in American companies, total proprietary employment, average annual rate of growth for employment, and the average size of security departments.

TABLE 6.20 HALLCREST ESTIMATES AND PROJECTIONS PROPRIETARY SECURITY 1980 - 2000							
Year	Annual Operating Costs	Average Annual Rate of Growth	Number of Security Departments*	Average Annual Rate of Growth	Number of Security Employees	Average Employees Per Company	Average Annual Rate of Growth
1980	$6,250,000,000	N/A	40,000	N/A	420,000	10.5	N/A
1990	$13,600,000,000	8.1%	50,000	2.3%	528,000	10.5	+2%
2000	$16,000,000,000	1.6%	60,000	1.8%	410,000	6.8	-2%

* The term "security departments" is intended to indicate the number of proprietary security elements within American companies and agencies; many security elements within private companies are not designated as departments.

Table 6.21 displays a breakdown of proprietary security employment on the basis of category of employment for the period 1982 to 2000. The base year, 1982, is used, rather than 1980, because the original composition of proprietary security employment was based on a Hallcrest survey conducted in 1982. The category "store detective" would only apply to retail establishments; otherwise the composition ratios are likely to be representative of most "average" security departments.

				TABLE 6.21					
			HALLCREST ESTIMATES AND PROJECTIONS						
			COMPOSITION OF PROPRIETARY SECURITY ORGANIZATIONS 1982-2000						
Segment	Employees 1982	Percent of 1982 Total	Employees 1990	Percent of 1990 Total	Average Annual Rate of Growth	Employees 2000	Percent of 2000 Total	Average Annual Rate of Growth
Guards	346,326	77%	393,360	74%	1.6%	280,000	68%	-3.3%
Managers/ Staff	60,332	13%	95,040	18%	5.8%	100,000	24%	+0.5%
Store Detectives	20,106	4%	26,400	5%	3.5%	19,000	5%	-3.2%
Investigators	10,000	2%	10,560	2%	0.7%	9,000	2%	-1.6%
Other	12,215	3%	2,640	0.5%	-17.4%	2,000	0.5%	-2.7%
TOTALS	**448,979**		**528,000**		1.6%	**410,000**		-2.5%

To amplify these tables, the following pages present a brief analysis of annual operating costs, numbers of companies with security elements, proprietary employment, and employment composition. This section also examines a similar analysis completed by *Security* for 1990 and attempts to explain variances with the Hallcrest data. The *Security* survey also identified other related statistics that would interest the reader who seeks to have a better understanding of the proprietary security sector.

Annual Operating Costs: Proprietary security annual operating costs in the United States (overseas costs are not calculated) comprised approximately 32% of all private security expenditures and revenues in 1980. By 1990 this dropped to 26% of all expenditures, and by the year 2000 Hallcrest projects that only about 16% will be spent by proprietary security organizations.

As shown in **Table 6.22,** the average annual rate of growth of total proprietary security expenditures will drop from 8% per annum in 1990 to approximately 2% per annum in 2000. It is believed that the greatest decrease will occur during the last half of the 1990s.

| TABLE 6.22 |
| HALLCREST ESTIMATES AND PROJECTIONS OF AVERAGE ANNUAL OPERATING BUDGETS FOR SECURITY ORGANIZATIONS 1980-2000 |

Year	Average Annual Operating Budget	Average Annual Rate of Growth
1980	$156,000	N/A
1990	$272,000	5.7%
2000	$267,000	-0.2%

Number of Companies: The number of companies with security units for the period 1980 to 2000, though a rough approximation, seems to be a reasonable estimate. There is a necessary mathematical balance among various statistical data that describe proprietary security organizations. Since estimates of annual expenditures by proprietary security organizations are thought to be generally reliable, other data (such as average annual budgets for security in American companies, annual payroll, number of employees for all proprietary organizations, and median employees per company) determine the number of companies that "balance" these numerical relationships. Probable error, however, could be as high as 25%.

The number of private companies and agencies with security departments or personnel was approximately 40,000 in 1980. The number of such proprietary organizations increased to 50,000 by 1990 at an average annual rate of 2.3% and should increase to 60,000 by the year 2000 at a slightly slower rate of 1.8%. In 1980, about 57% of all private security organizations were proprietary; this decreased to 47% by 1990. Hallcrest predicts that the number will further decrease to approximately 39% by 2000.

Employment: The Hallcrest study believes that trends in reductions of security staff will continue at many companies in America over the next decade. Some organizations will eliminate security departments, and more and more security requirements will be contracted to outside security companies.

Overall, the total of all employees in proprietary security organizations will decrease from 528,000 persons in 1990 to about 410,000 persons in the year 2000. In 1980 there were approximately 420,000 people employed in proprietary security organizations. Thus, within the 20-year period of 1980 to 2000, the average rate of annual growth will shift from +2.3%

211

in 1990 to -2.5% by the end of the decade. The average annual rate of growth of the 20-year period should be about -0.1%.

Another way to view this change is that in 1980, 43% of all persons working in security jobs were working in proprietary security organizations. By 1990 the percentage dropped to 35%, and at the turn of the next century, Hallcrest believes that less than 22% of security jobs will be in proprietary security organizations.

Composition: For the 8-year period (1982 to 1990), the average annual rates of growth for proprietary categories are described below:

Although it is projected that the overall size of proprietary security will shrink significantly over the next 10 years, it appears that American companies increased the percentage of their staffs comprised of managers and supervisors during the past 10 years. Managers and management staff grew at an average annual rate of 5.8%. By contrast, the rate of employee growth for all proprietary security organizations and all employment categories was only about 2.3%, and the rate for all private security personnel was 6.7%. This may reflect higher qualification requirements for proprietary security personnel, which ultimately allows more personnel to enter management or management staff categories.

While the number of guards increased from 1982 to 1990 at an average annual rate of approximately 2%, their percentage of the total security organization was reduced about 3%, and the management staff increased by 5%. Overall, it is likely that by the end of this decade, less than 68% of proprietary security personnel will be in the "guard" category. The rate of growth of guards is believed to be a negative 2% currently, and it should decline to a negative 3% by the year 2000. It would seem that companies will be hiring fewer guards but more managers--on a percentage basis. Overall employment figures should decrease. The reduction of personnel in the "other" category is possibly attributable to increased "contracting out" for specialized services, such as honesty and drug testing.

A valid prediction of the composition of proprietary security organizations in the year 2000 is difficult to make because of the uncertainty of the existing data and trends. There is no reliable way to forecast whether current trends in annual rates of growth for various proprietary employment categories will continue to decline or to properly account for the effect of the overall reduction in the size of proprietary security on the basis of changes in composition. Nevertheless, on the bases of maintaining a projected proprietary employee population of 410,000 in the year 2000 and allowing management and management staff categories to grow to about 24% of the composition of proprietary categories, the data presented in **Table 6.22** were generated.

1990 *Security* Estimates

Statistics on proprietary security were compiled in a *Security* report entitled "Security Forecast 1990." The data were based on a mail survey of 1,000 "end-user" security decision makers. Some of the key findings of this survey related to the size of average annual operating budgets and the average annual rate of growth of the budget are tabulated in **Table 6.23**. [13]

Security's estimate of the average operating budget in 1990 is roughly 1.5 times Hallcrest's estimate. It is believed, however, that this is primarily attributable to the effect of very large companies on such statistics. Moreover, it is conceivable that very small security departments may not have responded to the survey. It also needs to be pointed out that the *Security* data would result in average annual rates of growth of operating budgets at -8% in 1989 and +4% in 1990. Average annual rate of growth calculations can be inaccurate if computed for short intervals. Average annual rates are heavily influenced by compounding, which

TABLE 6.23 SECURITY ESTIMATES OF AVERAGE ANNUAL OPERATING BUDGETS FOR SECURITY ORGANIZATIONS 1988-1990		
Year	Average Annual Operating Budget	Average Annual Rate of Growth
1988	$460,208	N/A
1989	$423,571	-8.0%
1990	$439,667	+3.8%

does not show an effect for a 1-year period. Nevertheless, while Hallcrest's estimate of an average operating budget for 1990 is $272,000, *Security*'s is $424,000. On the other hand, although the 1-year rate estimated on the basis of *Security*'s data is 4% in 1990, Hallcrest's rate is higher at 6%. Over time the 2 estimates would approach one another.

The *Security* survey revealed additional data that provide interesting insights into proprietary security. A few of the key points follow:

- About 36% of a security budget goes to personnel and over-head. Approximately 27% is spent for outside security services, and 16% goes to maintenance and repair of equipment. About 12% is spent for new equipment, and 9% is used to replace equipment.

- The median budget figure for "outside services" is $44,100.

- The median size of security departments in 1989 was 11 persons. This correlates exactly with the Hallcrest estimate.

- On the basis of its 1990 survey, *Security* believes that staff reductions may have bottomed out. Only 6% of those surveyed planned to reduce staff, as compared to 17% in 1989.

COMPARISON OF HALLCREST 1985 AND
1990 PRIVATE SECURITY DATA

Primarily of interest to private security researchers and academicians, **Table 6.24** and **Table 6.25** present a comparative tabulation of Hallcrest estimates, first compiled in 1982 (and published in 1985) and the current estimates for 1990. **Table 6.24** displays a comparison of proprietary security employment composition for this period. **Table 6.25** compares service and manufacturing service employment. Since it was believed that researchers would compare *The Hallcrest Report* (1990) with the earlier Hallcrest study, the research staff decided to facilitate this process.

SEGMENT	EMPLOYEES 1982	PERCENT OF TOTAL 1982	EMPLOYEES 1990	PERCENT OF TOTAL 1990	CHANGE IN COMPOSITION 1982-90	PERCENT OF CHANGE	AVERAGE ANNUAL RATE OF GROWTH
Guards	340,026	77%	393,360	74%	-3%	14%	2%
Managers and Staff	60,332	13%	95,040	18%	+5%	58%	6%
Store Detectives	20,106	4%	26,400	5%	-1%	31%	3%
Investigators	10,000	2%	10,560	2%	0%	6%	1%
Other	12,215	3%	2,640	0.5%	-2.5%	-78%	-17%
TOTAL	**448,979**		**528,000**			18%	2%

TABLE 6.24
COMPARISON OF HALLCREST 1982 TO 1990 DATA
PROPRIETARY SECURITY EMPLOYEES

These comparative tables also provide some insights into the data beyond comparing the Hallcrest studies. **Table 6.24,** for example, suggests that the composition of proprietary security employment has remained substantially the same, with the exception of an apparent slight growth in managerial staff and a minor reduction in guard personnel. If the calculations of average annual rate of growth for these 2 employment categories are valid, it is likely that the trend will continue for the coming decade. Managerial personnel seem to be growing at about 3 times the rate of guard personnel. If true, this may reflect an increased interest among American companies in hiring security managers and directors with higher qualifications and experience. It may also reflect a trend toward increased use of contract security guards by private companies. On the basis of this table, it is estimated that proprietary employment is presently growing at an annual rate of 2%, only slightly higher than the national work force growth rate of 1.2%.

Table 6.25 provides a similar analysis of the contract and manufacturing sector. Variances for 1982 data are presented in this table with the tabulations provided in **Table 6.24.** The creation of new service categories (investigators, manufacturers, and locksmiths) necessitated a revision of 1982 data, which contributed to these variances. The only significant variance is in the guard company category. **Table 6.13** on **page 197** indicated that guard company employment represented about 59% of total service and manufacturing

215

sector employment, while the table below suggests that it is 67%. *The Hallcrest Report* (1990) refinement of 1980 data resulted in a higher estimate for guard personnel; about 485,000 were estimated by *The Hallcrest Report* (1985), and the current estimate is 520,000. The introduction of the new service segments and estimates of high employment in these categories brought the percentage of total estimates for guard employment down 8%.

TABLE 6.25
COMPARISON OF HALLCREST 1982 TO 1990 DATA FOR
SERVICE AND MANUFACTURING EMPLOYEES

SEGMENT	EMPLOYEES 1982	PERCENT OF TOTAL 1982	EMPLOYEES 1990	PERCENT OF TOTAL 1990	CHANGE IN COMPOSI-TION	PERCENT OF CHANGE	AVERAGE ANNUAL RATE OF GROWTH
Guards	484,600	67%	520,104	54%	-13%	7%	1%
Investigators*	57,000	8%	70,467	7%	-1%	24%	3%
Armored Car	26,300	4%	14,673	2%	-2%	-44%	-7%
Alarm	64,740	9%	119,697	12%	+3%	77%	7%
Consultants	3,000	0.4%	2,896	0.3%	nil	-3%	0%
Manufacturers*	31,000	4%	88,421	9%	+5%	185%	14%
Locksmiths*	48,400	7%	69,695	7%	nil	44%	5%
Other	5,000	1%	79,348	8%	7%	1487%	41%
TOTAL	720,000		965,300			34%	4%

* Not reported as a segment in the original 1985 Hallcrest Report

The salient information suggested by **Table 6.25** is that manufacturers showed the greatest rate of growth in employment for this 8-year period (14%), and armored car companies showed the highest rate of decline (-7%). The percentage of change and rate of growth for the "other" category should be largely discounted since it is primarily attributed to low estimates in 1982.

THE EFFECT OF LARGE COMPANIES
ON INDUSTRY STATISTICS

It is useful to look at contrasts between industry leaders in various segments and what portion of the industry they represent. One segment for which reasonably reliable data could be obtained was the guard industry. **Table 6.26**, from *Security Letter Source Book 1990-1991,*[14] provides a useful insight; the 10 largest U.S. security guard and patrol companies had revenues in 1988 totaling about $2.4 billion. A closer examination of the effect these largest companies have on the statistical averages reveals how misleading aggregate averages can be, as depicted in **Table 6.27**. Assuming the entire guard and patrol segment had revenues of approximately $7.94 billion in 1988, the top 10 companies comprised 30% of the total, although only representing 0.1% of all companies (10 out of 9,025). With regard to guard segment employment in 1988, the top 10 had 189,400 employees, which is 40% of the 469,300 employees for the entire guard segment that year.

TABLE 6.26 TEN LARGEST U.S. SECURITY GUARD AND PATROL COMPANIES		
Company/Head Office	*Employees*	*1988 Revenues*
Pinkerton's, Inc. Van Nuys, California	55,000	$652,000,000
Burns International Security Services, Paramus, New Jersey *(estimated)*	30,000	$435,000,000
The Wackenhut Corporation Coral Gables, Florida	35,000	$400,000,000
Wells Fargo Guard Services, Parsippany, New Jersey	21,500	$250,000,000
American Protective Services, Oakland, California	9,000	$151,000,000
Globe Security Deerfield Beach, Florida	10,000	$125,000,000
Stanley Smith Security, Inc. San Antonio, Texas	8,900	$120,000,000
Guardsmark, Inc. Memphis, Tennessee	8,000	$120,000,000
Allied Security, Inc. Pittsburgh, Pennsylvania *(estimated)*	6,000	$76,000,000
Advance Security, Inc. Atlanta, Georgia	6,000	$75,000,000
TOTALS	**189,400**	**$2,404,000,000**

Notes: Prepared from questionnaire responses for the *Security Letter Source Book* for revenues through December 31, 1988, except where "estimated" is indicated. Totals may include investigative and consulting services and also some revenues reflect sales of non-guard-related revenues.

SOURCE: *Security Letter Source Book 1990-1991*

Data from other segments on which to base similar analyses are more difficult to locate. Information is available, however, for gross annual revenues of major alarm companies. It should be recalled that this category includes those companies which sell, install, monitor, and service commercial and residential alarm systems. The top 10 companies in this segment earned about $1.2 billion in 1989.[15] The entire alarm company segment collected total revenues of approximately $3.9 billion in 1989. The 10 largest alarm companies represent about 31% of total industry segment revenues for 1989. Although this is the same ratio as reported for the guard segment, conclusions that these 2 segments are representative of the entire industry should not be drawn from this observation. *(Note: Because employment data were not available for the alarm companies, this analysis was not conducted.)*

Another useful insight into the influence of the largest companies on their individual industry segments is the effect on average gross annual revenues per company. Dividing the gross annual revenues for a segment by the estimated number of companies in a segment yields the average annual revenues for each company ($7.9 billion for 9,025 guard companies in 1988). Including the top 10 companies in the guard segment, the average annual revenue per company is about $880,000. Since the 10 largest companies capture 31% of the revenues, calculating the average annual revenues for the remaining companies reveals that the average drops to approximately $615,000, a substantial reduction. The same calculations for the alarm industry segment in 1989 result in average annual revenues per remaining company dropping from $404,000 to $280,000.

In the case of the guard industry, the average annual revenues for the remaining companies would drop further, from $615,000 (top 10 eliminated) to $550,000 (top 40 eliminated). In this same example, the 38 largest guard companies (2 companies did not report) had a total employment of 230,890 persons. Consequently, the average number of employees for the remaining companies is reduced from 31 employees (if top 10 eliminated) to 27 (if top 38 not considered). One might deduce, therefore, that the bottom 50% of guard companies possibly average less than $500,000 in average annual revenues and employ fewer than 25 persons.

TABLE 6.27 COMPARISON OF TOTAL GUARD SEGMENT AVERAGES FOR 1988 ANNUAL REVENUES AND EMPLOYMENT PER COMPANY IF TOP 40 COMPANIES NOT CONSIDERED		
Category	Average Annual Revenues	Average Number of Employees Per Company
ALL GUARD COMPANIES	$880,000	52
IF TOP 40 FIRMS ELIMINATED	$550,000	27

Conducting the same type of analyses on the average number of employees working for a guard or patrol company indicates that while the aggregate guard segment averages 52 employees per company, the elimination of the 10 largest companies reduces the average to 31 employees. The analysis could be extended by eliminating the top 40 companies. This would likely reduce the average of a "typical" company to 27 employees.

In summary, were a newspaper reporter to write an article on the security guard industry, it would make a substantial difference whether he or she viewed aggregate industry averages or the statistical profile of a typical company that was not among the 50, or so, largest guard companies. The total industry averages would misrepresent a typical guard company by 63% for revenues and 52% for employment. The same distortions are likely to occur were similar analyses to be conducted for some other service segments. A few segments may not have this problem, or at least not at the same order of magnitude. Private investigators and consultants may not be materially influenced by the largest firms in their individual categories.

THE "UNAMERICAN" GROWTH OF THE INDUSTRY

In the past 5 years (1985-1989), British, Swiss, Australian, and Japanese companies have invested over $4 billion in American security companies.[16] Other key countries involved in investment or acquisitions include Canada, Finland, and Sweden. The United Kingdom seems to dominate foreign investment within the American private security industry. According to Lee Jones, president, Support Services Group, who monitors the sale and acquisition of security companies, of 40 buyers completing 145 transactions, 23% involved foreign money.[17] Some of the major foreign investors and buyers are:[18]

England	**Hawley Group Ltd**
	Security Centres
	LEP Group PLC
	Automated Security Holdings PLC
	Valor PLC
	Securiguard Group PLC
	RHP Group PLC
Switzerland	**Cerberus AG**
	Inspectorate International Ltd

219

Japan	Secom Co. Ltd
	Chugai Boyeki Co. Ltd
Australia	Mayne Nickless Ltd
	Wormald International Ltd
Sweden	Inter Innovation AB
Canada	First City Industries

Many of the investment or acquisition transactions involved highly prominent American companies, including Arrowhead Enterprises Inc., Alarm Supply Company, Jewelers Protection Inc., Purolator Armored, National Guardian Corporation, Holmes Protection Inc., Sonitrol Corporation, Vicon Industries, Yale, Nutone, Kidde Inc., ADT Inc., Pyrotronics, and London House.

DEPARTURES AND VARIATIONS
FROM THE 1985 HALLCREST REPORT

Since comparisons and contrasts with *The Hallcrest Report* (1985) are likely, it is important to note the major changes in nomenclature and categorizations for this current effort. The most significant variation is that while the 1985 study included perhaps the most comprehensive and extensive surveys of the private security industry conducted, it was not possible to conduct such surveys for the 1990 update of the original report. Although some original data were derived and some unique analyses were conducted, this 1990 report is consequently narrower in scope.

Other major departures, variations, and explanations include the following:

1.   The service and product statistics are primarily limited to the United States. Revenues from overseas sales and operations are generally not considered since these data are not readily available. If they are included, it is inadvertent. This is not a departure from *The Hallcrest Report* (1985), but bears repeating.

2.   *The Hallcrest Report* (1985) included some fire equipment sales in product statistics. Upon reflection, it is probable that only a portion of the fire industry was

represented in that data and, therefore, the statistics were biased by these data. Further, many companies that provide fire equipment and services are entirely out of the private security industry; their inclusion would be inappropriate for a private security industry forecast. Although this study does recognize that many major private security companies are involved in fire protection services and equipment, this report made a conscientious effort to distill fire systems and services out of the data.

Service Sector Changes

3.	The Bureau of Labor Statistics reports that there were 646 armored car and courier companies in the United States in 1987. It is doubtful that there are more than 80 (and probably fewer) armored car companies operating today; thus, it appears that the BLS counted the remainder as courier companies. The question is whether the courier companies they counted were all primarily serving the security industry or whether they were the ordinary messenger services found in most major cities. For these reasons, the "couriers" category was deleted in *The Hallcrest Report* (1990). They are counted in the category "other," until more detailed information is available for this industry specialty.

4.	Also as previously noted, the criteria for alarm companies were narrowed and refined. This category is no longer named "central station alarm monitoring," because it includes monitoring, installation, and service revenues for both local and central station alarm businesses.

5.	Private investigators were separated from contract guards and investigators. Although most major sources of private security industry statistics lump these categories together (including the Bureau of Labor Statistics), for this report the private investigator industry is a separate category. Although many guard companies provide private investigation services, independent private investigators are a substantial element of the industry. This report attempts to recognize this fact. While great care was taken to avoid double-counting companies providing guard and investigative services by relying heavily on state government licensing data, such overcounting was probably not entirely eliminated.

6.	Locksmiths were added as a category. Even though some data about locksmiths were included in the 1985 study, they were not previously treated by any major industry study as a separate category in the aggregate statistics. The 1990 Hallcrest research staff determined that since locksmiths primarily serve security interests, they warrant separate inclusion. Most market research sources have ignored locksmiths, possibly because they have their own trade associations and aren't consistently members of private security professional and trade associations. The addition of locksmiths as a category resulted in major adjustments to *The Hallcrest Report* (1985) data since locksmiths had significantly increased the estimated number of security businesses, total industry revenues, and the number of security industry employees.

7.   Limited information is available about the size, composition, and financial parameters of the consulting profession. Virtually no information is available about the recent development of security engineering practices (security engineering is not presently recognized as a registered engineering practice), as either independent operating companies or as parts of traditional architectural and engineering firms and U.S. governmental and military departments. Some information about consultants (not engineers) was collected by *The Hallcrest Report* (1985). *Security* magazine reported additional statistical information about the security consulting field, as did The Freedonia Group. This report synthesizes these various sources of information and presents much more detailed information about this segment of the industry than was available in the original Hallcrest study.

8.   Another category in this study, "Manufacturers and Distributors," was added in recognition that a portion of the manufacturing and distributing segment generates revenue from services. A few manufacturers are involved in installation services; many gain revenue from maintenance and repair contracts. Moreover, some earlier studies did not recognize that many people are employed by manufacturers and distributors and that these people should be counted with private security employment estimates.

9.   The research staff found certain anomalies in some of the statistics for the private security industry. Searching for an understanding of why these irregularities were occurring revealed that the "other" categories in both service and equipment sale listings played a significant role. Individually, the uncounted products and services did not represent substantial revenues or high employment, but in the aggregate they were very significant. The 1990 research staff discovered that approximately 28 services are provided by private security or security-related companies that are not directly contained among the 7 major service areas listed in the data tables in this chapter. The staff also noted that there are at

222

least 560 unique security product types on the market and that the data tables only list 12 major product categories.[19]   While "other" was a category used in the first Hallcrest report, the interpretation of this miscellaneous classification was expanded for this study.

Equipment/Product Sector Changes

10.   *The Hallcrest Report* (1985), as well as a number of other market research reports, had an equipment category called "intrusion detection equipment." There were also product headings for monitoring and detection equipment, which had several variations. The current report attempts to gather all of these headings into one broad category called "alarms." Only security equipment is considered; fire system equipment is not intended to fall into this category in this report. The new category represents all alarm-related equipment, including detection, monitoring, annunciation, and control equipment, that is not clearly subsumed by other equipment categories.

11.   Termed "data encryption devices" in the 1985 study, the 1990 category is called "telephone security." The thought was to make the category broader rather than narrower. The category is intended to consider not only telephones but also other communications products that utilize telephone lines, such as facsimile and telex machines. This category does not include computer security encryption devices. The new category is not restricted to encryption devices but also includes pen recorders, wiretap detection and analysis equipment, call originator loggers, cut-line alarms, and other similar equipment and devices.

12.   A category new to Hallcrest research reports is "computer security/shielding." The need for a category for computer security is self-evident since it is currently a robust and rapidly growing market. Shielding,** however, is only loosely related, and the only reason it is linked to computer security is that computers have a higher requirement for shielding than most other electronic equipment. Moreover, there are too few market statistics on shielding equipment and materials to warrant a separate category. It was further determined that it would be inappropriate to relegate this equipment to the

---

**   "Shielding" is a security industry term designating a technology employed to protect electronic equipment, particularly computers, from electromagnetic emanations and interference. Some market research studies have used the industry jargon for shielding equipment and materials, "Tempest." Without such protection it is possible to receive the emitted radiation and reconstruct the information being processed by the computer--a technology utilized for foreign or industrial espionage.

miscellaneous "other" category since the value of shipments was high. Consequently, computer security sales data were melded with shielding market statistics.

13.   *The Hallcrest Report* (1985) included an equipment category termed "fixed security equipment," which was intended to classify many types of security storage and locking equipment. The 1990 report attempts to simplify this category by relating it to the major equipment items in this category, namely safes and vaults, as well as other types of secure storage containers.

14.   Another departure from the 1985 study is that this report attempts to estimate the number of original equipment manufacturers (OEMs) and distributors. This may be the only major market research report that has attempted to develop such an estimate.

15.   Some 1985 report data have been modified. Since new categories have been added and some categories have been reinterpreted, it was necessary to adjust data collected in 1982 as if the 1990 report changes had been in effect then. This allowed the research staff to compare growth trends and data relationships by evaluating comparable categories and compilations.

16.   In some instances the research staff identified data from other sources that were credible but that were presented for a year other than the years used for this report. It was occasionally necessary to use average annual rates of growth to adjust the data to the milestone years used in this report.

17.   As a final note, the service segments "manufacturers" and "locksmiths" only report service revenues for these categories. The revenues derived from the sale of security equipment and locks are listed in the table for equipment sales.

ENDNOTES

1.   Robert McCrie, editor, *Security Letter Source Book 1990-1991*, 4th ed., (New York: Security Letter, Inc., 1990), (Distributor and Sales Agent: Butterworths), pp. 337-339.

2.   *Guide To Security Industry Market Studies: 1986 - June 1989*, American Society for Industrial Security, 2nd ed., Arlington, Virginia, July 1989.

3.   McCrie, pp. 361-366.

4.   William Cunningham and Todd Taylor, *The Hallcrest Report: Private Security and Police In America*, 1985, p. 114.

5.   *Outlook 2000, Monthly Labor Review*, Vol. 112, No. 11, U.S. Department of Labor, Bureau of Labor Statistics, November 1989.

6.   Lester Thurow, *The Zero-Sum Society*, (New York: Basic Books, 1982), p. 88.

7.   Cunningham and Taylor, p. 114.

8.   Nicholas Beltrante, *Resource News*, January 1990.

9.   Kerry Lydon, "New Niche-Services Tailor Protection," *Security*, December 1989, p. 41.

10.   As noted in Cunningham and Taylor, p. 115.

11.   "Booming Consultant Market Balances Slumping Armored Car Services to Spearhead Solid Industry Growth," *Security*, September 1988, p. 17.

12.   "Security Products and Services," *Leading Edge Report*, Study LE7302, March 1990, p. 6.

13.   These estimates were reported in a study prepared by *Security,* entitled "Security Forecast 1990."

14.   *Security Letter Source Book 1990-1991*, p. 127.

15.   The source of this data is Lee Jones, Support Services Group, San Clemente, California, as report in the *Security Letter Source Book 1990-1991*, as well as in *Security Dealer*, February 1990. The top 10 alarm companies were reported as having annual gross

revenues of: ADT, $410 million; Honeywell, $180 million; Wells Fargo, $175 million; National Guardian, $137 million; Holmes Protection, $78 million; Security Link, $69 million; Westec/Secom, $59 million; Rollins, $50 million; Network/PSI, $42 million; and API Alarms, $35 million.

16.   Patrick Egan, "The Future is Now," *News and Views*, National Burglar and Fire Alarm Association, Vols. 8904 & 8905, 1989.

17.   "Foreign Dollars Fuel 1988 Buy-Ups," *Security Distributing & Marketing*, October 1989, p. 102.

18.   "Foreigners Think Longer-Term," *Security Distributing & Marketing*, May 1988, pp. 62-63.

19.   The number of product types was developed by the technical staff of the *Security Industry Buyers Guide*, published by C&P Telephone of Virginia (Bell Atlantic), in association with the American Society for Industrial Security.

CHAPTER 7
COMPARISONS OF PRIVATE SECURITY
AND LAW ENFORCEMENT
EMPLOYMENT AND EXPENDITURES

PRIVATE SECURITY SUMMARY

This chapter presents 3 decades of estimated growth and shifts in employment and expenditures for the 2 protective resources--private security and public law enforcement. Growth forecasts for employment and expenditures, based upon trendline extensions, are made to the year 2000. Protective service employment as a percent of the national work force is also projected to 2000. Further, this chapter graphically depicts the prominence of private security as the nation's protective resource. Also included is a brief discussion of possible reasons for the growth of private security over law enforcement, growth that will likely continue into the 21st Century.

Based upon the security market analysis reported in Chapter 6, the Hallcrest research staff predicts that the average annual rate of growth for revenues for the entire private security industry, including expenditures for the proprietary security sector, to the year 2000 will be approximately 7%. This growth rate is almost 3 times the estimates for the average annual rate of growth of the gross national product (GNP). The sales and revenues for the entire private security industry should continue to be robust. The rate of change in expenditures by the proprietary security sector is likely to continue to experience a slow-down in average rates of annual growth, even though there will be cumulative growth in terms of absolute dollars spent and people employed. The proprietary sector saw the beginning of a slight deceleration as early as the mid-1980s.

The average annual rate of growth in private security employment is forecast to be 2.3% over the next 10 years, higher than the 1.2% annual rate predicted for the entire U.S. work force by the Bureau of Labor Statistics (BLS). The Hallcrest research staff anticipates a gradual annual slowdown over the next 10 years due to a maturing of the industry.

LAW ENFORCEMENT SUMMARY

The Hallcrest research staff anticipates public expenditures for law enforcement will grow at an average annual rate of 4% from 1990 to 2000 (half the rate of growth of private security). This is a marked slowdown, considering that the average annual rate of growth for the period of 1980 to 1990 was about 8%. Law enforcement employment is predicted to grow at an average annual rate of approximately 1% over the next 10 years, just slightly slower than the U. S. Labor Department prediction of 1.2% for the national work force. Despite slow growth, the ratio of law enforcement officers to each 1,000 Americans should increase from the current ratio of 2.4 per 1,000 to 2.8 per 1,000 by the end of the decade.

COMBINED PROTECTIVE SERVICES SUMMARY

Currently, the combination of private security and law enforcement, as a national protective resource, has total employment of approximately 2.1 million people, representing almost 1% of the entire national population and almost 2% of the national work force. By the year 2000, combined employment should exceed 2.6 million people; the percentages of the national population and national work force would remain roughly the same. The average rate of annual growth for combined protective services employment is expected to be about 2%, which is 67% higher than the projected rate of growth for all American workers for the coming decade.

As predicted in **Table 7.1**, the combined expenditures for protective services will increase from the current level of $82 billion to about $147 billion by the year 2000 at an average annual rate of growth of approximately 6%. Spending for protective services may slow uniformly over the decade if current trends toward increasingly austere operating budgets for private and public organizations continue. A slight decline in the rate of annual growth could also occur if crime does not significantly increase over the coming decade--most authorities do not expect a significant increase--and if security and law enforcement protection goals are gradually achieved and protective measures approach an as yet undefined optimal level.

TABLE 7.1
HALLCREST ESTIMATES AND PROJECTIONS 1980 - 2000
SUMMARY OF PRIVATE SECURITY AND LAW ENFORCEMENT
EMPLOYMENT AND EXPENDITURES

Year	Private Security Employment (Millions)	Law Enforcement Employment (Millions)	Total Protective Services Employment (Millions)	Private Security Expenditures (Billions)	Law Enforcement Expenditures (Billions)	Total Expenditures (Billions)
1980	1.0	0.6	1.6	$20	$14	$34
1990	1.5	0.6	2.1	$52	$30	$82
2000	1.9	0.7	2.6	$103	$44	$147

Private security expenditures are presently about 1.7 times those of law enforcement; over the next 10 years the rate will increase to 2.4 times. In 1990 there are approximately 2.4 private security personnel for every law enforcement employee. By 2000 there will be more than 2.8 private security workers for each law enforcement officer--almost a 3-to-1 ratio. [1] In some cities and states, the ratio of private security to law enforcement employees is now--and will likely continue to be--as much as 4 or 5 to 1.

The following sections in this chapter examine the effect of treating private security and law enforcement as a single entity. This chapter also presents various comparisons of the 2 protective sectors for the milestone years of 1980, 1990, and 2000.

HALLCREST'S 5-SITE TEST

Statistical data related to employment in the public law enforcement sector are fairly extensive, even taking into account some differences in semantics and classification among

---

[1] Only sworn law enforcement personnel are considered in this study.

various analysts. The statistics on private security employment are less reliable, because the industry is highly fragmented and no central source of valid employment data is presently available. The Hallcrest research staff sampled 14 states and 2 major cities in an attempt to find reasonably reliable employment figures for private security.

TABLE 7.2
COMPARISON OF PRIVATE SECURITY AND LAW ENFORCEMENT EMPLOYMENT - 1989
Employment in Selected States and a Major City

State/City	Private Security Employment	Law Enforcement Employment	Ratio of Private Security to Police
California	201,000[2]	51,906[3]	3.9:1
Indiana	15,000[4]	8,826[5]	1.7:1
Michigan	36,264[6]	18,394[7]	2.0:1
Texas	110,000[8]	31,106[9]	3.5:1
St. Louis, Missouri	4,322[10]	1,528[11]	2.8:1
TOTAL	366,586	111,760	3.3:1

[2] Bureau of Collections and Investigative Services, State of California, February 1990.

[3] Sourcebook of Criminal Justice Statistics 1988, U. S. Government Printing Office, 1989, pp. 73-76.

[4] Indiana Professional Licensing Agency, August 22, 1989.

[5] Sourcebook of Criminal Justice Statistics 1988.

[6] Data collected from Michigan State Police, August 1989, and from interviews with Michigan corporate security directors, November 1989.

[7] Sourcebook of Criminal Justice Statistics 1988.

[8] Texas Board of Private Investigators, June 1989.

[9] Sourcebook of Criminal Justice Statistics 1988.

[10] St. Louis, Missouri, Metropolitan Police Department, June 1989.

[11] Crime in the United States 1988, U.S. Government Printing Office, 1989.

The 5 test sites depicted in **Table 7.2** were the only ones with minimally acceptable employment numbers for security workers. Actually, these sources are extremely conservative, since they represent licensed private security personnel and unquestionably leave out an unknown number of security workers who are not registered with the states or the test city.

TABLE 7.3 FIVE-SITE TEST DATA	
Population of five sites in 1990	56,700,000
Law enforcement population of five sites	111,760
Private security population of five sites	366,586
Percent of state population employed in law enforcement	.20%
Percent of state population employed in private security	.65%

The primary objective of this test was, therefore, to establish ratios between law enforcement employment and private security employment, as well as between police and private security employment and the national population. By establishing reliable estimates of public law enforcement employment on a national basis, it was hoped that the ratio of these test states (and 1 city) would predict the size of employment of private security on a nationwide basis. The assumption was that the ratio determined by these 5 test sites would predict the ratios for the United States. The baseline data for the 5-site test are presented in **Table 7.3**.

The use of these test ratios worked fairly well in predicting the size of private security employment but were less effective in projecting the employment levels of public law enforcement. **Table 7.4** lists the resulting national projections based on the ratios developed for the 5 sites. The 5-site test predicts that the ratio of private security employees to law enforcement personnel is approximately 3.2 to 1. This is in variance with other Hallcrest projections, which predict a ratio of 2.4 to 1. This represents a deviation of about - 25%.

TABLE 7.4 NATIONAL PROJECTIONS BASED ON FIVE-SITE TEST DATA	
Population of the United States in 1990	247,408,000
Predicted national employment in law enforcement	495,000
Predicted national employment in private security	1,608,000
Ratio of private security employees to law enforcement employees	3.2:1

The variances with *The Hallcrest Report* (1990) projections derived by other methods are tabulated in **Table 7.5**. One probable explanation for the variances is that 2 of the 4 test-site states, California and Texas, have such a high density of private security employment that they are not representative of the entire United States. Their estimated ratios of private security personnel to law enforcement personnel are 4 to 1 and 3.5 to 1, respectively. The Hallcrest staff estimates that the national ratio is approximately 2.4 to 1, significantly lower than these 2 states.

TABLE 7.5 HALLCREST PROJECTIONS FROM OTHER SOURCES AND COMPARISONS WITH FIVE- SITE TEST DATA PROJECTIONS	
Law enforcement employment	622,664
Variance with 5-site test	+26%
Private security employment	1,493,300
Variance with 5-site test	-7%
Ratio of private security employees to law enforcement employees	2.4:1
Variance with 5-site test	-25%

PRIVATE SECURITY PROFILE

Table 7.6 presents Hallcrest's estimates of industry-wide statistics for the private security industry, including contract services, manufacturing and proprietary sectors, in relation to the national population and the national work force. Total private security employment in 1990 is estimated to be 1.5 million people. The salient statistic from this table is the Hallcrest research staff estimate of the current ratio of private security personnel to law enforcement employment: 2.4 to 1. Another way of viewing this estimate is that there are approximately 6 private security employees for

TABLE 7.6 PRIVATE SECURITY CONTRASTS WITH NATIONAL POPULATIONS - 1990	
Private security employment	1,493,300
Percent of national population	0.6%
Ratio per 1,000 national population	6 per 1,000
Percent of national work force	1.2%
Ratio per 1,000 national work force population	12 per 1,000
Ratio to law enforcement employment	2.4:1

each group of 1,000 Americans and about 12 private security employees for each group of 1,000 workers in the nation.

The same data are presented in **Table 7.7** for the year 2000, except that the average annual rate of growth for employment over the 1990 to 2000 period is calculated, as is the percent change from 1980. While the information presented in the table is self-evident, it is worth noting that the ratio of private security to law enforcement personnel is expected to increase to 2.8 to 1, almost a 3-to-1 relationship. Total private security employment is expected to increase to 1.9 million by the decade's end. The percent of change in employment from 1980 to 2000 is approximately 193%. The annual rate of growth in employment is anticipated to be about 2.3%, roughly double the rate of employment growth for the national work force. By 2000 there will be 7 private security workers for each group of 1,000 Americans, an increase of 1 from 1990. Further, by 2000 there will be about 13 private security employees for each group of 1,000 workers in the nation--also an increase of 1 employee from the 1990 figure.

TABLE 7.7 PRIVATE SECURITY CONTRASTS PROJECTION - 2000	
Private security employment	1,882,700
Percent of national population	0.7%
Ratio per 1,000 national population	7 per 1,000
Percent of national work force	1.3%
Ratio per 1,000 national work force population	13 per 1,000
Ratio to law enforcement employment	2.8:1
Average annual rate of growth	2.3%
Percent change from 1980	193%

LAW ENFORCEMENT PROFILE

Similar to the tabulated information presented for private security employment, **Table 7.8** represents the profile of the law enforcement sector in relation to the national population and the national work force. For every 1,000 persons in the United States there are currently 2 law enforcement employees. The total of all federal, state, and local government law enforcement personnel in 1990 is approximately 623,000. Currently, there are 2.5 law enforcement officers for each group of 1,000 Americans, and 5 for each 1,000 workers.

TABLE 7.8 LAW ENFORCEMENT CONTRASTS - 1990	
Law enforcement employment	623,700
Percent of national population	0.25%
Ratio per 1,000 national population	2.5 per 1,000
Percent of national work force	0.5%
Ratio per 1,000 national work force population	5 per 1,000

233

Table 7.9 details the same information for the year 2000. The Hallcrest staff projects that by the end of the coming decade, approximately 684,000 sworn officers will be employed by law enforcement agencies, and the ratio to the national population will only barely increase to 2.6 per 1,000, an increase of 0.1 from 1990 data. Law enforcement employment is expected to grow at an average annual rate of 0.95%, which is close to the national average; the percent of change in employment between the years 1980 and 2000 will be about 117% (a 17% increase). The ratio of law enforcement personnel to the national work force is about 5 per 1,000, which is unchanged from 1990.

TABLE 7.9 LAW ENFORCEMENT CONTRASTS - 2000	
Law enforcement employment	684,400
Percent of national population	0.26%
Ratio per 1,000 national population	2.6 per 1,000
Percent of national work force	0.5%
Ratio per 1,000 national work force population	5 per 1,000
Average annual rate of growth in employment	1%
Percent change from 1980	117%

COMBINED PROTECTIVE SERVICES PROFILE

Table 7.10 presents the profile of combined protective employment in the United States for the year 1990. Currently, about 2.1 million people work either for private security or for public law enforcement. In combination, private security and law enforcement employment accounts for 9 protective service people for each group of 1,000 Americans. This amounts to 1.7% of the national work force, at a ratio of 17 protective service employees per 1,000 workers.

Table 7.11, on the following page, projects the combined protective services profile for the year 2000. The Hallcrest research staff estimates that over the next 10 years total protective employment will increase to approximately 2.6 million, an increase of 162% over 1990 figures. The ratio of protective service employees to the national population will increase to 10 per 1,000 and for

TABLE 7.10 COMBINED PRIVATE SECURITY AND PUBLIC LAW ENFORCEMENT CONTRASTS - 1990	
Combined employment	2,116,000
Percent of national population	0.9%
Ratio per 1,000 national population	9 per 1,000
Percent of national work force	1.7%
Ratio per 1,000 national work force population	17 per 1,000

the national work force to 18 per 1,000, an increase of 1 protective service employee for both ratios from the year 1990. The average rate of growth for employment for both sectors in combination should be approximately 2% per year, not quite twice the national average. Restating a significant perspective of the growth of protective services, it is noteworthy that by the end of the current decade, almost 1% of all people in the United States will be employed in protective services, and virtually 2% of all workers will be employed either by law

TABLE 7.11 COMBINED PRIVATE SECURITY AND PUBLIC LAW ENFORCEMENT CONTRASTS 2000	
Combined employment	2,567,100
Percent of national population	1%
Ratio per 1,000 national population	10 per 1,000
Percent of national work force	1.8%
Ratio per 1,000 national work force population	18 per 1,000
Average annual rate of growth	2%
Percent change from 1980	162%

enforcement agencies or by private security organizations. Clearly, the majority of the growth in protective services is attributable to the private security sector.

REASONS FOR PRIVATE SECURITY GROWTH

News articles often attribute the growth of private security to the simplistic theory that crime increases as unemployment increases, and security prospers through increased expenditures to control loss due to crime. One of the obvious myths in this theory is that all property crime is related to the state of the economy. The prevalence of many crimes in the business environment is more directly related to the opportunity to commit the crime--especially in the case of "white-collar" crime--and the lack of controls to address the threat potential. The Hallcrest surveys in the early 1980s disclosed that security program increases have not been automatic; rather, they are subject to the budgetary constraints of business recessions just like other organizational program budgets. Additions to, or upgrading of, security systems are generally treated as capital expenditures and as such have been subject to the same tightened controls placed upon other capital expenditures in many businesses in recent years.

235

After reviewing the literature covering possible reasons for the steady growth of private protection over the past 2 to 3 decades, the Hallcrest staff believes that 4 interrelated factors largely explain the greater employment and expenditure shift from public to private protection and the increasing growth of private security, while public protection has limited or no growth. These 4 major reasons for growth are: (1) an increase in crimes in the workplace, (2) an increase in fear (real or perceived) of crime, (3) the "fiscal crises of the state" has limited public protection, and (4) an increased public and business awareness and use of the more cost-effective private security products and services.

PRIVATE SECURITY AND LAW ENFORCEMENT EMPLOYMENT COMPARISONS

The following figures provide dramatic representations of the employment comparisons between the private security and law enforcement sectors. **Figure 7.1** shows almost a 3-to-1 ratio expressed in a pie chart.

FIGURE 7.1

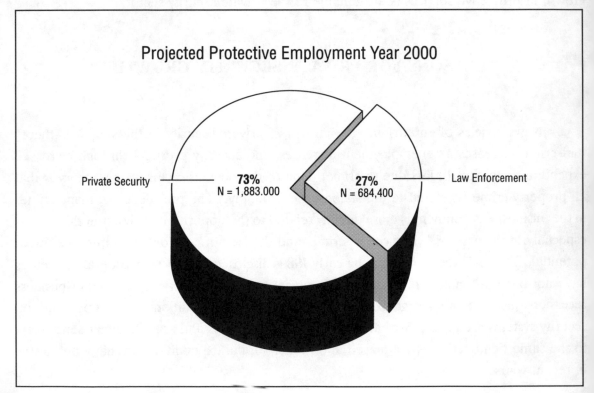

Projected Protective Employment Year 2000

Private Security — **73%** N = 1,883.000   **27%** N = 684,400 — Law Enforcement

Figure 7.2 shows the relative changes in employment in both sectors over the period of 1970 to 2000. This graph suggests that the point at which private security employment exceeded law enforcement employment may have occurred during the 1960s. Some authorities believe that the crossover happened during the early 1970s. In any event, the divergence of the 2 sectors since the crossover is clearly evident from the mid-1970s and beyond.

FIGURE 7.2

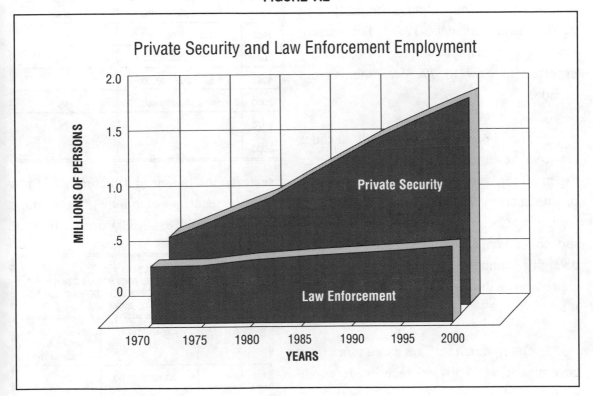

COMPARISON OF PRIVATE SECURITY AND
LAW ENFORCEMENT EXPENDITURES

Table 7.12 displays estimated annual public expenditures for law enforcement services. The statistical aberrations for the years 1975 and 1985 occurred because the figures were derived by rounding off and averaging prior and subsequent years. The average annual rate of growth for spending over this 30-year period is estimated to be 7%. The annual rate of growth for the period 1990 to the end of the decade is projected to be about 4%. A similar tabulation is presented in **Table 7.13**, which depicts private security revenues and expenditures for the same period. The average annual rate of growth of private security revenues for the entire period from 1970 to 2000 is estimated to be 12%. The current rate of growth is approximately 10%, and it is expected to slow to 7% over the current decade.

The 12% rate of growth incudes service revenues, proprietary security expenditures, and the revenues from the sale of security equipment and materials. If just private security services are considered (not the sale of security equipment), the average annual rate of growth for the same period is approximately 9%. Solely on the basis of services revenues, private security is still diverging annually from law enforcement expenditures, but at a much more gradual rate.

The research staff reviewed numerous government and private security research reports published over the past 20 years that provided relevant employment and expenditure data. Following analysis of this data, several graphics were prepared to depict the comparisons between and projections for private security and law enforcement employment and spending. Clearly the trend is toward more private security employment and expenditures.

TABLE 7.12 HALLCREST ESTIMATES AND PROJECTIONS OF LAW ENFORCEMENT EXPENDITURES 1970 TO 2000		
Year	Expenditure	Average Rate of Annual Growth
1970	$6,000,000,000.	
1972	$7,000,000,000	
1975	$11,000,000,000	
1980	$13,800,000,000	9%
1985	$22,000,000,000	
1990	$30,000,000,000	8%
1995	$37,000,000,000	
2000	$44,000,000,000	4%
1970 to 2000		7%

TABLE 7.13 HALLCREST ESTIMATES AND PROJECTIONS OF PRIVATE SECURITY REVENUES/EXPENDITURES 1970 TO 2000		
Year	Expenditure	Average Rate of Annual Growth
1970	$3,500,000,000	
1973	$4,400,000,000	
1974	$6,000,000,000	
1980	$20,000,000,000	19%
1985	$30,000,000,000	
1990	$52,000,000,000	10%
1995	$85,000,000,000	
2000	$103,000,000,000	7%
1970 to 2000		12%

A more descriptive illustration of the divergence of spending for private security and public law enforcement during the period 1970 to 2000 is presented as **Figure 7.3**. This figure suggests that a crossover occurred about 1977, when private security revenues and expenditures exceeded public spending for law enforcement services. On the basis of this line graph, both sectors appear to have run parallel from 1980 to 1985. Very rapid growth occurred in private security in 1985, and the divergence accelerates until the end of the decade.

FIGURE 7.3

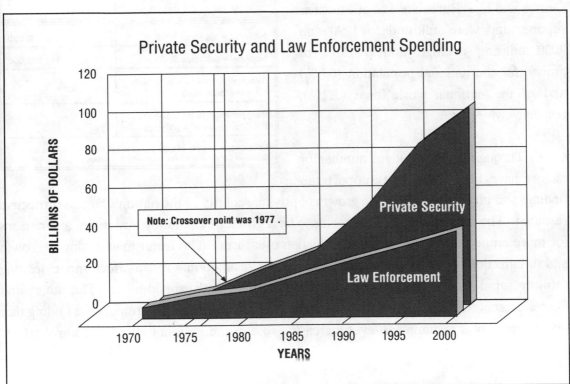

SUMMARY OF NATIONAL DATA

Table 7.14, the final table in this section, is primarily provided for other researchers who may wish to review the national population and work force statistics used to calculate various statistics previously presented in this section. The data were obtained from published U.S. Bureau of the Census and U.S. Bureau of Labor Statistics reports, and were adjusted to 1990 and 2000 utilizing average annual rates of growth for the national population (0.8%) and of the national work force (1.2%), respectively.

TABLE 7.14 NATIONAL EMPLOYMENT DATA SUMMARY	
National population 1990	247,408,000
National population 2000	267,990,000
Average annual rate of growth for national population 1990 to 2000	0.8%
Percent change from 1990 to 2000 for national population	108%
National work force 1990	124,730,000
National work force 2000	141,228,000
Average annual rate of growth for work force 1990 to 2000	1.2%
Percent change from 1990 to 2000 for national work force	113%

SOURCES: Derived by average annual rate of growth adjustments to Bureau of Census and Bureau of Labor Statistics data

Throughout this study a number of factors have been cited that support the findings and projections about the growth of private security as the nation's largest protective resource. The most significant fact seems to be a greater demand by businesses and citizens for more crime prevention and fear reduction measures. The trend toward slower growth and stabilization of law enforcement resources has resulted in a cause-effect impact leading to more rapid growth in private security employment and expenditures. The tables and figures presented in this section for the period 1970-2000 graphically support the finding that private security is assuming an ever increasing role in the national effort to control crime.

240

PART IV

PUBLIC
AND
PRIVATE
SECTOR
ISSUES

CHAPTER 8
RELATIONSHIPS AND
COOPERATIVE PROGRAMS

Before the mid-1980s, private security and public law enforcement functioned largely as mutually exclusive protective resources with relatively little interaction or cooperation between them. This section reviews the apparent void in public and private sector cooperative arrangements during the 1970s and before, and identifies significant changes in relationships during the 1980s. The emphasis in this section is on describing examples of private/public sector cooperative efforts that have emerged in recent years.

SECURITY AND POLICE RELATIONSHIPS
(BEFORE 1980)

As early as 1964, interest in this area was evident in 2 articles that appeared in *The Police Chief* on the topic of police/security liaison needs and opportunities.[1] Several years later, the Rand researchers surveyed police and security worker interaction and reported that 27% of private security personnel never had police contact and another 30% of security personnel had law enforcement contact only once or twice a year.[2] At this stage, it appears that the emphasis was simply on "speaking to one another" about crime-related events. The literature at this time contains no discussion of broad cooperative strategies.

In 1974, the Private Security Advisory Council (PSAC) to the Law Enforcement Assistance Administration (LEAA) formed a standing committee to study law enforcement and private security relationships. The Private Security Task Force (PSTF) in 1975 clearly recognized the need "to promote increased cooperation and the development of mechanisms to improve working relationships between public law enforcement agencies and the private security industry in their mutual objective of crime prevention."[3] Specifically, the PSTF adopted 3 standards and goals designed to improve understanding and cooperation between private security and the police.[4] Although the issues relating to meaningful interaction were being studied and discussed in the 1970s by the PSAC and the PSTF, among others, few broad-based cooperative programs emerged until the 1980s.

The thrust of the Hallcrest research in the early 1980s was to study interaction, relationships, and cooperative efforts involving private security and law enforcement. Through a series of national surveys of law enforcement and security executives and practitioners, the Hallcrest researchers assembled comprehensive information on obstacles to interaction and cooperation and, at the same time, identified steps to improve relationships between private security and law enforcement.

HALLCREST'S FINDINGS - EARLY 1980s

In the early 1980s, relationships between law enforcement and private security were rated fair to good, at best, by law enforcement executives. Just under one-half of proprietary security managers rated overall relationships excellent, and security employees were equally favorable in their ratings. For proprietary security managers, high ratings of relationships were moderately correlated with the number of cooperative programs established, the frequency of information sought from criminal justice agencies, and the degree of cooperation received from law enforcement on investigation and response to criminal incidents.

The prior research efforts by Rand and the PSAC had noted several impediments to interaction and cooperation, including role conflict, negative stereotypes, lack of mutual respect, and minimal knowledge on the part of law enforcement about private security. Hallcrest research confirmed the continuing existence of these obstacles.

Upgrading the selection processes and training of private security personnel will have the greatest impact on improved interaction and cooperation, based upon national and site survey respondent recommendations by both law enforcement and private security. Establishing licensing and regulation or improving existing regulatory controls was recommended by many survey respondents as a mechanism to upgrade private security.

Management and supervisory meetings and private security liaison officer positions in law enforcement agencies were recommended to expand law enforcement knowledge and appreciation of the role of private security, increase dialogue, resolve problems and exchange information. Information exchange and improved communications were the primary recommendations made for more effective use of combined resources. Operational security employees expressed a desire for closer interaction with law enforcement personnel--i.e., interacting with security personnel and familiarizing themselves with facilities and security policies in their patrol areas.

Chiefs and sheriffs reported few cooperative programs with private security except occasionally in crime prevention. Most police agencies did not even maintain a list of security managers or firms in their area. Some corporate security managers (less than half) reported cooperative programs or procedures with law enforcement for hazardous materials movement, VIP/executive protection, disaster management, traffic control, crowd control, terrorism countermeasures, and economic crime investigation. Few examples of cooperation in these or other areas emerged from a literature review.

COOPERATIVE PROGRAMS
(MID-1980s TO 1990)

Beginning in the mid-1980s, cooperative programs between the private and public sectors emerged at a faster pace than ever before. Led by a relatively small number of committed men and women in national groups and associations, major corporations and local organizations became the catalysts for new cooperative programs and interaction. Partnerships between private security and law enforcement groups will likely continue to be forged throughout the 1990s, creating an increasingly formidable coalition fighting crime and favoring joint solutions to issues affecting private security and law enforcement, the public, and the business community. This section identifies and briefly describes selected examples of cooperative initiatives that have recently emerged.

NATIONAL PROGRAMS

Joint Council

Throughout the 1980s, both the International Association of Chiefs of Police (IACP) and the American Society for Industrial Security (ASIS) had standing committees on private sector and law enforcement cooperation and liaison. Joint meetings and coordinated program dialogue began between these national organizations, along with the Private Security Industry Committee of the National Sheriffs' Association (NSA), in the mid-1980s. With initial leadership and staff from the NSA committee and financial support from the National Institute of Justice (NIJ), a Joint Council of Law Enforcement and Private Security Associations was established in 1986, comprised of representatives of NSA, IACP, and ASIS. At the 3 workshops of the Joint Council between 1986 and 1988, the representatives expressed common objectives in seeking improved communications and cooperative programs between public and private sectors.

At the first meeting of the Joint Council in August 1986, the members identified 15 areas for cooperative programs.[5] Needed programs and topics in rank order of importance to the Joint Council members were:

1. Developing public law enforcement and private security protocols or guidelines for cooperation

2. Cataloging and publishing success stories

3. Making criminal history information available to the private sector

4. Exchanging expertise, training, and technology between the private/public sectors

5. Enhancing working relationships between both sectors in crime prevention

6. Setting selection and training standards for private security

7. Suppressing drugs in the workplace

8. Improving understanding of private security role by law enforcement

9. Privatizing selected law enforcement functions

246

10. Conducting joint public/private operations (e.g., VIP protection, hazardous materials transport, overseas threat information)

11. Providing cooperation and honesty in background checks

12. Improving public/private sector operational communications

13. Reviewing polygraph legislation

14. Developing guidelines for police moonlighting in private security

15. Reducing false alarms

While productive linkages were achieved by the Joint Council, lack of continuous funding and staff support has caused this council to become dormant. Yet, an effective dialogue among these national associations and liaison committees has continued, duplication of programs has largely been avoided, and a subtle, but healthy, competition exists in conceiving and producing cooperative programs and "products."

IACP Private Sector Liaison Committee (PSLC)

The PSLC has been one of the most active and productive IACP committees over the past 5 years. It has developed new cooperative programs and has promoted, sought corporate and public funding for, and distributed innovative program documents nationwide. Also, the PSLC has helped create a greater awareness among police executives that the business community and private security resources are strong supporters of effective law enforcement. Within the past few years, this committee of police executives, business leaders, and senior security executives has initiated and/or participated in more than a half dozen national programs. Several significant PSLC programs are summarized below.

- **Product Tampering**

    With the encouragement of the PSLC and financial support from The Southland Corporation (owner of 7-Eleven Stores), Athena Research Corporation was retained to develop protocols or best practices for law enforcement response to product tampering threats and incidents. Upon review and approval of this document by the PSLC in 1987, the IACP adopted

247

these protocols as its model policy guide for law enforcement response to product tampering.[6] Concurring with a PSLC recommendation, the IACP staff distributed the product tampering policy document to law enforcement agencies nationwide. Additionally, a videotape for training law enforcement personnel about proper handling of product tampering threats was developed by Athena Research with the support of the Grocery Manufacturers of America and the Food Marketing Institute. These tapes have been widely distributed by the IACP.

- ## Operation Bootstrap

Conceived by Chief Michael Shanahan, co-chair of the PSLC and chief of police at the University of Washington in Seattle, Operation Bootstrap has become a highly visible national program of the PSLC. Operation Bootstrap is a clearinghouse at the University of Washington that provides tuition-free corporate management training programs to a cross-section of police managers across the country. It began in 1985 as a pilot program of the IACP, and now Operation Bootstrap reaches into 45 states and has received financial support from private foundations and the NIJ. It offers management training and self-help programs that range in length from a day to a week and cover subjects such as effective supervision, conflict resolution, group problem solving, and stress management.[7] Approximately 70 *Fortune* 500 companies donated nearly 1,000 seats in their executive education courses in 1989, absorbing tuition costs for law enforcement personnel and leaving participants responsible only for travel and per diem expenses through their departments. The estimated value of this corporate-donated training to the law enforcement sector was $500,000 last year.[8]

- ## Drugs in the Workplace

Model Substance Abuse Policy

Based upon the work of Maryland Governor William Schaefer's Drugs in the Workplace Committee in 1987-88 in developing a model substance abuse policy, the PSLC reviewed the policy document and agreed that it

248

should serve as a national model. In 1989 the IACP, with full acknowledge-ment to the State of Maryland for model policy development, published and distributed the document, *Drugs in the Workplace: Model Substance Abuse Policy*. The PSLC urged local law enforcement agencies and others to distribute this model policy to local businesses. Among others, Pinkerton's, the nation's largest security service company, has reproduced this drug abuse policy and has distributed the document to clients and others nationwide. Also, the Washington State Restaurant and Hotel Association funded the reproduction and distribution of this document throughout its state.

Workplace Drug Investigation and Prosecution

In 1990, a PSLC subcommittee of corporate security and law enforce-ment executives was formed to coordinate the development of standards and protocols for business and public sector coordination of the detection, investigation, arrest, and prosecution of drug trafficking and use in the workplace. Subcommittee members noted a variety of problems in this crime area. Most importantly, they noted a void in protocols dealing with private sector and law enforcement linkages in conducting workplace drug investiga-tions and achieving successful prosecution of offenders.

• Telecommunications Fraud

In 1989, the PSLC formed a subcommittee to address the growing national problem of telephone service thefts and fraud, estimated to cost subscribers and telephone companies $500 million a year. Working in cooperation with MCI, AT&T, Sprint, Northern Telecom, and other members of the Communications Fraud Control Association, this group is developing guidelines and protocols for public and private sector prevention and detection of this recently emerging crime.

- ### Project Honest Broker

    Another PSLC subcommittee was formed in 1989 to explore the feasibility of compiling a desk-top "workbook" or other rapid information source which summarizes successful private/public programs throughout North America. The objective of Project Honest Broker, an idea and program-sharing mechanism, is to catalog successful community policing and crime prevention efforts; corporate, state, and local programs which help curb crime; and programs involving partnerships between private security and law enforcement.

ASIS, Law Enforcement Liaison Council (LELC)

This council of both proprietary and contractual security executives and law enforcement officials is currently pursuing 4 primary programs:

- ### Private Sector Access to Criminal Records

    For nearly 5 years, this council, along with the PSLC of the IACP, has been seeking state approval for private sector employers, especially in private security, to have unrestricted access to criminal conviction records. Several years ago, the council compiled and published a review of state laws regarding availability of criminal conviction data in *Security Management*.[9] Using the Washington State statute on private sector access to conviction records as a model, the LELC and the IACP's PSLC hope to introduce legislation permitting record access in states which currently restrict such access.

- ### Operation Cooperation

    After several years of consideration and recommendation by the council and with the assistance of ASIS headquarters staff, a professional video production entitled *Operation Cooperation* was completed in 1989. In this video prominent security and law enforcement professionals stress the need for public and private sector cooperation for crime control and suggest steps for closer working relationships. Tapes are available through ASIS chapters nationwide, and the LELC intends that this video will be primarily for use by police agencies and training academies throughout the country.

- **Private Security/Police Partnership Models**

    This 1990 undertaking by the LELC has several parts. First is the development of an operational guide for the formation of security/police collaborative networks. The council intends this guide to stress the needs for mutual assistance programs as well as to provide suggestions for types of organizational structures, membership, etc. Another part to this project will list potential police/security cooperative programs and joint ventures that might be undertaken. Another component, already begun, and somewhat similar to the IACP's Project Honest Broker, involves the search for and compilation of "success stories" or partnership initiatives between private security and law enforcement, whether industry specific (e.g., hospital, transportation, retail, telecommunications, etc.) or cooperative ventures within a geographic area.

- **Accreditation for Security Management**

    The council has agreed to study the feasibility of an accreditation process for security organizations and security management similar to the Commission on Accreditation for Law Enforcement Agencies (CALEA). The council has also agreed to consider the process of standards development for private security management, though some ASIS members recognize it as a controversial topic.

National Burglar and Fire Alarm Association (NBFAA) and Central Station Alarm Association (CSAA)

In January 1990, representatives of NBFAA and CSAA suggested to the IACP's PSLC that these alarm associations produce a training video for law enforcement officers on alarm systems. Various members of the PSLC agreed to work with the alarm industry in producing and promoting such a training video in the hopes of achieving greater understanding of alarm systems by law enforcement officers.

National Crime Prevention Council (NCPC)

Since the mid-1980s, the NCPC has become involved in at least a half dozen cooperative crime-prevention ventures with the private sector. The NCPC is probably best known for its trenchcoat-clad dog, McGruff, and its "Take a Bite out of Crime" mass media campaign. Not as widely known is that this public awareness campaign is largely made possible because of NCPC's partnership with the Advertising Council which distributes messages about crime prevention through television, radio, print media, and outdoor advertising. The estimated value of donated space and air time is $40 million to $50 million a year.[10]

Other examples of corporate partnerships with NCPC include The Southland Corporation's distribution of more than 20 million McGruff crime prevention brochures and designation of over 1,700 7-Eleven stores as "McGruff Houses," places where employees are trained to make emergency telephone calls for people in trouble.[11] Another NCPC supporter, Texize, maker of household cleaning products, has conducted a nationwide campaign to educate children and their parents about safety and crime prevention. Texize has distributed 200,000 children's emergency phone books, and has led the implementation of an elementary school crime-prevention curriculum nationwide.[12]

Two other cooperative programs involving NCPC are noteworthy.

- ## Security Education/Employment Demonstration Project[13]

During 1986 and 1987, public high school students in Baltimore, Cleveland, and St. Louis participated in the pilot Security Education Employment Program developed by NCPC with funding from the American Can Company Foundation. The program's specific goal was to train teenagers from inner-city neighborhoods for careers in private security. The Security Education Employment Program taught young people basic skills needed to find and keep a good job. The program also fostered working partnerships between schools, businesses, local governments, and private security companies.

The roots of the Security Education Employment Program lie in an innovative project initiated by the American Can Company at Martin Luther King, Jr., High School in New York City. The company decided to hold its 1983 shareholders' meeting at Martin Luther King and to train students to provide security. Richard Post, then director of corporate security for American Can, worked with Burns International Security to develop a course in basic security practices and procedures. Because of the students' enthusiastic response and excellent performance as security guards, American Can and the school decided to continue the program.

A grant from the American Can Company Foundation and matching funds from local sources allowed the NCPC to test this model in Baltimore, St. Louis, and Cleveland. Local partnerships were a prerequisite: public high schools provided the site and the students; security professionals from local ASIS chapters taught classes; and security firms provided part-time and then, after completion of the course, full-time jobs for graduates who passed the firm's examination.

The 16-week (1 semester) curriculum covered the skills and responsibilities of a security officer including patrol, access control, report writing, security surveys, traffic control, and self-defense. Other training increased student awareness of the effects of substance abuse, and the crime risks faced by children, the elderly, women, and handicapped people.

Burns International Security Services and Advance Security served as lead firms. Following the second year of this demonstration project, NCPC staff evaluated the strengths and weaknesses of this project and documented the program.[14]

- ### Corporate Action Kit

ADT, the nation's largest alarm company, in cooperation with NCPC produced a comprehensive corporate and employee crime prevention resource manual.[15] Camera-ready security awareness materials are presented for 15 topics, including protection of company information, workplace substance abuse, travel and home security, frauds and con games, and community crime prevention tips. Copies of this manual are distributed by both NCPC and ADT.

253

The Overseas Security Advisory Council (OSAC)

Based upon recommendations from business, government, and security leaders, former Secretary of State George Shultz created the OSAC in 1985 to increase the information exchange between public and private sector security managers on overseas security threats and security programs. The purpose of the OSAC is to promote greater security for Americans and American business facilities abroad.

This Council has 25 members--4 from the federal government and 21 from American multinational corporations. The chairperson of OSAC is the director of the State Department's Diplomatic Security Service (DSS), and the vice chairperson is a private sector security executive. Professional staff support is provided by a senior State Department manager and a security executive on loan from his or her corporation.

Various OSAC committees take on assignments such as information exchange, physical security, and overseas security awareness. Council meetings are held quarterly. To promote cooperation abroad, the OSAC has formed mini-councils in business centers in Europe, the Middle East, South and Central America, and East Asia.

To collect and disseminate timely information on security threats overseas, the Council and DDS developed a data base on problem areas of the world. This data base provides American businesses with computerized, unclassified threat information and sources of help in most areas of the world.

Since its formation, OSAC has produced several publications. "Security Guidelines for American Families Living Abroad" offers suggestions on topics ranging from intrusion alarms to safe telephone answering. "Crisis Management Guidelines" includes procedures to follow in planning and meeting various types of emergencies. This publication was produced after surveys showed U.S. business representatives needed guidelines to cope with terrorist activity and other threats to their overseas personnel and facilities.

"Are You A-OK? (Alert Overseas Kids)," a videotape starring actor/comedian Chevy Chase, has been distributed by the Council. It demonstrates good security practices for children aged 5 through 12.

STATE/LOCAL PROGRAMS

Washington Law Enforcement Executive Forum (WLEEF)

The WLEEF, formed by key law enforcement officials and private sector executives in the early 1980s, is the only statewide public/private sector organization in the nation.[16] Foremost among its missions and goals has been the creation of an atmosphere of mutual understanding of problems facing law enforcement and the business community in an effort to identify and affect crime trends. Membership is composed of 26 individuals equally divided between the private sector and law enforcement executives, including sheriffs, chiefs, the state patrol chief, and special agents in charge of the Seattle offices of the FBI and Secret Service, as well as representation from the state attorney general's office. Close relationship and open communication exist between the WLEEF and the Washington Association of Sheriffs and Police Chiefs.

Numerous cooperative program accomplishments have been realized by the Forum. Examples of projects undertaken include:

- funding a statewide loaned-executive program to enhance management of local police agencies;

- providing support for the *Law Enforcement Executive Journal*, the nation's first law enforcement/business publication;

- supporting computer crime control legislation;

- funding and developing a state-wide toll-free hotline for reporting drunk drivers;

- sponsoring legislation for regulation and training of private security personnel;

- promoting a Business Watch program to prevent crimes against businesses; and

255

- creating an Economic Crime Task Force (1) to assess the nature and extent of white-collar crime in the state, (2) to develop strategies to reduce such crime, (3) to promote appropriate legislative initiatives and revisions, and (4) to collect and disseminate information on economic crime.

Dallas, Texas

Since 1983, an operational-level program called the Dallas Police/Private Security Joint Information Committee has accomplished a variety of cooperative activities.[17] Estimating in 1984 that private security employment was about 10,000 in Dallas compared to 2,100 police officers, the Dallas Police Department sought programs to enhance the crime-fighting capabilities of, and build greater cooperation with, private security. Over the next few years, the programs described below were developed.

- A series of 2-day seminars is still conducted by the Dallas Police for private security personnel, covering such topics as laws of arrest, bomb threats, alarm ordinances, and field operating procedures.

- A Joint Committee was formed, comprised of proprietary and contract security managers and several officials of the Dallas Police Department.

- Published and distributed by the Department, BOLO (Be On the Lookout) bulletins are issued to security organizations to relay city crime patterns and to describe suspects in recent crimes.

- Using a local private security executive as the instructor, information about the role and scope of private security is presented to all police recruits as a standard entry-level course.

- Security officers are invited to attend "roll call" briefings at various patrol division stations, and police officers often attend security officers' prior-to-duty meetings to share information and to become better acquainted.

- Workshops attended by about 100 security organizations are hosted by the Department twice a year to exchange information

256

on topical issues such as check and credit card theft and fraud, auto theft, search and seizure, criminal trespass, etc.

News of the Dallas program has been carried by at least 5 law enforcement periodicals, and requests for program information have been received by more than 20 police and security agencies.[18]

Detroit, Michigan

With the possible exception of Seattle and the State of Washington, Hallcrest's research found no area of the country more active in cooperative security and police programs than the Detroit metropolitan area. Four separate cooperative ventures have been established in the area over the past decade, and the reconnaissance interviews indicated a relatively high degree of public/private interaction throughout the State of Michigan. Two Detroit programs will be identified here, followed by 2 other cooperative programs, one in Southfield and the other in Dearborn.

Downtown Detroit Security Executive Council (DDSEC)

Begun in 1984 by a bank security executive and past president of ASIS, Carl Carter, and a widely respected crime prevention professional, Commander James Humphrey of the Detroit Police Department, the DDSEC with its 55 members has become a crime-prevention partnership among 35 major corporations and local, state, and federal law enforcement agencies and offices in downtown Detroit.[19]

The council's goals include:

- identification of security problems in the downtown area from police reports and incidents reported to private security;

- promotion of crime prevention through environmental design in new construction and renovation projects;

- development of open, continuous communications and information-sharing between private security and law enforcement;

257

- promotion of crime-reduction and crime-awareness programs throughout the Downtown Detroit Business District; and

- fostering cooperative efforts with other community groups and business associations on crime-prevention projects.

Projects sponsored by the DDSEC have included:

- a closed-circuit television street surveillance system designed and implemented in cooperation with the Detroit Police, Michigan Bell Telephone, and the Greater Detroit Chamber of Commerce;

- promotion of Business Watch and Vertical Watch crime-prevention programs;

- surveying the security resources--personnel, communications, vehicles, etc.--available throughout the downtown area;

- a Telephone Information Program (TIP) to promptly report to the proper city agency various area problems such as streetlight outages, potholes, missing traffic signs, and other indicators of neglect;

- a Security On Site (SOS) program which, through outdoor signs denoting participation in SOS by a downtown business, means that site is staffed 24 hours a day and is available to call for police, fire, or medical assistance, and, in some cases, provides safe access for persons in trouble; and

- quarterly training, through the council's educational arm, the Downtown Security Forum, covering a wide range of security-related topics such as workplace substance abuse, white-collar and other business crimes, executive protection, auto theft, and security liability. Attendees include not only downtown security practitioners, but also business leaders, building managers, and law enforcement officials.

Annual "Update" Seminars on Security and Crime Prevention

In an effort to bring about improved relationships between the public and private protection sectors, the Detroit Police Department's Crime Prevention Section and the

Detroit Chapter of ASIS have cosponsored an annual professional development seminar since 1984.

The annual series, called "Update," focuses on current trends and topics which are of interest to both sectors. The seminars are specifically designed to offer 2 days of security and crime-prevention training at an affordable price. Also, exhibits of security products and services are displayed by about 50 companies as an important part of these annual seminars. Since its inception the seminar has grown in attendance from 125 attendees in 1984 to more than 400 registered attendees in 1989, with about equal attendance between law enforcement and security.

One of the primary aspects of the seminar is the cooperation displayed between the 2 sectors in the development, planning, and coordination of the seminar. The law enforcement and security attendees network among themselves to form new relationships and to share common problems and work out mutual approaches and solutions.

Southfield, Michigan

One of the earliest cooperative programs, PRIDE (Pooling Resources In Defense of our Environment), was begun by the Southfield Police Department in 1981 to regularly exchange crime-related information, to integrate protective services wherever possible, and to form a better working relationship between the police and private security.[20] PRIDE has about 130 members from the public and private sectors, including representatives from major corporations, universities, high schools, hospitals, hotels, shopping centers, and private security organizations. To facilitate networking and to exchange information on security and law enforcement-related issues, bimonthly breakfast meetings are hosted by various member organizations.

PRIDE's meetings and programs are coordinated by a police lieutenant who is assigned full-time as a security liaison officer. This lieutenant serves as a contact person for the business and private security community on law enforcement-related issues and information.

In addition to the bimonthly information-sharing meetings and networking among PRIDE members, other significant programs are promoted by PRIDE:

- **Mall Enforcement Network (MEN)**

  This program disseminates information on criminal activity at shopping malls in the metropolitan Detroit area. Major retail crimes and trends are shared among about a dozen regional police agencies and the Michigan State Police via the state-wide computer system (LEIN), Law Enforcement Information Network. Local police promptly alert retailers and mall security departments to significant crimes and crime patterns.

- **Private Parking Enforcement**

  In Southfield, the police department has transferred the duty and authority of enforcing parking laws on private property to private security. Violations involving handicapped parking areas, fire lanes, and traffic congestion problems on private property are routinely handled by private security, allowing police officers to be redirected to other law enforcement functions.

- **Security Vehicles Marking and Police Vehicle Deployment**

  Another unique cooperative effort is to have security vehicles with markings similar to those of the police department. The purpose is to give higher visibility to law enforcement and security personnel in the community, and thereby enhance crime prevention. Another innovative program in Southfield is the retention of used police vehicles. Rather than trading them in, which is a traditional way of disposing of old police vehicles, they are put in parking lots, shopping malls, etc., as decoy vehicles. The private security operation that is responsible for the premises has the responsibility to maintain these vehicles.

Dearborn, Michigan

In 1989, the Dearborn Security Network was formed to share crime-related information more effectively between the Dearborn Police Department and private security.[21] The Network has more than 100 members, made up largely of corporate security personnel. Meetings are held monthly, and formal presentations are conducted on topics such as bomb threat response, automobile theft on corporate property, and others. The Network is coordinated and directed by a member of the police department.

With primary funding by Ford Motor Company, a computer bulletin board was installed to share crime-related information among Network members. This computer information system has a variety of "menus" for its users. Files such as armed robberies, frauds, stolen vehicles, commercial burglaries, "be on the lookout for," and others can be called up by Network members. These crime files are updated daily by the Network director at the Dearborn Police Department. The system also includes announcements of crime-prevention seminars and other programs of interest to security personnel. Another feature is an image scanner which can transmit mugshots and police reports to the computer systems of Network members. Also, through a satellite pickup, training programs can be received and shared with Network members.

Baltimore County, Maryland

Since the mid-1980s the Baltimore County Police Department (BCPD), working with the Maryland Chiefs of Police Association and the local ASIS chapter, has sought a closer and more productive relationship with private security and the business community. Among its activities are the following:

- appointing a command officer to serve as a liaison with private security firms and organizations;

- researching false alarms and helping to develop legislation to reduce false alarm calls to the police;

- forming a Baltimore County Police Foundation to foster improved relationships with the business community and to jointly develop crime control strategies with the private sector, such as a comprehensive "Drugs in the Workplace" program; and

- including businesses in the Department's fear reduction and community policing programs.

In 1986, following meetings between high ranking commanders of the New York City Police Department (NYPD) and prominent security directors in the city, the Area Police - Private Security Liaison (APPL) was started in Midtown Manhattan to enhance public/private cooperation in protecting people and property, to exchange information, and to help eliminate the "credibility gap" between police and private security.[22]

APPL started in 1986 with about 30 private security organizations in 3 police precincts and has grown to more than 350 security organizations employing 12,000 private security personnel in 4 APPL programs--Midtown, Downtown, Uptown, and Downtown Brooklyn. The program is currently being expanded city-wide, and a command officer has been appointed as private security coordinator.

APPL involves monthly meetings to coordinate personal and property protection efforts, traffic problems, emergency response, and security surveys. Quarterly training sessions have been held on topics such as drugs in the workplace, fire and emergency medical responses, bomb threats, and fraud and street scams.

Both the private security and law enforcement groups recognize the advantages of APPL. The police provide (1) information on crime trends, wanted persons, and stolen property; (2) training for security supervisors; (3) assistance to private security in protecting assets and clientele; and (4) an atmosphere conducive to establishing trust and cooperation. For its part, private security offers the police vital information and acts as "eyes and ears," provides technology and expertise in asset protection, and helps the police establish linkages with the private security and business community.

CORPORATE AND OTHER INITIATIVES

In addition to the many corporations that are participating in the cooperative programs mentioned above as well as other such programs, businesses throughout the country are funding and providing leadership for crime-fighting and security/police programs. Several examples are presented below.

Mobil/Federal Law Enforcement Training Center (FLETC)

At the encouragement of Mobil's corporate security manager, George Murphy, and with a grant from the Mobil Foundation, the FLETC hosted 2 conferences of security and law enforcement professionals in 1986 to determine the feasibility of, and curriculum for, a series of national seminars on private security and law enforcement roles and capabilities. The purpose of these regional seminars, later called "Project Partnership" by the IACP's PSLC, for senior law enforcement and security executives was to:

- build a better understanding of private security and law enforcement responsibilities and constraints;

- promote improved crime and loss control through greater interaction and sharing of resources; and

- serve as a catalyst to promote new and imaginative cooperative programs.

While the national committees of ASIS, IACP, and NSA involved in police/security liaison endorsed these regional seminars, funding has not yet been obtained. However, a facilitators' conference on police/security cooperative programs, again funded by Mobil, is planned for August 1990 at the FLETC.

International Business Machines (IBM)

For a number of years, corporate and group security managers at IBM have hosted a luncheon or dinner for law enforcement leaders at IACP annual conferences, including IACP officers and members of the Executive Board, members of the State Association of Chiefs of Police (SACOP), and members of the Private Sector Liaison Committee. The purposes of these meetings are: (1) to inform IACP's leaders of recent public/private sector cooperative programs, (2) to stress the need for continuing close cooperation between corporate America and public law enforcement, and (3) to express appreciation for the support of law enforcement agencies across the country in helping security organizations to prevent and solve crimes in the workplace.

Hoffman-La Roche

In 1988, this major pharmaceutical/diagnostic products and services company led in forming a private sector initiative to wage a campaign against drug abuse.[23] Hoffman-La Roche brought more than 250 business leaders together in Washington, D.C., to seek solutions to the problem of drug abuse in the workplace. President Reagan delivered the conference's keynote address. Hoffman-La Roche also commissioned the benchmark Gallup Survey on drug testing practices of companies nationwide.[24]

ADT

Realizing that police departments throughout North America are increasingly frustrated by the high number of false alarms, this major alarm company has adopted an innovative policy and is attempting to gain support for its position throughout the alarm industry. In an effort to reduce the costly burden of false alarm response by law enforcement agencies, ADT notes the following:

- False alarms tie up resources, endanger lives, and reduce the ability to respond to real emergencies.

- A solution to the false alarm problem can only be attained through the responsible cooperation of the customer, the police, and the alarm monitoring company.

- Alarm permits and false alarm fines alone will not significantly reduce false alarms.

- Telephone verification of alarms before dispatching the police is a proven method of reducing false alarms and should be required by police.

- Suspension of police response for 1 year after 4 "at fault" false alarms in a year's time is a necessary requirement of any police policy.

- Prompt reinstatement of police response after suspension must be possible after the alarm monitoring company and the customer certify that corrective action has been taken. Corrective action means things like repair of malfunctioning equipment, such as faulty sensors, and better education of the customer--since 60% to 80% of false alarms are caused by customers.[25]

Thus far, ADT's position on false-alarm reduction is a minority point of view with both major alarm industry associations, NBFAA and CSAA. Apparently, some dissenters believe that it would be unethical to advocate suspension of police response to alarms, and others fear that the ADT policy position might restrict their business practices.[26]

Arizona Community Watch

This cooperative program, a 1989 National Crime Prevention award winner, is an "observe and report" program begun by Arizona Public Service Company, Salt River Project, Southwest Gas Corporation, and U.S. West Communications in 1989. This venture allows the 4 organizations to work together to make their communities safer. Field personnel use their 2-way radios or cellular telephones to report suspicious activities, fires, and accidents to dispatchers. The appropriate agency is then notified. The program has achieved unity between the companies and has alerted public safety authorities on 328 occasions in its first 6 months of operation. In addition, it is a model for a potential state-wide organization.[27]

Mountain Fuel Supply Company

This Salt Lake City-based utility is also a 1989 National Crime Prevention award winner. Mountain Fuel entered into a partnership with the Utah Council for Crime Prevention (UCCP) to design and implement a McGruff Truck Program, using McGruff-labeled utility vehicles as protection places for children in trouble. Training materials for drivers and law enforcement were produced, and a comprehensive public awareness campaign was launched throughout the Utah-southwest Wyoming service area. Mountain Fuel helped UCCP provide instruction to schools and technical assistance to other utility companies nationwide. Mountain Fuel and 4 other sites are piloting a possible national McGruff Truck effort.[28]

SUMMARY

In just the past few years, the forging of cooperative crime and fear reduction ventures between the public and private sectors has begun--albeit slowly. The number of partnerships and the diversity of programs undertaken is evidence of the desire and need for enhanced communication and cooperation between the law enforcement, private security, and business communities.

END NOTES

1.   Raymond Atherton, "Units Maintaining Liaison," and Thad Brown, "Types of Assistance Available," *The Police Chief*, November 1964.

2.   James Kakalik and Sorrel Wildhorn, *Private Police In The United States*, Volume I (R-869) and Volume II (R-870) (Washington, D.C., U.S. Government Printing Office, 1971).

3.   *Private Security: Report of the Task Force on Private Security*, National Advisory Committee on Criminal Justice Standards and Goals, Law Enforcement Assistance Administration (Washington, D.C., U.S. Government Printing Office, 1976), p. 205.

4.   Ibid.

5.   Minutes of The Joint Council of Law Enforcement and Private Security Associations, Chicago, IL (National Sheriffs' Association), August 21 and 22, 1986, pp. 4-6. See also, Lauren Goin, "The Joint Council...The Beginning," *The National Sheriff*, October-November 1986.

6.   W. J. Crow and Rosemary Erickson, *Product Tampering: A Recommended Policy of the International Association of Chiefs of Police*, published by the IACP, 1987.

7.   For a more complete program description, see Bill Burns, "Operation Bootstrap: Opening Corporate Classrooms to Police Managers," *NIJ Reports*, National Criminal Justice Reference Service, No. 217, November/December 1989. Also, see Michael Shanahan, "Operation Bootstrap," *The Police Chief*, February 1987.

8.   Burns, p. 2.

9.   Charles Sine, Jr., "The Record Speaks," *Security Management*, September 1988.

10.   *Corporate Action Kit*, National Crime Prevention Council and ADT, Inc., October 1986, p. 13.

11.   Ibid, p. 3.

12.   Ibid.

13.   "Public/Private Partnership Trains Inner-City Teens For Security Careers," *Catalyst*, Vol. 6, No. 6, National Crime Prevention Council, August 1986.

14.   *Creating a Safe Community: The Young Security Officer's Guide*, National Crime Prevention Council, 1987.

15.   *Corporate Action Kit*, National Crime Prevention Council and ADT, 1986.

16.   Norman Kates, "A Forum on the Forum," *Washington Law Enforcement Executive Journal*, August 1988, p. 6.

17.   John Driscoll (Deputy Chief of Police), *Public and Private Security Forces Unite in Dallas*, Dallas Police Department, unpublished, circa 1985.

18.   Ibid.

19.   Carl Carter, "Downtown Security: A Partnership Between Public and Private Sectors," *International Marketplace*, Central Business District Association, Detroit, Michigan, Vol. 3, No. 8, August 1986.

20.   Correspondence from Lt. Michael Chapman, Southfield Police Department, Southfield, Michigan, July 13, 1989.

21.   Correspondence from Corporal Douglas Laurain, Dearborn Police Department, July 13, 1989.

22.   Anthony Voelker (Chief of Organized Crime Control), *Starter Kit: APPL Program*, New York Police Department, 1989.

23.   "Fighting Drug Abuse in Corporate America," *Special Report: The National Conference on Corporate Initiatives for a Drug Free Workplace*, Hoffman-La Roche (Nutley, NJ), 1988, p. 3.

24.   Ibid.

25.   *Industry Relations Update*, Vol. 2, No. 1, ADT Security Systems, March 1990, p. 13.

26.   Ibid.

27.   "National Crime Prevention Awards," *The McGruff Gala*, The Crime Prevention Coalition, 1990, p. 7.

28.   Ibid.

CHAPTER 9
MAJOR SECURITY AND POLICE ISSUES

This chapter reviews 4 topics--**privatization, false alarms, police moonlighting**, and **private justice**--that are considered by many law enforcement and private security practitioners to be pivotal in forging improved relationships and effective working arrangements between public and private sector protective resources. The first topic, privatization of law enforcement tasks, covers the practices of transferring police tasks to the private sector and contracting with private security for performance of selected activities. A few examples of privatization of noncrime police support tasks are provided.

The second and third topics, false alarms and police moonlighting in private security, are long-standing police and security problem areas. While both groups are concerned about the influence of these issues on their operations, police officer moonlighting is largely a complaint of contract security service companies, and the effect of false alarms on police workload is largely a police complaint. Continued growth in police moonlighting and false alarms keeps these issues at the forefront of public and private sector relationships.

Finally, the topic of private justice or private adjudication of business crime is addressed. The business community seems to rely less often on the public criminal justice system, favoring instead private settlement of illicit workplace behavior. The reasons for the apparent reliance on private justice systems are explored. This chapter also includes a brief discussion on the character of private justice.

PRIVATIZATION OF
LAW ENFORCEMENT ACTIVITIES

Having the private sector perform services once performed by the government sector is known as privatization. Global privatization has been gathering momentum in recent years from the Pacific Rim to Eastern and Western Europe, and throughout North America.

The President of the U.S. Chamber of Commerce, Dr. Richard Lesher, sees "...billions of tax dollars to be saved, and quantum leaps in efficiency to be had through privatization."[1] Bluntly, he notes:

> *There is no great mystery attached to the advantages of privatization. Government, by its very nature, is unable to make the hard decisions required to achieve economic efficiency. It cannot fire incompetent workers or reward productive ones; it cannot respond quickly to the marketplace; and it cannot innovate. In fact, governments' personnel rewards are based on growth in the bureaucracy, while in the private sector rewards are tied to getting the job done with less expenditure.*[2]

State and local government spending for private sector services over the past 15 years has been dramatic, growing from $27 billion in 1975 to $81 billion in 1982[3] and to an estimated $100 billion by 1988.[4] In addition, 1987 federal government spending for private sector goods and services was $197 billion.[5] All indications from the literature review are that privatization will continue its robust growth throughout the 1990s.

For purposes of this research, privatization refers to (1) transferring or shedding of law enforcement tasks, (2) contracting out, and (3) supplementing public safety services. Transferring public functions simply means that the services or activities which are "shed" must be provided privately by businesses and individuals. Contracting out means that a government agency enters into a contract with a private firm to perform one or more services and ensures that the private firm provides the desired quality of service. Supplementing the delivery of public safety means that citizens and businesses "... have voted with their dollars to supplement publicly provided protection services to achieve a greater sense of safety."[6] This supplement increasingly takes the form of citizen and business crime prevention efforts, including the increasing use of private security products and services for neighborhoods, shopping malls, industrial plants, financial institutions, and virtually every residential setting and work place.

TRANSFER OF POLICE TASKS

Gradually, from the early part of this century until the late 1970s, the police assumed more and more non-crime-related services such as assisting the mentally ill, the homeless, runaway children and animals; responding to street light outage, potholes, abandoned-vehicle, and lost-property calls; guarding public buildings and parking lots; and escorting funerals and bank depositors. By the late 1970s, studies of police workload consistently revealed that only about 20% of calls were crime-related.[7]

Faced with ever-increasing calls for service, tight budgets, and few additional personnel, police administrators during the 1980s sought ways to reduce the number of nonessential tasks. Many police departments began to limit investigations and follow-up on the basis of certain "solvability" or case-management factors. It seemed logical, therefore, that some departments might also be interested in transferring the responsibility for handling specific criminal incidents, especially those that have a low probability of clearance (such as theft from cars in employee parking lots of industrial and commercial complexes).

Table 9.1 shows how law enforcement executives and private security managers in the 1981 nationwide Hallcrest surveys rated the possibility of such a transfer in 6 specific law enforcement activities, with "yes" and "maybe" responses combined to give an indication of their willingness to discuss what is, after all, a radical departure from police tradition.

The 1981 survey of law enforcement executives showed a surprising level of interest in the possibility of transferring responsibilities, considering the relatively low ratings they

271

gave to private security performance and contribution to crime control. Overall, the greatest interest was in turning over responsibility for responding to burglar alarms and for completing incident reports where the victim declines prosecution or files for insurance purposes only. No statistically significant differences were found in the responses of municipal police, sheriffs' departments, and county police departments. However, when the data were controlled for size of department, it was clear, for all tasks except one, that the smaller the department, the greater the interest in transferring responsibility. The one exception was responsibility for responding to burglar alarms, which nearly 70% of large departments were interested in transferring to the private sector.

TABLE 9.1 POSSIBILITY OF TRANSFERRING RESPONSIBILITY TO PRIVATE SECURITY			
Activity	Law Enforcement Executives	Proprietary Security Managers	Contract Security Managers
Responding to burglar alarms	57%	69%	68%
Preliminary investigations	40%	88%	68%
Completing incident reports			
a) victim declines prosecution; for insurance purposes only	68%	87%	66%
b) misdemeanors	45%	81%	63%
Supplemental case reports	38%	78%	60%
Transporting citizen arrests	35%	32%	38%

Source: *Hallcrest Report* (1985).

CONTRACTING OUT

Additionally, in the 1981 Hallcrest survey, 40% of the responding law enforcement executives identified activities that "potentially might be more cost-effectively performed by contracting with private security." The most frequently identified activities were: public building security, parking enforcement, parking lot patrol, school crossing guards, public parks patrol, animal control, traffic control, noninjury accident investigation, special events security, city/county code violations, funeral escorts, court security, prisoner transport, and housing project patrol. Subsequently, law enforcement officers in the 2 field-study sites surveyed during the earlier (1981-82) Hallcrest research were asked for their opinion. Police officers in Baltimore County, Maryland, favored contracting out all listed activities except code violations and prisoner transport. Officers in Multnomah County, Oregon, favored contracting out all activities except public park patrol, court security, and prisoner transport.

Executives of major contract guard service companies said they were currently performing a number of these noncrime activities, including parking enforcement, parking lot patrol, housing project patrol, and traffic control. They also identified other areas of potential business growth such as court security, noninjury accident investigation, government building and public event security, jail security, and crime prevention services.

In the earlier Hallcrest study, a few examples of privatization of public safety services were found in the early 1980s: private paramedical services in Newton, Massachusetts; private fire-fighting services in Arizona and Oregon; and private policing of small communities in Ohio, Illinois, and Florida. *The Hallcrest Report* (1985) concluded that while much of the contracting out of government services helped reduce costs, actual contracting of crime-related police work posed a unique problem. Crime-related, law enforcement services are rooted in constitutional responsibilities and may be one of the few truly mandated functions that should not or cannot be contracted away.

More likely than contracting out crime-related law enforcement functions is a return of noncrime and nonemergency services to the private sector, thus removing extraneous activities from the workload of police agencies. Law enforcement officials might forge this sort of partnership with private security more readily if they felt that private sector alternatives gave their officers more time for "real" police work. As for the competence of private security to provide support tasks, the elements of supply and demand and tight contract specifications would probably produce a sufficient number of security firms qualified to handle the noncrime activities contracted out by law enforcement agencies.

RECENT TRENDS (1985 AND 1990)

The 1989-90 field and focus group interviews and the literature review revealed considerable evidence that privatization is emerging slowly in law enforcement and other criminal justice functions. Virtually all public and private sector interviewees predict that

273

the contracting of some criminal justice activities to private security will accelerate in the 1990s and beyond. Perhaps the most notable examples of privatization to date have been in corrections. By 1986, 13 private jails and prisons had opened in 9 states, including California, Colorado, Pennsylvania, Tennessee, and Texas.[8] Also, a 1986 study found that 18 out of 29 states surveyed reported 1 or more aspects of privatization of corrections then under consideration.[9]

A significant contribution to the literature on privatization is the 1987 NIJ-sponsored report, *Public Policing--Privately Provided*.[10] This report addresses issues related to contracts between local governments and private companies for the delivery of police support services such as guarding public buildings or sports arenas, providing court security, and conducting background investigations on job applicants. The authors, Marcia and Jan Chaiken, stress "support tasks" in their discussion of police contracting with private security; they view as "unrealistic and implausible" the contracting out of total police services.[11]

The Hallcrest staff concurs with the Chaikens that neither local law enforcement nor most contract security executives want to see contracting of the total police function. The field and focus group interviews revealed no widespread interest on the part of security guard and investigative firms in contracting for overall law enforcement and crime control within cities or counties. Apparently, the liability of assuming armed police duties coupled with the lack of trained and experienced personnel makes "full" policing contracts unattractive and unlikely. However, Hallcrest did find considerable interest among security guard companies in contracting with law enforcement agencies for non-crime-related support functions.

Moreover, the literature reviewed and interviews conducted by the staff indicated greater interest on the part of some federal, state, and local governments in contracting out selected tasks or functions than was found by the Hallcrest researchers in the early 1980s. Yet, the Chaikens report that several large national security companies are, for the time being, avoiding contracts with local governments, citing delays in payment, difficulties in avoiding corruption, and the risk of an incident which might result in negative publicity.[12] However, many managers and owners of private investigative firms expressed interest in contracting with the public sector to conduct a wide variety of investigative activities.

Despite reluctance by a few private security firms to contract with government agencies, the following 1987 list of jurisdictions which contract privately for various protective functions was assembled by the authors of *Public Policing--Privately Provided*:[13]

SITES WITH EXPERIENCE IN PRIVATE PROVISION OF PROTECTIVE SERVICES

STATE	JURISDICTION	TYPE OF SERVICE
Alaska	Anchorage	Parking meter enforcement Parking meter collection Parking lot security
Arizona	State Flagstaff Maricopa County Phoenix	Parking lot enforcement School crossing guards Building security Crowd control
California	Federal Hawthorne Los Angeles Los Angeles County Norwalk San Diego San Francisco Santa Barbara	US Department of Energy facility security Traffic control during peak hours Patrol streets surrounding private university Traffic and security for special events Building security Park security Park security Housing project security Park security Building security Airport security Prisoner transport
Colorado	Denver Fort Collins	Building security Building security
Connecticut	Hartford	Sports arena security
Florida	Dade County Fort Lauderdale Pensacola St. Petersburg	Courts, building security Airport, building security Airport security Park security
Hawaii	State	Parking lot enforcement
Idaho	State Idaho Falls	Regional medical center security School crossing guards
Kentucky	Lexington	Housing project security
Massachusetts	Boston	Hospital, courts, library security--city Library security--federal
Nevada	Federal	Nuclear test site security
New Jersey	Sports Authority	Sports arena security
New York	State Buffalo New York City Oneonta Suffolk School District	Response to burglar alarms in state office buildings Court security--federal Security compounds for towed cars Shelter security Human Resources Administration security Building security Locate cars with outstanding tickets Arrests for retail store theft Management training; police Campus security
Pennsylvania	State Philadelphia Pittsburgh	Unemployment offices security Welfare offices security Parking enforcement Court security--federal

SITES WITH EXPERIENCE IN PRIVATE PROVISION OF PROTECTIVE SERVICES
(Continued)

STATE	JURISDICTION	TYPE OF SERVICE
		Patrol city park
		High school stadium security
		School crossing guards
		Transfer of prisoners
Texas	Dallas/Fort Worth	Airport security including baggage checking
	Houston	Building security
Utah	State	Building security
		Training for transit police
Washington	Seattle	Building security
	Tacoma	Sports arena security
Washington, D.C.	District of Columbia	Planning and management
		Federal building security

In late 1985 according to *The New York Times*, about 36,000 of the estimated 1.1 million private security workers were assigned to government contracts: 11,000 in federal government, 9,000 in states, and 16,000 in local government.[14] Further, this publication indicated that security work for governments, along with the residential sector, was the fastest growing market in private security.[15] The current research effort was unable to validate these numbers or claims. Interviews conducted by the Hallcrest staff in 1989 and 1990 indicated new areas of contracting for security services. At the federal level, in addition to numerous contracts for building and facility security, private security firms have been contracted to:

- provide security at about 20 American embassies under construction where military guards are not required,

- conduct background investigations of job applicants,

- provide court security,

- transport prisoners, and

- maintain custody of hospitalized prisoners.

Some knowledgeable observers of police privatization speculate that economies and efficiencies for federal, state, and local governments might soon be realized through contracting for specialized and technical security services. Such services might include investigations of complex white-collar, computer, and other high-tech crimes; various investigations for Inspectors General, Attorneys General, District Attorneys, etc.; engineering of security, fire, and life-safety systems for public buildings; installation, monitoring, and maintenance of security equipment and systems; guarding of civil and military facilities; and transporting sensitive and high-value material via private armored vehicles. In the early 1980s, Thomas Wathen, the current president of the nation's largest security service firm, Pinkerton's, candidly addressed an International Association of Chiefs of Police (IACP) annual conference:

> *My guess is that for all the years of building the services you are currently trying to deliver, you've inherited (or grabbed) a fair share of jobs which aren't even related to the penal code. In other words, you're doing a lot of nonpolice-related work. You should be aware that many of these functions could actually be performed without any sworn police personnel being involved... .*
>
> *So many jobs could be "contracted"--not just "civilianized" (since you almost always end up paying police wages after a few years). I'm here to tell you that you'd have even greater "control" for a much lower cost to your city... .*
>
> *You need only write out the specifications and some definite performance guidelines (measuring tools for yourselves) and you'll have a nontraditional way to deliver traditional services at a much lower cost.*[16]

Evidently, this message has drawn the serious attention of some law enforcement and other governmental officials in their attempt to meet increasing demands for service with strained fiscal and personnel resources.

Recent examples of privatization include, among others:

• <u>Tacoma, Washington</u>

In response to widespread concerns by business leaders, workers, and patrons in downtown Tacoma regarding crime and fear, the Local Improvement District (LID), a special taxing district, raised the funds for additional protective services in the downtown corridor in 1987.[17] These funds were directed to the City of Tacoma, which supplemented the police budget to enable contracting with a private security company for additional protection.

The police department selected a regional security company, Northwest Protective Service, Inc., to provide 17 personnel, called Community Services Representatives (CSRs) to patrol the downtown corridor. These uniformed CSRs are trained and managed by the police department. They are unarmed but are equipped with radios to report situations requiring police response. The CSRs function largely as "eyes and ears" for the police while patrolling the downtown business corridor.

Although a thorough evaluation of this 2-year privatization effort has not been undertaken, it seems to be an acceptable and cost-saving alternative to adding more police officers in downtown Tacoma. Apparently, the police department is basically satisfied with contracting for and managing private security resources. The cost of contracting for the 17 CSRs is at least 50% lower than the cost of using more highly trained and more expensive police officers. Businesspeople, other workers, and customers reportedly feel safer from urban crime because of the presence of these private security CSRs in downtown Tacoma.

- <u>East Hills, Long Island, New York</u>[18]

Local officials contracted with a security firm to provide 30 unarmed, uniformed security officers to patrol the town 24 hours a day. The security firm, Eastgate Security and Investigations, Inc., works in cooperation with the Nassau County police to prevent crime and to enhance public safety in this town of 9,000. Residents of East Hills in voting for private security accepted a "tax-deductible tax increase."[19]

- <u>Wynstone, North Barrington, Illinois</u>

With no police force in North Barrington, the developers of Wynstone, a prominent residential community, contracted with Levy Security Consultants, Ltd., of Chicago to provide 24-hour access and traffic control, emergency response, loss prevention, and rule enforcement.[20] Three unarmed security officers per shift patrol in marked cars with the Wynstone crest. The cars have radar, sirens, public address equipment, and special lighting. Security costs are included in the residents' monthly assessments.

- Kansas City, Missouri

In the first test of its kind nationwide, the Kansas City Police Department has proposed to contract with private security firms to perform 22 tasks currently performed by police officers.[21] Although the proposed test of privatization has not yet been funded, the Kansas City Police Department has developed substantial justification for the project.

Noting that calls for service have increased by 61% while the number of officers has decreased by 12% since the early 1970s, former chief Larry Joiner established an internal task force to seek alternative methods of policing, including the feasibility of contracting out some non-crime-related tasks.[22] The departmental study group quickly ruled out the possibility of adding more police officers because of budgetary limitations. A survey of 262 Kansas City police officers revealed 56 non-law-enforcement-related tasks that might be performed by nonsworn personnel. Also, an analysis of 72 dispatch/call categories during August 1989 for the Metro Division revealed that the vast majority of calls and time spent by police officers was in response to noncrime events.[23] Interestingly, the second most frequent dispatch out of the 72 call-for-service categories was in response to intrusion alarms; the most frequent was for disturbance calls.

The internal study group also conducted a survey of 23 major police departments around the nation,[24] which yielded little new information on contracting with private security. Actually, this survey found only 2 out of 23 police departments that used private security, and these 2 provided building security only.

The Kansas City Police Task Force concluded that:

> *...most, if not all, of the non-law enforcement activities carried out by our department could be handled by private security organizations. The tasks in question could be handled just as effectively, at a lesser expense, and would not require a diminution of overall service to the public. The accomplishment of these tasks requiring relatively unskilled personnel could be met with the cooperation of the private sector. This would produce the desired effect of freeing up police officers for true law enforcement functions and would require less training for those private security personnel assigned to carry out the perfunctory tasks.*[25]

279

The task force recommended that 1 patrol division within the city be used as the test site for a 2-year experiment for 3 types of contracts encompassing 22 separate tasks. The first is a special-request contract for tasks that occur at irregular times, such as assisting with traffic and crowd control at special events and guarding prisoners at hospitals. The second contract type would initially include only 1 task: response to all intrusion alarms in the test patrol division, estimated to be about 30 per day.

The third contract type would involve performing 19 support tasks within 1 patrol division. The tasks proposed for unarmed private security personnel are the following:

- Transport prisoners
- Provide standby for owner on open window or door
- Provide standby for vehicles to be towed
- Assist at traffic, medical, or other emergencies
- Assist stranded motorists
- Perform school crossing guard duties
- Provide standby on road hazards
- Direct traffic on lights out or at barricaded positions
- Respond to 911 hang-up calls from outside pay phones
- Assist elderly and disabled people on minor problems (e.g., lockouts)
- Transport citizens (e.g., victims, witnesses, etc.)
- Assist lost juveniles or elderly people
- Deliver intradepartmental paperwork
- Respond to parking complaints
- Recover found property not involved in crimes (e.g., bicycles, purses, etc.)
- Take walk-in reports (e.g., minor traffic accident)
- Guard crime scenes
- Provide standby for arrival of police officers (e.g., traffic accident, injured person)
- Perform routine tasks (e.g., obtain building listings, provide community and crime prevention information, etc.)

The police department estimates that at least 10 security personnel will be needed to perform the above tasks on a regular basis during this test project. Also, the department projects that these tasks can be performed by private security at a 37% savings to the city.

The police department has requested financial support from the National Institute of Justice (NIJ) and from the Committee of National Security Companies (CONSCO) for the operations, monitoring, and evaluation of this privatization experiment to determine its cost-effectiveness and level of acceptance by police personnel and by the citizens.

THE FUTURE OF PRIVATIZATION

Well-planned privatization programs such as that in Kansas City, once implemented and if successful, will likely be replicated in many small and large law enforcement agencies. As the NIJ director, James Stewart, noted, "The responsibility of government to ensure security need not necessarily mean that government must provide all the protective services itself."[26]

Increasing privatization of criminal justice services will likely occur throughout the 1990s and well into the 21st Century. We agree with the view of criminal justice scholar Robert Trojanowicz on the future of privatization:

One question that need not be asked is whether the trend will persist. We are already too far down the road to turn back. Therefore, the ultimate question is not whether this change is good or bad, but whether these changes will occur piecemeal and poorly or thoughtfully and well.[27]

FALSE ALARMS

Can the police, the alarm industry, and the public tolerate double the current number of false and nuisance alarms? It could happen by the year 2000 if the number of false alarms corresponds with the projected growth of alarm systems, especially in the residential market. In the early 1980s, from 2% to 5% of residences had alarm systems;[28] by the mid-'80s that figure had increased to 7%.[29] By the end of the 1980s, the estimate was up to 10%, and residential alarm installations might double before the year 2000.[30]

The Hallcrest Report (1985) identified the burden of excessive false alarms on the police as a major problem in creating good working relationships between law enforcement and private security.[31] Police studies of alarm response consistently show that 95% to 99% of alarm calls are false and that alarm calls represent 10% to 30% or more of total calls for service. In the market analysis of the security industry, we found a rapid growth in alarm companies and alarm installations and a corresponding surge in false alarms. The alarm response workload has severely strained police resources and in some communities has reached a saturation point, i.e., police response is discontinued altogether or is suspended until corrective measures are taken.

The alarm industry in a given community is not a cohesive, easily identifiable group. Alarm systems differ widely in size and complexity, components used, clients served, and business practices. These factors combined with the proliferation of inexpensive retail (over-the-counter) alarm systems and do-it-yourself installations mandate a broad-based approach to minimize false alarms.

GROWTH OF ALARM FIRMS AND SYSTEMS

Hallcrest estimates that in the United States nearly 13,000 alarm firms are actively engaged in the sale and installation of intrusion and hold-up detection systems. In addition, about 2,200 locksmiths are engaged secondarily in the installation of alarm systems. The largest sales volumes for alarm companies are generated in the manufacturing, residential, and retailing markets.

The staff has identified 5 factors that could stimulate wider use of alarm systems, especially in the residential sector, and thus further compound the problem of alarm response intensifying police and alarm company workload: (1) the growth of retail (over-the-counter) sales of alarm systems and do-it-yourself alarm installations, (2) insurance premium reductions and possible tax credits for security expenditures, (3) improved alarm transmission capabilities to handle more alarm systems, including greater radio frequency access, (4) the potential for the Regional Bell Operating Companies (RBOCs) to enter the alarm systems field, and (5) the potential of car alarms installed as standard equipment on new vehicles. The combined implications and impact of these factors on police calls for service could be overwhelming.

CONTRACTING OUT ALARM RESPONSE

The transfer of alarm response to the private sector has been suggested as a possible solution to the burden of alarm response and false alarms on police workload. Transfer of alarm response to private security was favored by 57% of the nearly 400 responding law enforcement executives in the Hallcrest national survey in the early 1980s.[32] The staff sensed the same inclination by police to shed alarm response in its 1989 and 1990 field interviews. Again, in the national surveys in the early 1980s, the majority of central station managers favored or would have considered assumption of alarm response. Today, some of the major national firms see contracted alarm response as a potential area of growth. Eight of 10 local managers of guard and patrol companies were also receptive to contracted alarm response.[33]

ALARM RESPONSE - A PIVOTAL ISSUE

The Hallcrest research staff believes that alarm response may well be a pivotal issue in the overall relationship between law enforcement and private security in the next few years--an issue not limited to just the law enforcement/alarm company relationship. This belief is based upon 2 observations.

First, some law enforcement officials view alarm response (especially residential) not as police business, but as a special consideration for the few citizens who can afford alarm systems, or as a free service for the alarm companies who make a profit at the expense of the police. Second, limited law enforcement personnel availability in some agencies may be a motivating force to transfer alarm response to private security. Regardless of personnel availability, however, the 5 factors cited previously for burgeoning alarm installations would cause the current false alarm problem to take a quantum leap. Alarm response would then become a major rather than a nagging problem for law enforcement and the alarm system subscribers expecting response.

DEFINITIONAL ISSUES

Alarm companies generally define a false alarm as an alarm signal transmission when there is not a situation or equipment condition on the protected premises that creates vulnerability, or when there is not an actual or attempted penetration of the protected premises. As noted by the National Burglar and Fire Alarm Association (NBFAA) and other groups who have studied the issue, there are 3 major and several minor causes of false alarms: (1) between 50% and 70% are caused by customer/subscriber misuse of their alarm systems; (2) between 10% and 20% are caused by alarm company personnel in the installation and servicing of alarm systems; and (3) between 10% and 20% involve faulty equipment. Lesser causes of false alarms include telephone line problems and extreme weather conditions. Some alarm studies list an "unknown" or "undetermined" category of causes that can be as high as 25%, depending upon the degree of specificity in other categories.

Many false alarms are caused by using alarm sensor devices in applications for which they were never intended--a result of poor selection of system components or improper sales practices. Most modern alarm systems also are subject to a variety of ambient environmental conditions.

False alarms caused by customer/subscriber misuse of the system could be reduced through better user training or fines imposed on the user and/or the alarm company. Problems with alarm installation and servicing have been addressed more attentively in recent years through improved engineering design of equipment. The emergence of "smart sensors" with self-diagnostic capabilities and alarm verification might help reduce nuisance and false alarms. In addition, today's alarms are better shielded against electromagnetic interference than previous systems were.

Police Definitions

To the law enforcement administrator and patrol officer alike, the cause of the false alarm is immaterial; their concern is the substantial amount of patrol time consumed in responding to alarm calls. The police define false alarms as any burglary or hold-up alarm signal that does not involve an actual perpetrator or attempt, i.e., a false call for police service when no police response was warranted by the alarm condition. Accordingly, the impact on police workload is measured by a false alarm rate based on total calls for police service.

Alarm Industry Definitions

Alarm companies, however, measure false alarms against a base of total alarm systems in operation in a city or metropolitan area. Using the alarm industry definition of false alarms per 100 alarm systems results in a fairly good performance record for most alarm systems. A growing number of alarm companies use devices to detect tampering with the alarm system. These devices deter some intrusion attempts, and the perpetrator leaves before committing a theft, inflicting damage, or leaving evidence of an attempted entry.

Alarm companies feel that some alarm conditions considered false by the police are indeed attempts at intrusion, and that negative attitudes by patrol officers toward alarm

285

systems account for many of the unknown causes not attributed to environmental conditions. Additionally, alarm personnel frequently complain that police officers often are slow to respond and perform only a cursory check when they find no readily apparent sign of forced entry.

EFFECTIVENESS OF ALARM SYSTEMS

Alarm systems are generally perceived by security practitioners and users as having both deterrent and detection value. Two different police department-initiated studies of alarm system effectiveness determined that residences with alarm systems were 6 times less likely to be burglarized than homes without alarm systems. One of the studies also showed that the burglary rate for alarmed business premises was one-half that of nonalarmed businesses.[34] These studies should be extended to use a more scientific methodology to test the actual effectiveness of alarm systems before widespread acceptance of these limited findings.

Studies by the NBFAA and the Western Burglar and Fire Alarm Association also indicate that alarm systems are responsible for the capture of thousands of suspects annually, resulting in high conviction-to-arrest ratios. This offsets additional criminal justice expense and resolves a large number of other burglaries through "clearance by arrest."

MANAGING THE PROBLEM

Efforts to control the false alarm problem primarily have involved enactment of alarm control ordinances and development of customer education and awareness programs by alarm companies. The NBFAA, which in early 1990 announced the publication of its model alarm ordinance, estimates that more than 2,000 communities have alarm control ordinances. These alarm ordinances typically include (1) alarm system permits, (2) allowance for 3 to 5 false alarms per system per year, (3) punitive action in the form of a graduated scale of fines, and (4) ultimately nonresponse to problem locations.[35]

Some departments (Cincinnati; Miami; Oakland; Multnomah County, Oregon; and Fulton County, Georgia, among others) have reported impressive results on false alarm reduction for both total alarm systems and police alarm-response workload. User or subscriber training campaigns usually include instruction on the proper use of the alarm system.

The Hallcrest staff's review of alarm control ordinance programs suggests that they are most successful when they foster cooperation among the user, the alarm company, and the law enforcement agencies rather than placing undue hardships on the user and the alarm companies. The most effective programs appear to be those which were initially developed in conjunction with the alarm companies, and those which continue to involve the alarm companies in follow-up customer training.

A NATIONAL STRATEGY NEEDED

Because so many dimensions of the false alarm problem transcend community or state-level efforts, the solution to this problem demands a national strategy. As noted earlier, the problem of false alarms and alarm response could well become one of the most significant issues in public law enforcement and private security relationships in the 1990s, especially as public safety agencies struggle to maintain current service levels while new alarm system installations might accelerate at an unprecedented pace. An initial step in developing this national strategy might be to gather comparative empirical data on alarm system effectiveness and false alarm impact on police services. Ideally, studies would evaluate different alarm system types and equipment in communities of varying sizes and different patrol and alarm response policies. Such data are not currently available.

Multi-city studies in different regions should be conducted on the false alarm problem and alarm system effectiveness in deterring property crime and reducing the level of police burglary and robbery investigations. A comprehensive assessment of the false alarm problem is especially critical because of the potential for increased market penetration through the former Bell Telephone operating companies and increased sales of low-cost retail and do-it-yourself alarm systems.

RECENT DEVELOPMENTS

Without question, during the 1980s prominent alarm companies (ADT and Honeywell, among others) and the major alarm industry association, NBFAA, have taken significant steps to reduce the wasteful costs of false alarms. Through improved engineering and systems design, some alarm companies have made their alarms more difficult to "false." Also, many alarm companies have substantially increased alarm system user training for their customers, which helps reduce misuse and false alarms. In the late 1980s, the NBFAA introduced the National Training School for training and certifying alarm technicians. This training program is offered through NBFAA chapters throughout the United States. One objective is to minimize the occurrence of false alarms through better trained alarm technicians.

Responsible alarm industry members are making diligent efforts to control the problem of false alarms. Les Brualdi, president of ADT (the nation's largest alarm company), in speeches to industry leaders over the past 2 years, has called for a "zero defect mentality" with regard to false alarms.[36] Similarly, an editorial in a monthly publication of a major state alarm association forcefully stated the case:

> *We call on all alarm companies to a renewal of our commitment to reduce false alarms to their minimum. We say it is time that we stopped making excuses for false alarms; that it is time for each alarm company owner and each alarm company employee to make an extra effort to eliminate unwanted alarms.*[37]

POLICE MOONLIGHTING IN PRIVATE SECURITY

BACKGROUND

Businesses frequently hire an off-duty law enforcement officer to perform guard, patrol, traffic direction, crowd control, order maintenance, and other security functions. Fast- food restaurants and convenience stores, for example, may retain an off-duty police officer to discourage loiterers and disorderly persons and to deter robbery attempts. Building contractors and utility companies will often secure the services of a police officer (on- or off-duty) to direct traffic at a construction or repair site. Civic centers, shopping malls, and sports facilities frequently use off-duty police personnel for security.

For more than 15 years, secondary employment or "moonlighting" by law enforcement officers in private security has evoked negative feelings on the part of most contract security company owners and managers, who see this practice as unfair competition. The Private Security Advisory Council (1972-77), the Private Security Task Force (1975-76), and *The Hallcrest Report* (1985) identified police moonlighting in private security as a major source of conflict between law enforcement and private security, especially among guard and patrol businesses.[38] Despite security industry displeasure, all indications are that moonlighting is "alive and well" and continues to grow, as will the demand for private protection throughout the 1990s.

A recent article notes that "public law enforcement is going private."[39] At first glance, this article in *Security* seemed to address the topical issue of privatization or contracting out of police services to private security. But instead, it suggests that private security employers consider hiring off-duty police officers as a means of obtaining qualified personnel: "After all, they are armed with police badges, radios, uniforms, guns, and the full power of arrest."[40]

None of the earlier studies of private security and police relationships in the 1970s attempted to determine the scope of off-duty police moonlighting in private security, though they noted its pervasiveness. Hallcrest's research in the early 1980s included survey respondents in 3 groups directly involved in and knowledgeable about police moonlighting: (1) law enforcement executives representing 384 departments covering all 50 states, (2) corporate or proprietary security executives from 676 businesses, and (3) 557 contract security managers and executives representing local, regional, and national security companies. This was the first national--and to date, possibly the only--survey of these groups to assess respondent perceptions on a variety of security and police topics, including moonlighting by police.

These surveys revealed that 81% of the law enforcement administrators indicated that their department's regulations permit officers to moonlight in private security, while 19% prohibited or severely restricted private security moonlighting. Law enforcement administrators estimated that about 20% of their personnel have regular outside security employment to supplement their police salaries. Nationally, the Hallcrest researchers estimated that at least 150,000 local law enforcement officers in the U.S. are regularly engaged in off-duty employment in private security. The 3 most common methods of obtaining off-duty officers for security work, in rank order, are: (1) the officer is hired and paid directly by the business, (2) the department contracts with the business firm, invoices for the officer's off-duty work, and pays the officer, and (3) off-duty security work is coordinated through a police union or association.

Three-fourths of the departments allow moonlighting officers to use their police uniforms, and many also permit personnel to use other equipment, especially radios and police vehicles. In many departments, this outside employment is not perceived as moonlighting since the jobs are often regularly scheduled, and officers simply view them as "paying details" and "special duty" assignments. The security jobs are frequently scheduled through the department, and officer payment is handled as part of the normal internal payroll procedure. Police officers seek secondary security employment (1) to supplement income, and (2) to develop a second career for full-time employment upon resignation or retirement.

In some departments, collective bargaining agreements mandate the right of the union or employee association to coordinate outside employment, the number of hours per week, and the wage structure. In the Hallcrest national and site surveys, however, law enforcement administrators, police officers, and proprietary security directors believed that obtaining the services of off-duty police officers in uniform and using department equipment should be an available option for additional protection. Provided that officers are hired through the police agency or hired directly by the business, the law enforcement executives did not see a major conflict of interest. However, they do consider that potential conflict-of-interest situations exist when: (1) private security firms hire police officers, (2) individual officers and deputies contract services, and (3) police unions or associations obtain employment for their members. Conflict-of-interest issues primarily involve, first, the use or misuse of authority or police records for personal or financial gain, and second, the provision of selected services that are normally part of an officer's publicly paid responsibilities.

Liability issues connected with moonlighting are well founded, based upon a growing body of tort actions. In general, the officers must be acting within the "scope of their employment," and must be "furthering the purposes of their employer." Just because police officers are in uniform, or are otherwise identified as police officers, does not mean their actions are justified under the "color of their authority." In some situations the courts have held that the scope of an officer's employment passes to his private employer, especially when he is paid directly by the business. The courts have also noted that many of the security actions expected of the moonlighting police officer are outside the normal scope of employment until the actual exercise of police authority is required. Liability issues are influenced by both statutory and department expectations that the officer is vested with 24-hour authority under the law.

Police executives have also expressed concerns about the effects of outside employment on an officer's physical, mental, and emotional fitness for duty. The courts have generally upheld department regulations that limit the amount of off-duty employment, since public safety personnel must be available when needed and able to perform efficiently. In addition to 40 hours as a police officer, some officers work another 40 hours a week in off-duty security positions; for others, security employment is a second, continuous career. Thus, fatigue is a genuine concern for some department administrators.

Some law enforcement administrators have attempted to address the problems of moonlighting in private security (1) by clearly specifying in department rules and regulations

291

that all off-duty police actions of officers carry the full authority of regular on-duty officers, (2) by assigning officers to extra-duty assignments for security-related jobs through the department and keeping the payment mechanism within the department, (3) by obtaining a third-party waiver of liability from the officer and his off-duty employer, and (4) by placing an upper limit (generally 20 hours per week) on outside employment. These policies have not been simple solutions to the problem of moonlighting in security. The first 2 policies, for example, can work at cross-purposes with attempts to shift liability and workers' compensation claims to the individual officer and his private employer, since every move to increase the department's control also appears to increase its liability. Also, some department limits of 20 hours of off-duty work pertain only to the regular 5-day work period (exclusive of days off and vacation days), potentially allowing another 20 to 30 hours per week in a private security position.

Also, in the 1981-82 Hallcrest national surveys, one-fifth of the proprietary security managers reported receiving informal bids for security services from law enforcement agencies, and about one-third reported receiving bids from individual officers or deputies. This form of competition should be formalized, with the department or officers subject to the licensing required of other contract security services in their state. Of greater concern, however, is the practice of police officers controlling or operating security firms. This was not an infrequent practice, and some of these firms openly flaunted a quasi-police status in their advertising. More than one-third of municipal police departments in the national surveys permitted their officers to be directly involved in the operation of a contract security firm as either an owner or corporate officer. Most private security managers feel that police ownership or control of security firms is direct and unfair competition with contract security firms.

The Hallcrest staff has similar concerns about the involvement of police officers in private investigative work, where they could be in a position to compromise department information, to obtain police records illegally, or to overlook criminal involvement of a client. Four out of 10 departments permitted moonlighting in private investigations; 6 out of 10 departments in jurisdictions of greater than 500,000 permitted this practice. One-half of the private investigative firms and guard and patrol firms surveyed reported using off-duty officers for investigative work--an ambiguous position for contract firms which criticize uniformed police officer moonlighting.

Proprietary or corporate security managers and contract security firms also commonly use off-duty police officers who wear public police uniforms when functioning in a primarily private security capacity.   These managers questioned the propriety of police officers performing private investigations.   Law enforcement administrators do not always approve of this widespread practice and share many of contract security's concerns.

RECENT TRENDS IN MOONLIGHTING (After 1985)

As the security market has grown, so has secondary employment of law enforcement officers in private security, and controversy concerning this established practice continues. As Jane Pauley, former co-host of NBC's "Today" show, noted in her introduction to a debate on police moonlighting, "It's a good deal for cops, but some think it's not so good for the country."[41] That "some" includes most contract security company CEOs, managers, and sales representatives who see police moonlighting as a factor that limits their security sales opportunity and market share.   Other objections were suggested in *The Lipman Report*, which cited 5 reasons police officers should not moonlight as security guards and "certainly should not do so in police uniforms:"[42]

- Training (enforcement orientation vs. confrontation avoidance)
- Impaired effectiveness (double-duty, overworked, etc.)
- Legal liability
- Conflict of interest
- Guns--(the authors contend that, except in unusual cases, security guards do not need guns)[43]

Seemingly, the opposite view of police moonlighting is taken by Professor Albert Reiss of Yale, who undertook a "snapshot" study of this topic in 13 police agencies.[44] His study supports police moonlighting and suggests that police departments might consider "opening shop" in the contract security business:

Given the adjunctive role that secondary employment plays in augmenting police manpower and visibility for all police departments, and given the fact that most departments can count on a minimum demand for such service, the question can be raised as to whether departments might not hire more regular police officers and organize a contract service to private employers. Although such a service might be regarded as competitive with private security services, that seems insufficient grounds to preclude its consideration. If the public police can satisfy a private employer demand for police service in ways that are both superior to that provided by private security while at the same time increasing the preventive and deterrent capability of the public police, there may be good reasons for organizing to meet at least some of that demand through regular rather than secondary employment of their police officers.[45]

The opposite position is taken by Professor Mark Moore, a Harvard criminal justice researcher, who finds moonlighting dangerous.

At first it sounds great, more police out there at no more public cost. But in the long run, private financial relationships with public agencies undermine the notion of a public police force with equal protection for all.[46]

Reminiscent of the negative stereotyping of "private police" by the Rand study in 1972, Professor Reiss also concludes that "at most, private security is complementary to the public police service."[47] He also disagrees that police moonlighting is "unfair competition" with private security, and says that "a major advantage of off-duty police employment is that it meets a demand for police service at private rather than public expense."[48] Evidently, he ignores the significant expenses of taxpayer-funded police recruitment, training, fringe benefits, uniforms, weapons, handcuffs, radios, vehicles, and other publicly supported items and services that accompany most moonlighting police officers.

Interestingly, some law enforcement officers earn more from moonlighting than from their regular jobs.[49] Hallcrest's 1989 field interviews in 12 metropolitan regions revealed a range of off-duty rates from $15 to $25 per hour. During his study, Professor Reiss observed that "in many police departments the actual number of off-duty uniformed officers performing police duties exceeded by a substantial number those officially on duty."[50]

Apparently, the number of moonlighting police increased dramatically in the 1980s. The Hallcrest 1981-82 national surveys indicated that about 20% of law enforcement officers were regularly engaged in off-duty security work. By 1987, Professor Reiss found 47% of Seattle's police officers moonlighting, and 53% in Colorado Springs. Hallcrest's field study in 1989 revealed moonlighting by more than 50% of the law enforcement officers in Seattle, in the Washington, D.C. area, and in Dade and Lee Counties in Florida. It is interesting to compare this level of law enforcement moonlighting (40-50%+) with the national level for secondary employment of 6.2%, according to the Bureau of Labor Statistics.[51]

If, as the staff estimated earlier, 150,000 law enforcement officers are engaged in private security work just 15 hours per week at $15 per hour (the low end of the off-duty pay range), total annual earnings would be about $1.8 billion. This makes police moonlighting income equal to the combined 1988 revenues of the nation's 4 largest security guard companies: Pinkerton's, Inc. ($652 million), Burns International Security Service ($435 million), The Wackenhut Corporation ($400 million), and Wells Fargo Guard Service ($250 million).[52] Further, the total estimated level of police secondary employment in private security represents about 56,000 full-time-equivalent positions.

The Hallcrest research staff's reconnaissance efforts throughout the nation in 1989 support the observation of Professor Reiss that "there seems to be a shift toward the department contract system among police departments in municipalities with 100,000 or more inhabitants."[53] Yet, the Hallcrest staff suspects that, by far, most law enforcement officers still contract with and are paid directly by the private business. Whatever the method of police moonlighting, the practice is growing, and more law enforcement agencies have established formal policies and procedures to govern secondary employment. Recently, the International Association of Chiefs of Police developed and distributed a model policy on moonlighting.[54]

The Hallcrest staff has concluded that there are no simple solutions to police officer moonlighting in private security. It is here to stay. In some cases the use of police officers in uniform, using department equipment, is a clearly preferable option when small and large businesses require additional protection. Unfortunately, police administrators will have to live with the liability problem when they permit moonlighting. The main concern of the Hallcrest researchers is that public law enforcement agencies, as taxpayer-supported institutions, should not actively solicit security employment and place themselves in direct competition with the private sector--contract security.

PRIVATE JUSTICE

Without exception, the staff's 1989 reconnaissance interviews in 12 metropolitan areas confirmed a major finding of the Hallcrest 1981 national surveys of security and police executives: Much economic crime is resolved privately rather than through the public criminal justice system. As Joseph Rosetti, a well-respected security consultant and former corporate director of security for IBM, has said, "If all the crimes against business were dumped on the criminal justice system, it would collapse in a day." Yet, relatively little is known about the extent, the effectiveness, or the fairness of private adjudication of workplace crime.[55]

NONREPORTING OF CRIME

The earlier studies of private security in the 1970s clearly noted the problem of nonreporting of crime by the private sector.

Almost half of the [survey] respondents stated that there are some criminal activities that are handled by the employer and [are] not reported to the police.

> *Private Police in the United States: Findings and Recommendations*, Volume I (R-869), *The Rand Report*, 1971.

Eighty percent of the employers indicated there were certain types of criminal incidents which were not reported to the police.

> *Private Security and The Public Interest*, Institute for Local Self Government (Berkeley, California) 1974.

It would appear that a large percentage of criminal violators known to private security personnel are not referred to the criminal justice system. A logical conclusion would be that there is a 'private' criminal justice system wherein employer reprimands, restrictions, suspensions, demotions, job transfers, or employment terminations take the place of censure by the public system.

Report of the Task Force on Private Security, 1976.

Although conceding that some would consider its standard on reporting crime unrealistic, the Private Security Task Force (PSTF) established Standard 3.3 (1976):

All felonies and serious misdemeanors discovered by private security personnel should be reported to appropriate criminal justice agencies. Private security personnel should cooperate with those criminal justice agencies in all subsequent actions relating to those crimes.[56]

Based on Hallcrest's research in the 1980s, this standard has been largely ignored, perhaps because it was simply too idealistic.

The results of Hallcrest's 1981 national surveys of police and corporate security managers indicated that nonreporting was not a source of conflict between law enforcement and private security. These surveys also revealed that the workplace crimes most frequently reported to law enforcement generally were external or UCR index crimes such as arson, burglary, robbery, etc. For internal crimes such as fraud, employee theft, computer crimes, etc., the majority of security managers in the 1981 surveys reported that these incidents were resolved internally (e.g., by firing the employee, obtaining restitution, absorbing the loss) or that these crimes were directly reported to the prosecutor--not to the police. For the latter crimes, private resolution was reported almost twice as frequently as public prosecution.

The 1989 Hallcrest reconnaissance and focus group interviews with security executives revealed the same pattern of nonreporting of crime as was found in the early 1980s. Also, this research found that workplace crime increasingly is being privately adjudicated. For the most part, only UCR index and external crimes are referred to public authorities for investigation or prosecution.

BYPASSING PUBLIC CRIMINAL JUSTICE

Why does the private sector tend to report external, UCR index crimes to law enforcement, but seemingly avoid or bypass the police in the resolution of internal, economic crimes? Perhaps an important reason for lack of police involvement in economic crime is the workload of street crime and other calls for service, which place heavy demands on limited police resources. In 1981, law enforcement survey responses indicated that economic crimes were simply a lower priority for police resources; in addition, law enforcement agencies seem to be more interested in dealing with violent crime and offenses that are more visible to the community. Moreover, police officers often are ill-prepared to deal with economic or business crime because they lack the training and the resources.

In a comprehensive study of police and prosecutor relationships, William McDonald *et al* found that the more people and agencies involved in collecting, processing, and communicating case information, the greater the chance for distortion of communication, i.e., the greater the chance for error.[57] The quality of information available "affects the speed and related efficiency of case processing."[58] For maximum communication--and, in turn, maximum prosecutor efficiency and effectiveness--McDonald *et al* assert that the best possible arrangement is to have the police officer who "made" the case (i.e., who knows the most about the case) bring it directly to an experienced prosecutor for preliminary case review.

These observations have some direct parallels in police and private security interactions in pursuing economic crime. Cases brought to the police by private security are usually well developed by the time law enforcement is notified, often leaving the police as intermediaries or "information processors" between private security and the prosecutor. Since private security often has a strong case (in its opinion) before it seeks prosecution, little is to be gained by bringing the police and the prosecutor into the case at the initial stages. Aside from the few specialized economic crime investigation units in major police departments or partial mergers of police and prosecutor personnel in such units, police agencies generally do not have the expertise to investigate many types of economic crimes.

When public prosecution occurs, many cases are disposed of by plea bargaining, which many police officers do not support because they believe criminals should be prosecuted to the full extent of the law. Yet, for the business that is more interested in the deterrent value to other employees of a criminal prosecution for a theft or other crime, it may not be worth involving police officers, especially when it is possible to deal directly with a prosecutor who is willing to plea bargain.

Typically, private sector reservations about public adjudication center around 6 areas: (1) charging policies of prosecutors, (2) administrative delays in prosecution, (3) prosecutorial policy objectives, (4) differing "output goals" of criminal justice and business, (5) the Freedom of Information Act and rules of discovery, and (6) an unsympathetic attitude by the courts concerning business losses due to crime.

Prosecution of economic crime cases, especially complicated cases of fraud, can result in delay of trial dates and postponements that stretch over months, as well as the costly involvement of corporate legal counsel, and investigative, accounting, and operational personnel. For cases involving minimal monetary loss, but flagrant violations of company rules and internal controls, the end result could be a prosecution process that is more costly and time-consuming than the incident itself. Many cases involve confidential or proprietary information that the company does not want revealed through discovery or trial.

Often prosecutors feel hampered by lack of resources, specific knowledge, and trial experience in the prosecution of complex business crimes. Also, prosecutors may be tempted to categorize crimes of internal theft, fraud, and embezzlement as "company" problems and encourage the business to resolve the crime internally, since the offender is not part of the normal criminal element to whom the court system is routinely exposed. The prosecutor may encourage the organization to pursue only civil restitution and damages rather than a criminal prosecution. A few negative experiences by business organizations with public criminal justice realities may condition security managers to forgo prosecution except in the most flagrant circumstances.

If either the criminal justice system or the business is not willing to prosecute a case, the business may direct its own internal resources toward civil restitution. The company then has an opportunity to recover some or all of its actual losses and investment in investigative resources. Hallcrest's 1989 reconnaissance interviews reveal that more large and small businesses are instituting civil actions for restitution (and often, for damages as well) against alleged offenders--employees, competitors, contractors, or others.

Another reason for not reporting or prosecuting business crimes is fear of negative publicity. A positive public image for a business is a vital asset, and most corporations devote substantial efforts to protecting and enhancing their corporate image. Certainly, then, many businesses would prefer to settle crimes internally rather than risk adverse public and stockholder relations over employee theft, management fraud, or other crimes which may reveal a lack of internal controls. Further, businesses may be reluctant to publicize a crime case for fear of a possible increase in insurance premiums. In some cases, it might be more cost-effective to absorb a loss than to report it, since the increase in the premium can often exceed the value of the loss. Reporting the loss also alerts the insurance underwriter that the organization might have greater potential exposure to crime than was apparent when the policy was issued. In addition, some organizations have no incentive to report certain losses because they are self-insured or because policies they carry have high deductibles which preclude the ability to recover the loss.

James Calder (1980) suggests that there is a certain amount of indifference to crime in business, since "an all-important yet often ignored reality is that much crime committed is viewed as a cost of doing business for which there are numerous ways of distributing responsibility."[59] One very subtle but frequent method of distributing the responsibility and the cost burden for the loss is to increase consumer prices. The construction and retailing industries are good examples of this practice. An official for the Association of General Contractors stated that "some contractors routinely add 5% to their estimates to cover the cost of internal and external theft."[60]

An official of Burns Security Service estimated that shoplifting costs each U.S. household an additional $200 annually for its purchases.[61] Thus, the cost and expense of pursuing criminal prosecution might be forgone--notwithstanding any deterrent effects--if the loss could be recovered by redistributing the cost burden to the consumer through increased prices. As Calder (1987) points out, "...private justice is normally responsive to the economics of corporate self-interest."[62]

CHARACTERIZING PRIVATE JUSTICE

Business crime is most effectively attacked through sound management controls. When a loss occurs, private security, in conjunction with other internal control and audit functions, reexamines policies, controls, and security measures. Greater attention is focused on preventing and deterring future losses resulting from similar incidents than on the "offender" involved in the incident. The emphasis on loss prevention in private sector criminal incident response is a distinguishing characteristic of private security.

Calder (1987) correctly points out that "corporations are under no legal obligation to provide substantive and procedural justice resembling that which is found in the public sector."[63]   He mentions that some "progressive corporations" have fairly sophisticated adjudication-like processes, but that standards of justice are nonexistent within most *Fortune* 500 companies.[64] Therefore, the treatment of the offender can be expected to vary greatly. For some companies, collective bargaining contracts may guide the options available to the employer. For "guilty" employees, the options include suspension without pay, dismissal, job reassignment, job redesign (elimination of some job duties), civil restitution agreements, or criminal prosecution.

The Hallcrest staff supports the position that a fundamental shift in protection resources has occurred from public policing to the private sector. Clifford Shearing and Phillip Stenning (1983) feel that this shift in protection resources has also been accompanied by a shift in the character of social control; in many ways, private security and the private justice system exert far greater control on citizens than the public criminal justice system.

The shift from public to private systems of policing has brought with it a shift in the character of social control.   First, private security defines deviance in instrumental rather than moral terms: protecting corporate interests becomes more important than fighting crime, and sanctions are applied more often against those who create opportunities for loss rather than those who capitalize on the opportunity--the traditional offenders. Thus, the reach of social control has been extended.

Second, in the private realm, policing has largely disappeared from view as it has become integrated with other organizational functions and goals, at both the conceptual and behavioral levels. With private security, control is not an external force acting on individuals; now it operates from within the fabric of social interaction, and members of the communities in which it operates are simultaneously watchers and the watched. They are the bearers of their own control.

Third, this integration is expressed in the sanctioning system, in which private security draws upon organizational resources to enforce compliance.[65]

Yet, little is known about the structure and dynamics of private justice systems, especially in different types of businesses and institutions. Shearing and Stenning (1981), after years of studying private security in Canada, indicate that private justice systems do not conform to any uniform model, but share relatively informal negotiated procedures and outcomes as common characteristics.[66]

As yet, we have little knowledge about the structures and dynamics of such systems, the way they shape the activities of private security, and their impact on the relationships between private security and the public police and public criminal justice systems.[67]

Calder (1987) also notes that "judicial decisions, corporate law, and the sacred tradition of public-private separation sustain inaccessibility to information about the private sector [justice system]," and that "a precise assessment of the corporate inquisitorial process is unavailable as is carefully drawn national data on the rate of internal crime or rule violations."[68] Calder, among others, is especially concerned with the lack of fairness and due process in private justice systems and whether the private sector can "...install such protections before litigation and legislation impose them broadly."[69]

If, in fact, as much crime is resolved through the private justice systems as the 1981 Hallcrest national surveys and the current interviews seem to indicate, then some valid concerns could be raised regarding the fairness and consistency of these private justice systems. Research in this area would help to (1) delineate the common characteristics of private justice systems, (2) evaluate their reduction of public justice system workload, (3) determine the significant amount of underreported crime which accompanies use of the private justice system, and (4) assess the deterrent value of public versus private adjudication of economic crimes.

END NOTES

1.   Richard Lesher, "The Privatization Bandwagon," *The Voice of Business*, U.S. Chamber of Commerce, Washington, D.C., January 29, 1990.

2.   Ibid.

3.   *Report to the Nation on Crime and Justice*, 2d. ed., NCJ-105506, Bureau of Justice Statistics, U.S. Department of Justice, March 1988, p. 118.

4.   This $100 billion estimate is contained in promotional material for a new magazine, *Partnership Focus* (Sponsored by The Privatization Council), Vol. 1, No. 1, (Little Falls, N.J.: Maxco Publications), June 1990.

5.   "Private Delivery of Public Services," *The Lipman Report*, November 15, 1989, p. 1.

6.   James Stewart, "Public Safety and Private Police," *Public Administration Review*, Vol. 45, November 1985, p. 760.

7.   Eric Scott, *Calls for Service: Citizen Demand and Initial Police Response* (Bloomington, Indiana: Workshop in Political Theory and Policy Analysis, Indiana University, 1981), p. 6.

8.   *Report to the Nation on Crime and Justice*, p. 119. See also, Charles Logan and Bill McGriff, "Comparing Costs of Public and Private Prisons: A Case Study," *NIJ Research in Action; NIJ Reports*, September-October 1989.

9.   *Report to the Nation on Crime and Justice*, p. 119.

10.   Marcia Chaiken and Jan Chaiken, *Public Policing--Privately Provided*, National Institute of Justice, U.S. Department of Justice, June 1987.

11.   Ibid., p. 3.

12.   Ibid., p. 15.

13.   Ibid., Appendix D, pp. 43 and 44.

14.   Martin Tolchin, "Private Guards Get New Role in Public Law Enforcement, "*The New York Times*, November 29, 1985, p. 1.

15.   Ibid.

16.   Thomas Wathen, Private Security Workshop, 88th Annual Conference of International-al Association of Chiefs of Police, in *Police Chief*, January 1982, p. 38.

17.   Staff interview with Raymond Fjetland, Chief of Police, Tacoma, Washington, June 28, 1989.

18.   "Private Security Takes to the Streets," *Security*, September 1989, p. 19.

19.   Ibid.

20.   Ibid.

21.   Larry Joiner, Chief of Police, *Contracting Police Support Services to Private Security*, a federal grant application submitted by the Kansas City Police Department to the National Institute of Justice, January 22, 1990. See also, Lola Butcher, "KC Police May Buy Backup Help from Private Security Firms," *Kansas City Business Journal*, November 27, 1989.

22.   Ibid.

23.   Ibid.

24.   Ibid.

25.   Ibid.

26.   James Stewart, "Public Safety and Private Police," *Public Administration Review*, Vol. 45, November 1985, p. 760.

27.   Robert Trojanowicz, "Public and Private Justice: Preparing for the 21st Century," *Criminal Justice Alumni Newsletter*, Vol. V, No. 1, Michigan State University, fall-winter 1989, p. 2.

28.   William Cunningham and Todd Taylor, *The Hallcrest Report: Private Security and Police In America*, p. 137. (See Chapters 5 and 10 for a detailed discussion of the alarm industry and the false alarm problem.)

29.   *Crime Prevention Measures*, Bureau of Justice Statistics, U.S. Department of Justice, 1986.

30.   Interview with Charles Lavin, Jr., Executive Director, National Burglar and Fire Alarm Association (NBFAA), October 10, 1989. See Andrew Buck and Simon Hakim, "Burglar Alarms in the Community," *The Bellringer* (official publication of the Pennsylvania Burglar and Fire Alarm Association), March 1989, p. 13. These authors estimate that between 17% and 25% of suburban Philadelphia residences have alarm systems.

31.   Cunningham and Taylor, Chapter 10.

32.   Ibid, p. 294.

33.   Ibid, p. 319.

34.   Ibid, p. 212.

35.   Kenneth Kirschenbaum, "False Alarms," *Security Dealer*, February 1990, p. 21. The author notes that in New York City and other jurisdictions police response will be terminated if a subscriber experiences 3 false alarms within a 3-month period.

36.   *ADT Industry Relations Update*, Vol. 2, No. 1, March 1990, p. 2.

37.   "Editorial," *The Bellringer*, (Pennsylvania Burglar and Fire Alarm Association) November 1989, p. 3.

38.   See, for example, *Law Enforcement and Private Security Sources and Areas of Conflict and Strategies for Conflict Resolution*, Private Security Advisory Council, Law Enforcement Assistance Administration, U.S. Department of Justice, June 1977; *Report of the Task Force on Private Security* (Standards 6.7, 6.8, and 6.9); National Advisory Committee on Criminal Justice Standards and Goals, U.S. Department of Justice, 1976; and William Cunningham and Todd Taylor, *The Hallcrest Report: Private Security and Police In America*, 1985, Chapter 12.

39.   Leigh Gaines, "Police, Inc." *Security*, December 1989, p. 29.

40.   Ibid.

41.   Jane Pauley, "Off-Duty Cops and Moonlighting," *Today*, NBC-TV, March 6, 1989.

42.   "Moonlighting Police and Private Security," *The Lipman Report*, August 15, 1986, p. 1.

43.   *The Lipman Report*, pp. 1-4.

44.   Albert Reiss, Jr., *Private Employment of Public Police*, National Institute of Justice, U.S. Department of Justice, February 1988.

45.   Reiss, p. 80.

46.   Andrew Malcolm, "When Private Employers Hire Public Police," *The New York Times*, February 26, 1989, p. 22.

47. Reiss, p. 76.

48. Reiss, p. 78.

49. Malcolm, p. 1.

50. Reiss, p. 2.

51. Bureau of Labor Statistics as reported in "USA Snapshots," *USA TODAY*, December 14, 1989, p. B-1.

52. *Security Letter Source Book 1990-1991.*

53. Reiss, p. 80.

54. Malcolm, p. 22.

55. James Calder, "New Corporate Security: The Autumn of Crime Control and The Spring of Fairness and Due Process," *Journal of Contemporary Criminal Justice*, Vol. 3, No. 4, December 1987.

56. *Report to the Task Force on Private Security*, National Advisory Committee on Criminal Justice Standards and Goals, Law Enforcement Assistance Administration, 1976, p. 128.

57. William McDonald, Henry Rossman, and James Cramer, *Police-Prosecutor Relations in the United States: A Final Report* (Washington, D.C.: Institute of Criminal Law and Procedure, Georgetown University Law Center,) December 1981, p. 263.

58. Ibid, p. 275.

59. James Calder, "The Security-Criminal Justice Connection: Toward the Elimination of Separate-But-Equal Status," *Journal of Security Administration*, Vol. 3, No. 2, spring 1980, p. 43.

60. Lynn Adkins, "The High Cost of Employee Theft," *Dun's Business Month*, October 18, 1982, p. 72.

61. *The Wall Street Journal*, September 17, 1981, p. 1.

62. Calder (1987), p. 1.

63. Calder (1987), p. 4.

64. Ibid.

65. Clifford Shearing and Philip Stenning, "Private Security: Implications for Social Control," *Social Problems*, Vol. 30, No. 5, June 1983, pp. 503-504.

66.   Clifford Shearing and Philip Stenning, "Modern Private Security: Its Growth and Implications," *Crime and Justice: An Annual Review of Research, Vol. 3*, Michael Tonry and Norval Morris, eds., Chicago: University of Chicago Press, 1981, p. 334.

67.   Ibid; for a useful discussion see Steven Spitzer, "Dialectics of Formal and Informal Justice," in *Politics of Informal Justice: Vol. I: The American Experience*, 1981.

68.   Calder (1987), p. 6.

69.   Calder (1987), p. 22.

PART V

AGENDA
FOR
CHANGE

CHAPTER 10
FINDINGS, RECOMMENDATIONS, FORECASTS,
AND RESEARCH NEEDS

This chapter summarizes major findings, recommendations, forecasts, and research needs. In many ways, it is an agenda for making greater use of the resources available in the national effort to control and reduce crime. The ultimate goal of such an agenda is a safer America. This chapter generally follows the same topic order as the report and is divided into 2 sections. The first reviews the key findings, recommendations, and forecasts on issues that have a national scope or that comment on the protective services community--that is, public law enforcement and private security. The second section reiterates the Hallcrest staff's observations on the shortcomings of existing data and statistics about the protective services community, as well as suggestions for further research. This summary format is intended to help readers identify the major concepts and issues addressed by this research effort. Because certain observations and conclusions are derivative, not all of the following comments are explicitly addressed in the body of the report.

FINDINGS, RECOMMENDATIONS, AND FORECASTS

GENERAL AND ECONOMIC CRIME

• **Fear of Crime.** The increased use of locks, security lighting, burglar alarms, citizen patrols, and a wide array of private and public security measures indicates the fear Americans--individuals and businesses--have of crime. Indicators suggest strongly that fear of crime is increasing even while some statistics indicate that crime itself is stabilizing or declining. The coproduction of security resources by public law enforcement, private security, and citizens is necessary to reduce the fear of crime.

• **Decline in Household and Some Property Crime Rates.** According to the National Crime Survey, the percentage of households touched by crime declined 23% between 1975 and 1988. Despite an upturn in violent crime rates in recent years, this was an encouraging finding since it indicates that many of the activities of public law enforcement, private security, and citizens can have a positive influence on crime in America. Unfortunately, recognition of the role of private security products and services in this decade-long, slowing crime trend has been conspicuously absent.

To the reasons put forth by other researchers for a decline in household crime-- (1) community crime prevention, (2) jailing of more career criminals, and (3) fewer teens, who are the most crime-prone group--Hallcrest adds the massive use of private security resources, that is, equipment and personnel selected and paid for by individuals and businesses.

• **Lack of Control of Economic Crime.** While economic crime can never be eradicated, business and governmental efforts are not effectively preventing, detecting, prosecuting, or otherwise controlling it. Thus the frequency and cost of economic crime continue to rise.

312

• **Failure to Measure Economic Crime.** Neither business nor government is making a systematic, national attempt to measure accurately economic crime--the cost of which may exceed 2% of the gross national product.

• **Economic Crime Reporting Problem.** Four primary obstacles prevent the development of an ongoing program of reporting crime and loss data by business and industry: (1) no uniform definitions exist, (2) no data base exists on which to build and measure trends, (3) corporations and most industry groups have not developed effective internal reporting systems for crime-related losses, and (4) businesses are generally reluctant to release loss data that could reflect adversely on them.

Only when top corporate management insists on accurate collection and complete reporting of crimes within their businesses will meaningful, corporation-wide measurement of economic crime costs begin. Then, perhaps, accurate crime loss measurement by various industry segments and trade associations can be accomplished, providing, in turn, more accurate assessments of workplace crimes on the economy. Business crime control strategies can then be realistically designed, and various types of economic crime can be more accurately measured.

• **Economic Crime Research Center.** Clearly, a national clearinghouse for the collection and study of economic crime is warranted. Presently, no such entity exists. Establishment of a nonprofit Economic Crime Research Center or Institute with private and federal funding would help:

- standardize terminology and definitions;
- develop indices for measuring economic crime and its impact on the nation;
- coordinate the collection of crime loss data by trade and industry associations;
- fund research on the nature, perpetrators, and adjudication of economic crimes; and
- promote awareness of and countermeasures for economic crime through publications and seminars.

- **Economic Crime Trends.** During the 1990s, private security and law enforcement practitioners will be confronted with more sophisticated and technical white-collar crimes, which will have a higher dollar loss per incident than previously experienced. All the research conducted for this report leads to this forecast. Increased use of computers coupled with innovations in financial transactions will have tremendous reverberations in the future. The recent insider trading and other securities and thrift frauds are indicative of the problems that will likely continue throughout the decade.

- **Direct Costs of Economic Crime.** The cost of economic crime is not precisely known. The updated estimates are, to a large degree, based on earlier estimates and trend-line projections. The "best" estimates for the direct annual costs of economic crime are about $40 billion for the mid-1970s, $67 billion for the early 1980s, and $114 billion for 1990. Hallcrest projects an economic crime cost of $200 billion by the year 2000.

- **Indirect Costs of Economic Crime.** Assessing the indirect or secondary costs of economic crime is even more difficult than arriving at direct costs. Attempting to establish a dollar cost is simply impossible, given the data limitations and lack of reporting of economic crime. Yet, the indirect impact or costs of economic crime can be grouped into 3 categories: costs to business, government, and the public. Among other costs, businesses suffer reduced profits, loss of productivity, increased costs of insurance, overhead, and security and audit functions. For small businesses, survival itself is threatened. The effects on government include the costs of investigation and prosecution and loss of tax revenue (e.g., loss of sales tax, untaxed income of the perpetrator, and tax deductions allowed business for crime losses). Finally, the public is affected because it pays for most economic crime through increased costs of goods and services to offset business crime losses. Also, the public suffers because of increased taxes, loss of investor equity, and reduced employment due to business failures.

- **Litigation.** A major indirect cost of economic crime has been the increase in civil litigation and damage awards over the past 20 years. The field and focus group interviews indicate a growing concern over lawsuits. This concern is manifesting itself in a variety of security management issues such as the hiring, training, and equipping of private security personnel and the deployment of systems. By some estimates, security and crime-related lawsuits have risen 17 times higher than the inflation rate. This litigation usually claims security was inadequate to protect customers, employees, or the public from crimes or injuries.

- **Litigation as a Measure of Effectiveness.** During the 1990s, as a secondary outcome of litigation, evaluative measures of crime prevention effectiveness will emerge regarding the use of security guards, alarms, locks, cameras, lighting, security training, etc. to see what works in controlling crime. The evaluation criteria will help in implementing security strategies to combat specific crime losses. The litigation process has been a driving force in focusing attention on various security measures and their impact on controlling crime.

SELECTED CRIME CONCERNS

Business Ethics

- **Ethical Breaches.** The past decade has seen individual and corporate greed as well as unethical behavior unparalleled in recent history by business and government officials. One survey found that about 25% of the 500 largest corporations had been convicted in the past decade of at least 1 major crime or had paid penalties for serious misbehavior.

- **Public Perceptions.** Unethical, illicit behavior not only causes economic crime losses for businesses, government, and consumers but also contributes to the increasing use of and expenditures for private security. A number of national studies have indicated concern among the general public about the perception of honesty and ethical standards in business activities. A lack of a strong code of ethics not only in published form but also in practice have negative consequences on a company's viability and credibility.

- **Ethics and Private Security.** In the 1990s, corporate security personnel will increasingly be involved in testing adherence to corporate ethics policies. Research has indicated that there can be a positive cause-effect relationship between careful investigation of ethical behavior and better ethical practices in corporations. Active involvement of security personnel in enforcing the policies and procedures will increase as corporate leaders continue to recognize the positive influence of ethics. With proper direction from the corporate board room, corporate security personnel will be more involved in ensuring ethical practices.

Drug Abuse

• **Drug Use in America.** One in 7 Americans has used an illegal drug. Moreover, 1 in 4 American workers has knowledge of coworkers using illegal drugs on the job. The estimated annual cost of drug use to the United States ranges from $60 billion to $114 billion or more.

• **Correlation Between Drugs and Crime.** A high correlation exists between drug abuse and crime trends in America. Some studies have indicated that more than 80% of persons arrested for serious crimes tested positive for drug use. There is a reasonable expectation that the crime rate will decrease if Americans can reduce the availability and use of illegal drugs.

• **Mostly Large Companies Have Drug Programs.** The larger a company is, the more likely it is to have some form of substance abuse prevention or treatment program. This reflects the growing concerns of business leaders who recognize that workplace drug abuse is a significant problem. However, relatively few small companies have any form of drug testing or prevention program. When the largest corporations are not considered, there is some evidence that most other companies in America have limited involvement in drug prevention or treatment programs. According to some studies, only 2% of companies with fewer than 50 employees have drug abuse programs. Moreover, only 1 employee out of 100 is tested for drugs annually. Further, many corporate security organizations lack the resources and training to manage drug abuse prevention and detection programs.

Computer Crime

• **Extent of Computer Crime.** The annual cost of computer crime is unknown. Estimates range from a low of $1 billion to an unbelievable high of $200 billion. Money thefts account for about 36% of all computer crimes. The second highest rate of occurrence is for theft of telecommunications services, accounting for 34% with losses amounting to $500 million annually. More than 90% of known computer crimes are not prosecuted.

Computer crimes are committed by employees in much greater frequency than outside sources. Media coverage of "hackers" and illegal fund transfers has not reflected the true problem. One study has indicated that 80% of computer crimes involve employees.

• **Value of Computer Security Market.** Hallcrest estimates that 1990 revenues for computer security are $244 million, accounting for 2% of all security equipment revenues, and that they are growing at an average annual rate of 17%. By 2000, the value of the private computer security market will be about $864 million, with an average annual growth rate of about 13%, representing 3% of all security equipment sales. Other studies estimate the value of this market segment to be $1.4 billion or higher.

• **Corporate Programs.** In 1990, 12% of the average corporate security budget and 4% of the average data processing department budget is allocated to computer security. The average annual rate of growth appears to be approximately 25%. However, the rate of growth may slow significantly over the next 10 years, as most companies with major data processing departments will have implemented computer security measures.

• **Security Managers Ill-Equipped.** Most private security managers are ill-equipped, personally and organizationally, to counter the computer security threat. Many of these managers were trained and educated prior to the rapid increase in the use of computers. Managing computer security may be one of the greatest challenges facing private security managers in the next 10 years. They must meet this challenge by obtaining the necessary information system security training and education and by establishing effective working relationships with data processing managers to implement countermeasures. In addition, managers of information systems are often not security conscious.

• **Electronic Intrusion and Eavesdropping.** The extent of electronic intrusion and eavesdropping is not known. If it is a credible threat, many security and data processing department managers ignore the threat, or are ill-prepared to address it, or lack the resources for countermeasures.

• **Internal and External Attacks.** Although the methods and means to counter external and internal computer threats are available, there is scant application today.

317

Therefore, computer security risk levels will likely increase over the next few years. By the middle of the 1990s, however, most networks and systems will be protected. Overall, with the exception of attacks by disgruntled or dishonest employees, computer security is likely to become a diminishing problem.

- **Industrial Espionage.** Little is known about the amount of industrial espionage that may be occurring in the United States, and less is known about how pervasive electronic intrusion may be in industrial espionage. A 1984 study found that up to 54% of company market research managers were willing to engage in practices directed against competitors that might be regarded by others as dubious, bordering on industrial espionage.

Terrorism

- **Terrorism Displaced But Not Curtailed.** Expenditures for security may displace terrorist incidents but have minimal effects on reducing the number of incidents. Law enforcement has known for many years that saturation patrols can move crime to other locations but cannot eliminate crime. The same situation exists for preventing terrorist attacks. The attacks are merely displaced to unprotected or less protected facilities and targets.

- **Terrorist Threat in U.S. Minimal.** There is little evidence of a serious international terrorist threat in America. The "hype factor" is misleading. No international, political terrorist incidents have occurred in the United States since 1983.   About 0.3% of all worldwide incidents occur in North America. Of incidents specifically directed against U.S. interests, only 2% occur in North America. On a worldwide basis, the chance that an American traveling overseas will be involved in a terrorist incident is approximately 1 in 86,000--about 1/150 of the likelihood of contracting cancer.

- **Terrorism Not Defined.** A practical or legal definition of terrorism that represents a general consensus does not exist. Many organizations and authorities have attempted to obtain an accepted definition, but none has been developed. Some officials define terrorist incidents on the basis of political or ideological motivation behind the incident. Other sources often describe a wide variety of violent acts committed by criminals and lunatics as terrorism.

- **Expenditures Out of Balance With Benefits.** While the terrorist threat is real and is deadly, government and private industry have not attempted to address the problem dispassionately. Vast sums are being spent for counterterrorism programs, resulting in benefits that are generally out of balance with the expenditures.

- **American Companies as Targets.** The best-known companies are the most likely targets of international, political terrorism. Twenty of the top 25 American firms have already been attacked.

- **Counterterrorism Market.** Less than 1% to 2% of gross annual revenues and expenditures for private security can be attributed to counterterrorism. The current value of the domestic market segment probably ranges from $500 million to $1 billion. The value of the overseas market is not known. The private security counterterrorism market is probably small and is likely to shrink by the end of the decade.

DIMENSIONS OF PROTECTION

- **Shift in Turf.** A shift (measured in terms of spending and employment) in the primary responsibility for protection from public law enforcement to private security has occurred. This shift suggests a need for realignment of roles and greater cooperation between the public and private sectors. The traditional approach by law enforcement of working independently of citizens and businesses will change. Greater coproduction of neighborhood (residential, business, etc.) security by citizens, law enforcement, and private security will occur as the members of various communities take a larger stake in decision making about their protective options.

- **Police Service Assessment.** An assessment should be conducted of the basic police services the public is willing to support financially, the types of police tasks that should be transferred to the private sector, and which activities might be performed at a lower cost by the private sector with the same level of community satisfaction. The assessment should examine which police activities actually require the training, skill and sworn authority of a police officer and which tasks private security could handle.

319

•   **Special Taxing Districts.** Creating special assessments or taxing districts for different levels of protective services would allow funding of both police and security services at desired levels.   Also, efforts should be directed at the state and local level to reduce corporate and property taxes for significant expenditures on security goods and services that offset the need for additional public police services.

•   **Brokering Protective Services.** Police administrators should become "brokers" of protective service throughout the community, negotiating a variety of public and private protective arrangements in different areas on a cost-effective basis. Residential developments, commercial and industrial districts, developers, property owners, and residents should select the mix of protective services that best suits their protection needs and ability to pay.

•   **Special Police Authority.** Security personnel with special police powers should be used to free police from the tasks of apprehension, prisoner transport, report writing, evidence preservation, and court testimony for the large volume of shoplifting, trespassing, vandalism, and other minor criminal offenses against retailers and shopping malls.

SECURITY PERSONNEL ISSUES

•   **Private Security Younger and Better Educated.** Private security personnel in 1990 are younger and better educated than previously. Several local research efforts around the nation strongly support this finding. Further, more women and minorities are being employed by private security than before.

•   **Personnel Screening.** Especially in the guard and other service sectors of the security industry, screening of prospective employees to insure qualified workers devoid of criminal backgrounds needs upgrading. Further, all security employers should be granted access to criminal history records for purposes of screening applicants.

•   **Technology Replacing Few Personnel.** Emerging security technology will lead toward a small replacement of security personnel with security systems. The rapid growth of closed-circuit television, sophisticated alarm systems, access control, and other technology will have a bearing on the growth of private security personnel, especially guards. The primary outcome will not necessarily reduce the number of personnel but will change the functions they perform. This change of function may be one of the most dynamic changes in the private security industry by the 2lst Century.

• **Guard Wages.** For at least 20 years, the starting wage for most contract security guards has been slightly above the minimum wage. These low wages have led to high turnover and the employment of minimally qualified workers. Proprietary security guards have consistently received higher pay than contract guards. In 1990, Hallcrest estimates the mean wage for proprietary and contract unarmed guards to be $7.70 per hour.

• **Private Security Managers' Compensation on Par.** Salaries for the top corporate security executives in the 1990s will likely stay on par with managers of other corporate support functions. An important consideration in this forecast is that, especially in proprietary security functions, there will be a trend toward consolidating corporate security functions into such units as human resources, internal audit, facilities management, and environmental, safety, and risk management. Historically, support functions within corporations tend to have lower salaries than, for example, research, production, and sales.

• **Private Security Managers' Compensation to Increase Faster Than in Law Enforcement.** Throughout the 1990s, salary increases for both corporate and contract security executives will be greater than those for federal, state, or local law enforcement managers. This research reported a mean base salary of $52,000 for corporate security managers and $45,000-$50,000 for contract security managers.

• **Armed Personnel.** A dramatic decrease in the carrying of firearms by security personnel has occurred in the past 20 years. An estimated 50% of security guards carried firearms in 1970, dropping to about 10% by the mid-1980s. By the year 2000, perhaps only 5% of security personnel will be armed. This substantial reduction in armed personnel came about for 3 reasons: high insurance premiums for armed workers, higher liability and greater risk for employers, and stricter state and local government regulation of armed security personnel.

• **Security Training.** Hallcrest estimates that the typical security guard receives only 4 to 6 hours of preassignment training. While improved training materials and programs are available, the security guard industry has been slow to improve entry-level training. Only 14 states require any training for unarmed guards. The Private Security Task Force recommendation 15 years ago for 8 hours of preassignment training is still reasonable and an absolute minimum for operational security personnel.

While entry-level training for security personnel is generally lacking, notable expansion of training programs has occurred over the past 10 to 15 years for security specialists and managers. Training workshops and seminars conducted by the American Society for Industrial Security (ASIS) and the International Security Conference and Exposition (ISC EXPO) have increased at least 100% since 1977.

- **Security Education.** Growth in security academic programs has been significant. Nationwide, there were 33 certificate and degree programs 15 years ago. By 1990, the total had increased to 164.

- **Few Major Changes in Standards and Regulation.** The security industry has not taken the lead in promoting, discussing, or adopting standards. Further, few changes have occurred in the past 15 years in the number of states that license and regulate security. According to this and previous research, security executives support state licensing and regulation and strongly oppose local licensing. Hallcrest agrees that licensing and regulation processes in the United States are essentially the same as the Private Security Task Force found them 15 years ago: "Some good, some of limited value, and most lacking uniformity and comprehensiveness."

- **Statewide Regulation and Reciprocity Needed.** More effective licensing and regulation for the private security industry can be attained by statewide preemptive legislation and interstate licensing agency reciprocity. With the number of national private security companies, the legislatures must address these 2 critical components of the licensing and regulation process. In states with a proliferation of local licensing ordinances, legislatures must take a leadership role in establishing uniform and fair state-level legislation.

In addition, states must enter into interstate licensing reciprocity similar to that used by public law enforcement agencies in such matters as auto licenses, driver's licenses, and similar regulation. Currently, the national security companies are required to be licensed in many states. This is not cost-effective either for the security companies or ultimately to the users of security services. The same burden is experienced by many smaller security companies that operate in several jurisdictions in adjacent states.

• **Industry-Imposed Standards.** The British Security Industry Association (BSIA) has demonstrated that industry-imposed standards can be developed at a national level and can contribute to upgrading private security. If security standards were to be adopted along the lines of the BSIA's and if effective self-regulation by the security industry could be realized, there would be little need for state or local government regulation except for armed or deputized security personnel.

• **Accreditation Program Needed.** Some form of accreditation should be developed for private security similar to those developed by the Commission on Accreditation for Law Enforcement Agencies (CALEA) and the British Security Industry Association (BSIA). Since 1983, a consensus standard setting and accreditation process for law enforcement agencies has been in operation. While less than 10% of the nation's law enforcement agencies have completed the accreditation process, it can serve as a useful model for private security. The key issue in this recommendation is the call for meaningful self-regulation rather than a government-imposed process.

SECURITY SERVICES AND PRODUCTS

• **Nomenclature and Definitions.** The obvious difficulties in establishing a universally accepted definition of private security are indicative of the fragmentation and overlapping that exist in private security. Various security groups, researchers, and authors have debated the basic definition of private security for 20 years. There is little consensus as to the specific components of private security. One example is the locksmith industry, which is considered part of private security by some but not others. Another example of the difficulty is that many guard companies provide guards and patrols, conduct private investigations, monitor alarm systems, sell security equipment, and service and maintain such equipment. The "hybridization" of the security industry, reflected in the lack of acceptable definitions, is a major factor in misunderstandings as to the functions and duties in private security. Thus, data collection efforts are hampered by this nonagreement on a definition of private security.

- **Private Security Revenues.** Business and citizens currently spend $52 billion annually for security products and services to combat crime and prevent losses. This finding does not include the expenditures of federal, state, and local governments to control economic crime. By 2000, private security revenues and expenditures may exceed $103 billion.

- **Rate of Growth.** The growth of combined private security industry revenues/expenditures to the year 2000 will be about 7%, down from 10% for the 1980s, but still about 3 times the GNP's average annual rate of growth. Contract service and manufacturing service revenues currently are growing at an average annual rate of 11%, slowing to 9% by the year 2000. Proprietary security expenditures are presently growing at an annual rate of 8% but should slow to 2% by the end of the decade.

- **Revenues/Expenditures.** The sales and expenditures for the entire private security industry should continue to be robust, outpacing most other service revenue categories. However, because of market maturation revenues may be sluggish in such segments as armored car, locksmith, and security fencing.

- **Private Security Employment.** The average annual rate of growth in private security employment is forecast to be 2.3% until the year 2000, much higher than the 1.2% annual rate predicted for the entire U.S. work force. The Hallcrest research staff anticipates a gradual slowdown over the next 10 years due to a maturing of the industry, market saturation by some industry segments, and continued consolidation of the industry due to mergers, acquisitions, and business failures.

- **Alarm Company Employment.** The rate of employment growth in the alarm company segment will be about 6 times the national rate. This research concludes that about 120,000 persons are currently employed by alarm companies and that over the next 10 years the employment will increase to 250,000. Considering the distinct possibility of a dramatic decrease in the cost of residential security systems, this projection may be conservative. This segment of the private security industry is one of the most active in terms of growth in employment and expenditures.

• **Turnover of Companies.** The security business annual turnover, including failures, is at least 20%. It is important to note that some projections of the failure rate of American businesses is 33%; thus this is not necessarily an alarming figure.

• **Foreign Ownership.** Foreign ownership or investment in the private security industry is significant. Research indicated that British, Swiss, Australian, and Japanese companies have invested over $4 billion in American security companies over the last 5 years. No comprehensive listing of foreign ownership and investment could be found that would provide for an accurate estimate of the total investment in American firms. Hallcrest anticipates a growing trend toward foreign ownership and investment in American security companies.

• **Proprietary Security Shrinking and Changing.** Over the next decade membership in the American Society for Industrial Security (ASIS) will shift from primarily proprietary security managers to mostly contractual security managers. That shift will reflect the decrease in the number of proprietary security organizations in comparison to the growth in contract security companies. Hallcrest concludes that the contract security and manufacturing sectors employ twice as many people as the proprietary security sector. In the year 2000, the contract security and manufacturing sectors will employ 3 times as many people as the proprietary sector. The proprietary sector's expenditures will drop from an average annual rate of growth of 8% in 1990 to 2% in 2000, slightly less than the rate of growth of the GNP, due to increasing contracting of security services.

• **Growth of Contract Service Companies Greater.** New contract security businesses will begin at twice the rate of proprietary security organizations. This will be a major factor in the 1990s, representing the fifth consecutive decade of private security industry growth. Some researchers indicate that private security is a maturing industry and that there will be a gradual slowdown, especially in the growth of new private security organizations. However, the forecast is a switch from 29,600 contract security organizations in 1980 compared to 40,000 proprietary security organizations to 79,300 contract security companies in 2000 compared to 60,000 proprietary security organizations.

• **Shifts in Employment.** By the year 2000 there will be 750,000 contract guards compared to 410,000 proprietary security personnel. This represents a dramatic shift in the

325

employment of private security personnel. Employment in proprietary security will experience a substantial reduction over the next 10 years; annual growth will average out to be negative by the end of the decade, mostly due to increased contracting out of security services.

COMPARISONS OF
PRIVATE SECURITY AND LAW ENFORCEMENT

• **Almost 3-to-1 Ratio.** In 1990 the ratio of private security employees to public law enforcement employees is about 2.4 to 1. It is expected to increase to 2.8 to 1 by 2000.

• **Combined Employment and Expenditures.** The combined expenditures for protective services (private security and federal, state, and local law enforcement) will increase from the current level of $82 billion to about $147 billion by the year 2000 at an average annual rate of growth of approximately 6%. Spending for protective services may slow uniformly over the decade if current trends toward increasingly austere operating budgets by private and public organizations continue. A slight decline in the rate of annual growth could also occur if crime does not significantly increase over the coming decade--most authorities do not expect it to--and if security and law enforcement protection goals are gradually achieved. Currently, the combination of private security and law enforcement has total employment of approximately 2.1 million people, representing almost 1% of the entire national population and almost 2% of the national work force. By the year 2000, combined employment should exceed 2.6 million people; the percentages of the national population and national work force would remain roughly the same. The average rate of annual growth for combined protective services employment is expected to be about 2%, which is 80% higher than the projected rate of growth for all American workers for the coming decade. By the year 2000 there will be 10 protective workers (7 in private security and 3 in public law enforcement) for every 1,000 persons in the United States.

• **Expenditure Ratios.** Private security expenditures are presently about 1.7 times those of law enforcement; over the next 10 years they will increase to 2.4 times.

- **High Turnover Rate for Private Security to Continue.** Until significant improvements are made in training, salary, promotional opportunities, marginal personnel, and ineffective performance (commonly referred to as the "private security vicious circle"), there will continue to be a high attrition rate.

- **Law Enforcement Profile.** The total of all federal, state, and local government law enforcement personnel in 1990 is approximately 623,000. Currently, there are about 2 law enforcement officers for each 1,000 Americans, and 5 for each 1,000 people in the work force. By the end of the coming decade, approximately 684,000 sworn officers will be employed by law enforcement agencies, and the ratio to the national population will increase to 3 per 1,000, an increase of 1 from 1990 data. Law enforcement employment is expected to grow at an average annual rate of 1%, which is roughly the national average.

- **Private Security Profile.** Total private security employment in 1990 is estimated to be about 1.5 million people. The current ratio of private security personnel to law enforcement employment is 2.4 to 1. There are approximately 6 private security employees for each 1,000 Americans and about 12 private security employees for each group of 1,000 workers in the nation. Total private security employment is expected to increase to 1.9 million by the decade's end. The annual rate of growth in employment is anticipated to be about 2.3%, approximately double the rate of employment growth for the national work force. By 2000 there will be 7 private security workers per 1,000 Americans and 13 per 1,000 workers.

- **Reasons For Private Security Growth.** Four major reasons account for the increasing growth of private security and the limited growth of public law enforcement: (1) increasing workplace crime, (2) increasing fear of crime, (3) decreasing rate of government spending for public protection, and (4) increasing awareness and use of private security products and services as cost-effective protective measures.

327

RELATIONSHIPS AND COOPERATIVE PROGRAMS

• **Relationships Fair to Good, at Best.** Hallcrest found that law enforcement personnel rated their relationships with private security as fair to good in both the early and late 1980s. Upgrading the selection processes and training of private security personnel will have the greatest impact on improved cooperation, based on recommendations by both law enforcement and private security executives. Establishing licensing and regulation or improving existing regulatory controls was recommended by many as a mechanism to upgrade private security. Management and supervisory meetings and private security liaison officer positions in law enforcement agencies were recommended to increase dialogue, resolve problems, and exchange information. Information exchange and improved communications were also the primary recommendations for more effective use of combined resources. Operational security employees expressed a desire for law enforcement personnel to interact more closely with them and familiarize themselves with facilities and security policies in their patrol areas.

• **More Cooperative Programs Needed.** Beginning in the mid-1980s several model cooperative programs between private security and public law enforcement were initiated. Law enforcement and private security associations should expand their efforts to foster such programs in every metropolitan area.

• **Increase Police Knowledge of Private Security.** Seminars, training materials, inventories of security firms, and other mechanisms are recommended to develop a greater awareness by the police of the role and resources of private security in their communities.

MAJOR SECURITY/POLICE ISSUES

Privatization

• **Contracting Out Police Support Tasks.** During this research, federal and local law enforcement executives displayed more interest in contracting with private security for selected, noncrime support tasks than they did in the Hallcrest study in the early 1980s.

Strained police and other criminal justice budgets will make privatization a more popular and viable alternative during the 1990s and into the 21st Century. Private security generally offers an enormous resource for cost-effectively performing many routine, noncrime activities that are presently performed by more costly public law enforcement officers.

• **Task Transfer.** For those locations and organizations that have private security, the interests of the public will be best served if law enforcement transfers responsibility for certain minor incidents and crimes to private security.

False Alarms

• **Police Response Will Be Curtailed.** Initial alarm response by law enforcement agencies will be reduced or terminated in the next decade, especially in large urban areas. The growing desire among law enforcement administrators is to "shed" this service, and the most obvious provider of alarm response service will be private security. The problem of false alarms and alarm response will be one of the most significant issues in public law enforcement and private security relationships in the 1990s.

• **National Strategy Needed.** So many dimensions of the false alarm problem transcend community or state-level efforts that it demands a national strategy. Local ordinances and reliance on penalties for false alarms may be counterproductive.

Moonlighting

• **Police Moonlighting.** As the security market has grown, so has secondary employment of law enforcement officers as private security resources. Total annual earnings from police moonlighting in security are estimated at $1.8 billion (equivalent to the combined 1988 revenues of the nation's 4 largest security guard companies). Police moonlighting in private security will not abate but may grow throughout the 1990s.

Private Justice

• **Private Adjudication.** Most economic crime will be privately adjudicated rather than brought to the public justice system throughout this decade. There is general agreement that the majority of economic crime is resolved privately rather than through the public criminal justice system. Some feel that the public justice system could not handle the volume of cases. For the most part, businesses refer only UCR index and external crimes to public authorities for investigation and prosecution.

RESEARCH NEEDS

•   **More Economic Crime Research Needed.** There is a need for a consensus among researchers, the business community, and law enforcement on the definitions, classifications, and measurement (frequency and severity) of economic crime as well as the cost of each type of economic crime. The Uniform Crime Reports offer a frame of reference for such research. However, there are obvious limitations in using the Uniform Crime Reports since they do not, for the most part, include the types of offenses that generally would be defined as economic crime. Workplace drug trafficking and use, computer crime, employee theft and fraud, electronic intrusion, and industrial espionage are some examples of classifications of economic crime that warrant research. After the definitions have been established and the classifications made, future researchers can begin a more accurate measurement of each classification of economic crime.

•   **Economic Crime Reporting Poor.** Crime loss reporting by business and industry is incomplete or nonexistent. There is a need for centralized compilation of economic crime statistics similar to the FBI's compilation of statistics on street crime in its Uniform Crime Reports. Although there are limitations to the thoroughness and accuracy of the reporting of street crime in the United States, at least the definitions are agreed on and increases or decreases in certain types of crimes can be discerned. The Hallcrest staff have attempted to review the pertinent literature and make predictions and projections on the status of economic crime in the United States. However, without a centralized compilation of economic crime statistics, this research was, and further research efforts will be, greatly hampered.

•   **Studies of Private Adjudication Needed.** Research is needed to determine the fairness and effectiveness of private justice systems. In general, private justice systems are characterized by informal negotiations and procedures, which vary greatly from one organization to another. Few people understand the workings of such systems, and many feel there is little fairness or consistency throughout the private justice system. Research in this area would help to (1) delineate the common characteristics of private justice systems, (2) evaluate their reduction of public justice system workload, (3) determine the amount of underreported crime that accompanies use of the private justice system, and (4) assess the deterrent value of public versus private adjudication of economic crimes.

• **Deterrent Value of Prosecution.** Some studies have noted relationships between lower incidents of employee crimes and perceptions of aggressive prosecution policies. Further research is needed to document the deterrent value of aggressive, moderate, or selective criminal prosecution and civil litigation policies for different crimes across different organization types--especially for employee theft and fraud, drug sales and use, and computer crimes.

• **Improved Federal Reporting Needed.** Data from the U.S. Bureau of Labor Statistics, the Bureau of the Census, and other government sources are hard to analyze for research in private security. The Hallcrest staff note that these government agencies continue to use archaic nomenclature, categorization, and groupings. The U.S. Bureau of Labor Statistics and the Bureau of the Census should take the initiative in forming a study group composed of private security practitioners and researchers to assist in developing realistic and reliable data.

• **Measures of Effectiveness.** Empirical research should be conducted on the cost- effectiveness of specific security measures. Many people find it difficult to make objective decisions on security expenditures; instead they must rely on general advice from their security director, security vendor, or local police. Security managers, organization executives, and police crime prevention specialists could greatly benefit from knowing the actual and perceived benefit of implementing a single security measure or a mix of measures to combat 1 or more types of crime and loss.

331

- **Security Industry Research.** A comprehensive nationwide survey and census needs to be conducted. Detailed profiles should be developed for each security industry segment, including data on:

  - Employment
  - Wages
  - Revenues
  - Rates of growth
  - Services and products produced
  - Clients served
  - Export and import trends
  - Merger and acquisition activity
  - Foreign ownership or control

This level of market research is essential to assess empirically the dimensions of private security.

- **Risks to Private Security Officers.** Empirical data do not exist on the extent and causes of work-related injuries and deaths to private security workers. Surprisingly, some preliminary information indicates that security officers work in a relatively high-risk occupation. A national assessment of line-of-duty injuries and deaths to private security officers in comparison with law enforcement officers and other occupations should be undertaken. Further, this research should evaluate the intervention or protective measures taken by private security and law enforcement officers to avoid or minimize work-related injury or death.

- **National Study of False Alarms and Alarm Effectiveness.** Comparative data do not exist on either alarm system effectiveness or false alarm impact on police services for different alarm system types in communities of varying sizes and different alarm response policies. Multi-city studies should be conducted on the false alarm problem and alarm system effectiveness in deterring property crime and reducing the level of police burglary and robbery investigations. This is especially critical given the potential for increased market penetration through regional telephone companies and the growing sales of low-cost retail and "do-it-yourself" alarm systems.

332

- **Level of Public's Acceptances of Private Security.** Extremely limited research exists on the public's attitude toward greater private security involvement in fear abatement, crime prevention, property protection and performance of some noncrime police support tasks. National research is needed to assess the public's acceptance of private security as a major supplier of protective services.

SELECTED
BIBLIOGRAPHY

GOVERNMENT PUBLICATIONS

"Annual Wages Survey." U.S. Department of Labor. Bureau of Labor Statistics. 1975 through 1988.

Baker, Michael and Westin, Alan. *Employer Perceptions of Workplace Crime*. U.S. Department of Justice. Bureau of Justice Statistics. May 1987.

"BJS Data Report, 1988." U.S. Department of Justice. Bureau of Justice Statistics.

Burns, Bill. "Operation Bootstrap: Opening Corporate Classrooms to Police Managers." *NIJ Reports*. U.S. Department of Justice, National Institute of Justice. November-December 1989.

Chaiken, Marcia and Chaiken, Jan. *Public Policing--Privately Provided*. U.S. Department of Justice. National Institute of Justice. June 1987.

"Communication Equipment, Including Radio and TV." *1982 Census of Manufacturers*. U.S. Department of Commerce. Bureau of the Census.

Conly, Catherine and McEwen, J. Thomas. "Computer Crime." *NIJ Reports*, U.S. Department of Justice. National Institute of Justice. January-February 1990.

Crime in Retailing. U.S. Department of Commerce. 1975.

Crime Prevention Beliefs, Policies, and Practices of Chief Law Enforcement Executives: Results of a National Survey. National Crime Prevention Council. Washington, D.C. February 1989.

Crime Prevention Measures. U.S. Department of Justice. Bureau of Justice Statistics. 1986.

"Current Business Reports." *1987 Service Sector Annual Survey*. U.S. Department of Commerce. Bureau of the Census. Washington, D.C.: Government Printing Office. September 1988.

Directory of Criminal Justice Information Sources. U.S. Department of Justice. National Institute of Justice. 6th ed. September 1986.

"Drugs and Crime." *NIJ Reports*. U.S. Department of Justice. National Institute of Justice. March-April 1987.

Drugs and Crime Facts. U.S. Department of Justice. Bureau of Justice Statistics. Washington, D.C. 1989

"Drug Use Forecasting Update." *NIJ Reports*. U.S. Department of Justice. National Institute of Justice. No. 215. July-August 1989. p.8.

Edelhertz, Herbert. *The Nature, Impact, and Prosecution of White Collar Crime*. U.S. Department of Justice. National Institute of Law Enforcement and Criminal Justice. 1970.

"Experiments Help Shape New Policies." *NIJ Reports*. U.S. Department of Justice. National Institute of Justice. September-October 1988.

Feins, Judith. *Partnerships for Neighborhood Crime Prevention*. U.S. Department of Justice. National Institute of Justice. 1983.

"Final Report." The White House Conference for a Drug-Free America. June 1988.

"Foreign Protection of International Property Rights." International Trade Commission. Reported by the National Center for Computer Crime Data. 1988.

Goalder, James and Hormachea, C. *The Second Decade: A Study on Regulation of the Private Security Industry in Virginia*. Center for Public Affairs. Department of Criminal Justice Services. Virginia Commonwealth University. 1988.

Graham, Mary. "Controlling Drug Abuse and Crime: A Research Update." "Drugs and Crime. " *NIJ Report* SNI 202. U.S. Department of Justice. National Institute of Justice. March-April 1987.

Green, Gloria and Eptein, Rosalie. *Employment and Earnings*. U.S. Department of Labor. Bureau of Labor Statistics. Vol. 36. No. 1. Washington, D.C.: Government Printing Office. January 1989.

Households Touched by Crime, 1988. U.S. Department of Justice. Bureau of Justice Statistics. June 1989.

Innes, Christopher. "Drug Use and Crime." State Prison Inmate Survey-1986. U.S. Department of Justice, Bureau of Justice Statistics. 1986.

Joiner, Larry (Chief of Police), Kansas City Police Department. *Contracting Police Support Services to Private Security*. A grant application to the U.S. Department of Justice, National Institute of Justice. January 1990.

Justice Expenditure and Employment Extracts. U.S. Department of Justice. Bureau of Justice Statistics. Washington, D.C.: Government Printing Office. 1980 through 1985.

Kakalik, James and Wildhorn, Sorrel. *Private Police in the United States (The Rand Report)*. Vols. 1 through 5. U.S. Department of Justice. National Institute of Law Enforcement and Criminal Justice. Washington, D.C.: Government Printing Office. 1971.

Kelling, George. "Police and Communities: The Quite Revolution." *Perspectives on Policing*. U.S. Department of Justice. National Institute of Justice. June 1988.

Kelling, George and Stewart, James. "Neighborhoods and Police: The Maintenance of Civil Authority." *Perspectives on Policing*, U.S. Department of Justice. National Institute of Justice. May 1989.

Law Enforcement and Private Security Sources and Areas of Conflict and Strategies for Conflict Resolution. Private Security Advisory Council. U.S. Department of Justice. Law Enforcement Assistance Administration. June 1977.

Logan, Charles and McGriff, Bill. "Comparing Costs of Public and Private Prisons: A Case Study." *NIJ Reports*. U.S. Department of Justice, National Institute of Justice. September-October 1989.

McEwen, J. Thomas, Manili, Barbara, and Connors, Edward. "Employee Drug Testing Policies in Police Departments." *Research in Brief*. U.S. Department of Justice. National Institute of Justice. October 1986.

Morris, Norval and Tonry, Michael. "Computer Crime: The New Crime Scene." *NIJ Reports*. U.S. Department of Justice. National Institute of Justice. January-February 1990.

"National Crime Prevention Awards." *The McGruff Gala*. The Crime Prevention Coalition. Washington, D.C. 1990.

"The National Industry-Occupation Employment Matrix, 1970, 1978, and Projected 1990." Vol. 1. U.S. Department of Labor. Bureau of Labor Statistics. Bulletin 2086. Washington, D.C.: Government Printing Office.

"NIDA Capsules: Highlights of the 1988 National Household Survey on Drug Abuse." National Institute on Drug Abuse.

"Outlook 2000," *Monthly Labor Review*. Vol. 112. No. 11. U.S. Department of Labor. Bureau of Labor Statistics. November 1989.

Patterns of Global Terrorism. Department of State, Office of the Secretary of State. 1989 and 1990.

Peloso, D. "Future Role of Local Police In Economic Crime." California Commission on Police Officer Standards and Training. Sacramento, CA. 1985.

Private Sector Involvement in Prison-Based Business: A National Assessment. U.S. Department of Justice. National Institute of Justice. Washington, D.C.: Government Printing Office. November 1985.

Profile of State and Local Law Enforcement Agencies, 1987. U.S. Department of Justice. Bureau of Justice Statistics. March 1989.

Reiss, Albert, Jr. *Private Employment of Public Police*. U.S. Department of Justice. National Institute of Justice. February 1988.

Report of the National Advisory Commission on Law Enforcement. General Accounting Office. Washington, D.C. U.S. Government Printing Office. February 1990.

Report of the Task Force on Private Security. National Advisory Committee on Criminal Justice Standards and Goals. U.S. Department of Justice. 1976.

Report to the Nation on Crime and Justice. 2d. ed. NCJ-105506. U.S. Department of Justice. Bureau of Justice Statistics. March 1988.

Rosenbaum, Dennis, Lurigio, Arthur, and Lavrakas, Paul. "Crime Stoppers - A National Evaluation." *Research in Brief*. U.S. Department of Justice. National Institute of Justice. September 1986.

Sherman, Lawrence. "Police Crackdowns." *NIJ Reports*. U.S. Department of Justice. National Institute of Justice. March-April 1990.

Sourcebook of Criminal Justice Statistics. U.S. Department of Justice. Bureau of Justice Statistics. Washington, D.C.: Government Printing Office. 1982 through 1988.

Stahl, Stan, ed. *Commitment to Security*. National Center for Computer Crime Data (NCCCD). 1989.

Terrorism in the United States, 1987. Counterterrorism Section. Terrorist Research and Analytical Center. U.S. Department of Justice. Federal Bureau of Investigation. December 1987.

"Terrorist Attacks on U.S. Businesses Abroad." U.S. Department of State. March 1986.

U.S. Department of Commerce. *Crime in Service Industries*. Washington, D.C. Government Printing Office. 1977

"Victims of Crime." U.S. Department of Justice. Bureau of Justice Statistics. November 1981.

Wasserman, Robert and Moore, Mark. "Values in Policing." *Perspectives in Policing*. No. 8. U.S. Department of Justice. National Institute of Justice. November 1988.

White Collar Crime: The Problem and the Federal Response. Committee on the Judiciary. House of Representatives. Ninety-Fifth Congress. Library of Congress. June 1978.

PERIODICALS

Adams, James. "The Bank Dicks' Dirty Linen." *The Wall Street Journal*. February 15, 1989. p.A14.

Adkins, Lynn. "The High Cost of Employee Theft." *Dun's Business Month*. October 18, 1982. p.72.

ADT Industry Relations Update. Vol. 2. No. 1. March 1990. p.2.

Allison, John. "Five Ways to Keep Disputes Out of Court." *Harvard Business Review*. January-February 1990. p.166.

Anthony, Andrew and Thornburg, Frederick. "Security on Trial." *Security Management*. February 1989. pp.41-46.

Armer, Anne, ed. "Forecast 1989: More Growth Ahead." *Security Distributing and Marketing*. January 1989. p.48.

Associated Press. "Few Workers Tested for Drugs, Study Says." *The Seattle Times*. January 11, 1989. Section F.

Atherton, Raymond. "Units Maintaining Liaison." *The Police Chief*. November 1964.

Bacas, Harry. "To Stop a Thief." *Nation's Business*. June 1987. p.16.

Bacon, Donald. "Business Moves Against Drugs." *Nation's Business*. November 1989. p.82.

Bates, Norman. "Reducing Liability's Toll." *Security Management*. October 1988. pp.75-77.

Beltrante, Nicholas. *Resources News*. January 1990.

Bologna, Jack. "High-Tech Crime is Here to Stay." *The White Paper*. National Association of Certified Fraud Examiners. Vol. 3. No. 1. spring 1989. pp.3-4.

Bensinger, Peter "Drug Testing in the Workplace." *The Annals*. American Academy of Political and Social Science. July 1988.

"Booming Consultant Market Balances Slumping Armored Car Services to Spearhead Solid Industry Growth." *Security*. September 1988. p.17.

Bottom, Norman, Jr. and Kostanoski, John. "An Informational Theory of Security." *Journal of Security Administration*. Vol. 4. No. 1. spring 1981. p.1.

Brody, Michael. "The 1990s." *Fortune*. February 2, 1987. p.22.

Brown, Carl P. "Crimes of the Vault." *Security Management*. January 1990.

Brown, Thad. "Types of Assistance Available." *The Police Chief*. November 1964.

Buck, Andrew and Hakim, Simon. "Burglar Alarms in the Community." *The Bellringer*. Pennsylvania Burglar and Fire Alarm Association. March 1989. p.13.

Buckelew, Alvin. "The Threat of Technoterrorism." *Security Management*. November 1983. pp.38-46.

Bureau of Labor Statistics. "USA Snapshots." *USA Today*. December 14. 1989. p.B1.

Bureau of National Affairs. *The Wall Street Journal*. August 30, 1988.

Burgess, John. "Computer Virus Sparks a User Scare." *The Washington Post*. September 17, 1989.

_____. "Hong Kong Authorities Seize Computer Disks, Books in Raid." *The Washington Post*. November 18, 1989. p.D1.

_____. "Race to Secure Computers Threatens Free Exchange of Data." *The Washington Post*. March 4, 1989. p. D11.

"Business Ethics Get Renewed Push." *The Wall Street Journal*. February 6, 1990. p.1.

"Business Travel Management in the Nineties." *Fortune*. March 26, 1990. p.196.2.

Butcher, Lola. "KC Police May Buy Backup Help From Private Security Firms." *Kansas City Business Journal*. November 27, 1989.

Calder, James. "New Corporate Security: The Autumn of Crime Control and The Spring of Fairness and Due Process." *Journal of Contemporary Criminal Justice*. Vol. 3. No. 4. December 1987.

_____. "The Security-Criminal Justice Connection: Toward the Elimination of Separate-But-Equal Status." *Journal of Security Administration*. Vol. 3. No. 2. fall 1980.

Canton, Lucien. "Limiting Liability Exposure: Have We Gone Too Far?" *Security Management*. January 1990. pp.71-72.

Carter, Carl. "Downtown Security: A Partnership Between Public and Private Sectors." *International Marketplace*. Central Business District Association. Detroit, Michigan. Vol. 3. No. 8. August 1986.

Christman, John. "History of Law and Private Security." *The Protection Officer*. Vol 2. No. 4. p.30.

Churbuck, David. "Desktop Forgery." *Forbes*. November 27, 1989. pp.246-253.

"Computer Crime Survey." *Data Processing & Communications Security*. spring 1989. p.5.

"Computer Data Locks, Keys Market to Reach $1 Billion Annually in U.S. by 1993." *Corporate Security Digest*. August 1, 1988. p.3.

Cook, James. "The Paradox of Antidrug Enforcement." *Forbes*. November 13, 1989. p.105.

Corbett, William. "A Time to Redefine Policy?" *Security Management*. June 1990. p.40.

"Corporate Espionage Spreads." *American Business*. summer 1984. p.2.

Crow, W. J., Erickson, Rosemary, and Scott, Lloyd. "Set Your Sights on Preventing Retail Violence." *Security Management*. September 1987. pp.60-64.

Cunningham, William and Gross, Phillip. "National Research Efforts on Private Security - What There Is, What It Covers, & Where to Get Copies." *Security Management*. September 1977.

Cunningham, William and Taylor, Todd. "Doing More with Less: Private Security Options for Decreasing Police Workload." *The Police Chief*. May 1985.

de Bernardo, Mark. "Employers' Role in War on Drugs." *The Drug-Free Workplace*. Institute for a Drug-Free Workplace. Washington, D.C. fall 1989.

Derr, Kenneth. "Security Management in Transition." *Security Management*. October 1982. p.31.

"Drug Testing at Work." *The Drug-Free Workplace*. Institute For A Drug-Free Workplace. Washington, D.C. summer 1988.

"Editorial." *The Bellringer*. Pennsylvania Burglar and Fire Alarm Association. November 1989. p.3.

Egan, Patrick. "The Future is Now." *News and Views*. National Burglar & Fire Alarm Association. Vols. 8904 & 8905. 1989.

"An Ethical Double Standard." *Business Month*. December 1989. p.7.

"Ethics: Business Standards Viewed as Healthy," *Security*. March 1988. p.12.

Feldcamp, Robert. "Bush Drug Strategy Has Something for Everyone, But Not Nearly Enough." *Narcotics Demand Reduction Digest*. Washington Crime News Service. Vol. 1. No. 4. September 1989. pp.1-3.

"Financial Times." *Security Management*. January 1990. p.15.

"Foreign Dollars Fuel 1988 Buy-Ups." *Security Distributing & Marketing*. October 1989. p.102.

"Foreigners Think Longer-Term." *Security Distributing & Marketing*. May 1988. pp.62-63.

Gaines, Leigh. "Police, Inc." *Security*. December 1989. p.29.

"Getting Drugs Out of the Workplace." *Business Month*. November 1989. p.18.

Goin, Lauren. "The Joint Council...The Beginning." *The National Sheriff*. October-November 1986.

Gourley, Douglas. "Police-Public Relations." *The Annals*. The American Academy of Political Science. Newbury Park, CA: Sage Publications. 1954.

Green, Larry. "Combatting Terrorism: Designing the Shield - Part II." *Consulting-Specifying Engineer*. February 1987.

Hanselman, Richard. "A CEO's Perspective." *Security Management*. December 1981. p.40.

Hogan, John. "Thwarting the Information Thieves." *IEEE Spectrum*. July 1985. p.32.

Huchins, Sam. "Chapter News." *ASIS Dynamics*. January-February 1990. p.30.

Industry Relation Update. Vol. 2. No. 1. ADT Security Systems. March 1990.

International Trade Commission . *The Wall Street Journal*. March 16, 1989. p.1.

Inwald, Robin. "How to Detect Those 'Little White Lies' or 'Seven Deadly Sins' of Honesty Test Vendors." *Corporate Security Digest*. Vol. 3. No. 6. September 11, 1989.

Kates, Norman. "A Forum on the Forum." *Washington Law Enforcement Executive Journal*. August 1988. p.6.

Kelly, Jack. "Poll: On Job Drug Use is Significant." *USA Today*. December 13, 1989. p.1.

Kelly, Orr. "Corporate Crime: The Untold Story." *U.S. News and World Report*. September 6, 1982. p.25.

Kirschenbaum, Kenneth. "False Alarms." *Security Dealer*. February 1990. p.21.

Kuhn, Ryan A. "The Attack of Employer's Rights." *Security Journal*. Vol. 1. No. 2. 1990. pp.74-75.

Lesher, Richard. "The Privatization Bandwagon." *The Voice of Business*. U.S. Chamber of Commerce. Washington, D.C. January 29, 1990.

Levine, Art. "Watch Those Watchdogs." *U.S. News and World Report*. July 11, 1988. pp.36-38.

Lipman, Ira, ed. *The Annals*. The American Academy of Political and Social Science. Newbury Park, CA: Sage Publications. 1988.

Lipson, Milton. "Private Security: A Retrospective." *The Annals*. The American Academy of Political and Social Science. Newbury Park, CA: Sage Publications. July 1988.

Lydon, Kerry. "Forecast 1989: Hoping for a Soft Landing." *Security*. January 1989. p.46.

_____. "Who Makes Security Decisions for U.S. Business?" *Security*. September 1987.

_____. "New Niche-Services Tailor Protection." *Security*. December 1989. p.41.

Malcolm, Andrew. "When Private Employees Hire Public Police." *The New York Times*. February 26, 1989. p.22.

"Managing Today's Guards." *ASIS Dynamics*. November-December 1989. p.4.

Marx, Gary and Archer, Dane. "The Urban Vigilante." *Psychology Today*. January 1973. p.45.

McAfee, John. "Managing the Virus Threat." *Computerworld*. February 13, 1989. p.89.

McAllister, Bill. "Counterfeit Shoe Ring Uncovered." *The Washington Post*. December 30, 1989. p.B1.

McCrie, Robert. "The Growing Crisis in Civil Liberty." *Security Letter* Vol. XVI. No. 21. Part II. November 3, 1986.

McQueen, Michael and Shribman, David. "Battle Against Drugs is Chief Issue Facing Nation, Americans Say." *The Wall Street Journal*. September 22, 1989. p.1.

Meadows, Robert. "It's 1990 - Do You Know How Liable You Are?" *Security Management*. January 1990. pp.55-62.

Moffett, Matt. "Fear of Terrorists Directs New Attention to Illegal Immigrants." *The Wall Street Journal*. May 14, 1986. p.1.

Moore, Arthur Cotton. "Yes, We Have to Beef Up Security, But Ugly Barriers Hand Terrorists Their First Victory. There are Better Ways." *The Washingtonian*. July 1986. p.87.

Moore, R. H. "Licensing and the Regulation of Private Security." *Journal of Security Administration*. Vol. 10. No. 1. June 1987. pp.10-28.

Moore, Richter and Spain, Norman. "No Joke: Training Cuts Liability." *Security*. July 1989. p.31.

"Moonlighting Police and Private Security." April 15, 1989. *The Lipman Report*.

"Multinational Firms Act to Protect Overseas Workers From Terrorism." *The Wall Street Journal*. April 29, 1986. Section 2. p.1.

Murphy, Ian. "Who's Listening." *Data Processing & Communications Security*. 1988 and 1989.

Murray, Thomas. "Can Business Schools Teach Ethics?" *Business Month*. April 1987. p.24-25.

"New Streets, Paved With Gold." *Business Week*. October 16, 1989. p.92.

"1989 Facts and Figures." *Security Sales*. September 1989. p.14.

Omang, Joanne. "Businesses That Offer Defense Against Terrorism Are Booming." *The Washington Post*. January 3, 1986. p.A22.

"One in Four Florida Business Organizations Victims of Computer Crimes, Study Finds." *Corporate Security Digest*. June 19, 1989. p.1.

O'Toole, Thomas. "U.S. Tightens Guard on Nuclear Facilities." *The Washington Post*. August 27, 1985. p.A5.

Partnership Focus Vol. 1. No. 1. Little Falls, N.J.: Maxco Publications. June 1990.

Passero, Kathy. "Fearing Terrorism, Firms Limit Use of U.S. Carriers." *Corporate Travel*. May 1989.

Pasztor, Andy and Wartzman, Rick. "How a Spy for Boeing and His Pals Gleaned Data on Defense Plans." *The Wall Street Journal*. January 15, 1990. p.A1.

President's Commission on Organized Crime and Wharton Econometric Forecasting Associates, Inc. *The Washington Post*. April 2, 1986. p.A3.

"Private Business to Benefit From Security Bulletin Board." *Security*. January 1989. p. 20.

"Private Delivery of Public Services." *The Lipman Report*. November 15, 1989.

"Private Security Takes to the Streets." *Security*. September 1989. p.19.2.

"Public/Private Partnership Trains Inner-City Teens For Security Careers." *Catalyst*. Vol. 6. No. 6. National Crime Prevention Council. August 1986.

Purbrick, Anthony. British Security Industry Association. "A Tale of Two Counties." *Security Management*. January 1990. pp. 77-81.

"A Record Year for Terrorism in 1988." *Security Management*. May 1989. p.116.

Revell, Oliver. "International Terrorism in the United States." *The Police Chief*. March 1989. pp.16-22.

Robert Half International. *Nation's Business*. Vol. 75. No. 6. June 1987. p. 23.

Russell, Rebecca. "Changing Times for Contract Officer Pay." *Security*. February 1990. p.37.

_____. "Officer Training: Identify Your Options." *Security*. May 1990. p.49.

"Safeguarding Against Computer Crime." *The Lipman Report*. November 15, 1988.

Schwadel, Francine. "Chicago Retailers' Sting Aims to Put Shoplifting Professionals Out of Business." *The Wall Street Journal*. June 5, 1990. p.B1.

Scott, Thomas and McPherson, Marlys. "The Development of the Private Sector of the Criminal Justice System." *Law and Society Review*. Vol. 6. No. 2. 1971. pp.273-274.

"Security Forecast 1990." *Security*. January 1990.

"Security Survey: Liability Issues Lead to Growing Concern." *Security*. January 1990. p.12.

"Security's Paycheck: An Inside Look." *Security Distributing & Marketing*. September 1988. pp.45-48.

"Security Wrap-Up: Drug Testing, Crime Trends." *Security*. April 1990. p.9.

Shanahan, Michael. "Operation Bootstrap." *The Police Chief*. February 1987.

Shearing, Clifford and Stenning, Phillip. "Private Security: Implications for Social Control." *Social Problems*. Vol. 30. No. 5. June 1983.

Silk, Leonard. "Does Morality Have a Place in the Boardroom?" *Business Month*. October 1989. p.11.

Silver, Michael. "Negligent Hiring Claims Take off." *American Bar Association Journal*. May 1987. pp.72-78.

Sine, Charles, Jr. "The Record Speaks." *Security Management*. September 1988.

Skrzycki, Cindy. "Taking a Risk on Rehabilitation." *The Washington Post*. April 6, 1989. p.C1.

Slovak, Julianne. "Technology in the Year 2000." *Fortune*. July 18, 1988.

"The Specific Case Inventory Measuring Respondents' Information For Single-Theft Investigators." *Security Journal*. Vol. 1. No. 2. 1990. p.81.

Spitzer, Steven. "Dialectics of Formal and Informal Justice." *Politics of Informal Justice: Vol. I. The American Experience*. 1981.

Strauchs, John. "Living with Violence Abroad." *Security Management*. June 1984. p.30.

Stuart, James. "Police and Drug Testing: A Look at Some Issues." *The Police Chief*. October 1986. pp.27-32.

_____. "Public Safety and Private Police." *Public Administration Review*. Vol. 45. November 1985.

Swisher, Kara. "Lawyers Coordinate Myriad Suits Against EXXON." *The Washington Post*. January 30, 1990. p.C.9.

Tafoya, William. "Into the Future: A Look at the 21st Century." *Law Enforcement Technology*. September-October 1987.

"Target: United States." *The Lipman Report*. April 15, 1989.

Thomas, Max. "Classroom Conundrum: Profits + Ethics = ?" *Business Month*. February 1990. p.6.

Thornburgh, Richard, Attorney General of the United States. *The Police Chief*. April 1989. p.10.

Tolchin, Martin. "Private Guards Get New Role in Public Law Enforcement." *The New York Times*. November 29, 1985. p.1.

Trojanowicz, Robert. "Public and Private Justice: Preparing for the 21st Century." *Criminal Justice Alumni Newsletter*. Vol. V. No. 1. Michigan State University. fall-winter 1989. p.2.

True, Warren. "Drug Testing Arrives." *Oil & Gas Journal*. November 27, 1989. p.13.

"U.S. International Trade Commission." *The Washington Post*. December 30, 1989. p.B8.

"Visions of Tomorrow." *Life*. February 1989.

Vodak, Warren. "Security's Crystal Ball." *Security Dealer*. Vol. 12. No. 1. January 1990. p.32.

Walsh, William. "Private/Public Police Stereotypes: A Different Perspective." *Security Journal*. Vol.1. No. 1. 1989. pp.21-27.

Warner, David. "Firms Urged to Fight Drug Abuse." *The Business Advocate*. U.S. Chamber of Commerce. July 1988. p.1.

Wathen, Thomas. Private Security Workshop. 88th Annual Conference of International Association of Chiefs of Police. *The Police Chief*. January 1982. p.38.

Weiss, Stuart. "Locked Out." *Business Month*. October 1989. pp.44-49.

"White Collar Crime Costs." *Business Month*. August 1989. P.15.

Zalud, Bill. "Spy Business." *Security*. January 1989. pp.52-55.

_____. "Charting Security's Course." *Security*. January 1990. p.29.

_____. "1990 Directory of Products and Services." *Security*. November 1989.

Zendek, Gregory and Werner, Steven. "Retailers on the Defensive," *Chain Store Age Executive*. February 1983. p.16.

BOOKS

Albrecht, W. Steve, et. al. *How to Detect Business Fraud*. Englewood Cliffs, N.J.: Prentice-Hall. 1982.

Bennett, Georgette. *Crime Warps: The Future of Crime in America*. Garden City, NY: Anchor Press/Doubleday. 1987.

Brock, Randolph. "The Guard in the Year 2000." *Security in the Year 2000 and Beyond*. Louis Tyska, ed. Palm Springs, CA: ETC Publications. 1987.

Butcher, Brian. *A Movable Rambling Police*. Norfolk, England, Police Constabulary. 1989.

Clark, John and Hollinger, Richard. *Theft by Employees in Work Organizations*. Minneapolis: University of Minnesota. 1981.

Compensation in the Security/Loss Prevention Field. Abbott, Langer, and Associates. Editions 1 through 6.

Creating a Safe Community: The Young Security Officer's Guide, National Crime Prevention Council. Washington, D.C. 1987.

Crimes Against Business: Recommendations for Demonstration, Research, and Related Programs Designed to Reduce and Control Non-Violent Crimes Against Business. The American Management Associations. New York, NY. December 1977.

Crow, W. J. and Erickson, Rosemary. *Cameras and Silent Alarms: A Study of Their Effectiveness as a Robbery Deterrent*. Sioux Falls, SD: Athena Research Press. 1984.

Cunningham, William and Gross, Philip. *Prevention of Terrorism: Security Guidelines For Business and Other Organizations*. McLean, VA: Hallcrest Press. June 1978.

Cunningham, William and Taylor, Todd. *The Hallcrest Report: Private Security and Police in America*. McLean, VA: Chancellor Press. 1985.

Dinitz, Simon. "Multidisciplinary Approaches to White-Collar Crime." *White-Collar Crime: An Agenda for Research*. Herbert Edelhertz and Thomas D. Overcast, eds. Lexington Books. 1982.

Edwards, Paul, editor in chief. *Encyclopedia of Philosophy*. Vol. III. New York: McMillian Company and The Free Press. 1967.

Green, Gion. *Introduction to Security*. 3rd ed. Stoneham, MA: Butterworth Publishers, Inc. 1981.

Jackson, Carl. "The Need for Security." *Datapro Reports on Information Security*. Datapro Research Corporation. Delran, N.J.: McGraw-Hill. 1987.

Jacob, Herbert and Robert Lineberry. *Governmental Responses to Crime: Executive Summary*. Evanston, IL: Center for Urban Affairs and Policy Research. Northwestern University. 1982

McCrie, Robert. ed. *Security Letter Source Book 1990-1991*. 4th ed. Stoneham, MA: Butterworth Publishers. 1990.

Ricks, Truitt, Tillett, B., and Van Meter, Clifford. *Principles of Security*. 2d. ed. Criminal Justice Studies. Cincinnati, OH: Anderson Publishing Company.

Post, Richard and Kingsbury, Arthur. *Security Administration: An Introduction*. Springfield, IL: Charles Thomas. 1977.

Scott, Eric. *Calls For Service: Citizen Demand and Initial Police Response*. Bloomington, Indiana: Workshop in Political Theory Analysis, Indiana University. 1981.

Scott, Eric. *Police Referral in Metropolitan Area*. Bloomington, Indiana: Workshop in Political Theory and Policy Analysis. Indiana University. 1981.

Security Industry Buyers Guide. Published by C&P Telephone of Virginia, Bell Atlantic and the American Society for Industrial Security. Bethesda, MD. 1989-1990.

Shackley, Theodore, Oatman, Robert, and Finney, Richard. "A Look into the Future." *You're the Target*. New World Publishing. 1989.

Shearing, Clifford and Stenning, Philip. "Modern Private Security: Its Growth and Implications" in Michael Tonry and Norval Morris, ed. *Crime and Justice: An Annual Review of Research*. Vol. 3. Chicago: University of Chicago Press. 1981.

Thurow, Lester. *The Zero-Sum Society*. New York: Basic Books. 1982.

Tyska, Louis and Fennelly, Lawrence. *Security in the Year 2000 and Beyond*. Palm Springs, CA: ETC Publications. 1987.

Wilson, James. *Varieties of Police Behavior*. Cambridge: Harvard University Press. 1968.

OTHER

Albrecht, W. Steve, McDermott, and Williams, Timothy. *Organization Structures to Deal with Employee Fraud.* A research project funded by the ASIS Foundation, awaiting publication, 1990.

Commitment to Security. National Center for Computer Crime Data. 1989.

Corporate Action Kit. National Crime Prevention Council. Washington, D.C. and ADT. New York, NY. 1986.

Crow, W. J. and Erickson, Rosemary. *Product Tampering: A Recommended Policy of the International Association of Chiefs of Police (IACP).* Gaithersburg, MD. 1987.

Donovan, Edwin and Walsh, William. *An Evaluation of Starrett City Security Services.* A research project conducted by the Pennsylvania State University with a grant from Starrett Realty Corporation. Brooklyn, New York. April 1986.

Driscoll, John, Deputy Chief of Police. *Public and Private Security Forces Unite in Dallas.* Dallas Police Department. Unpublished. Dallas, TX. circa 1985.

"The Drug Monitoring and Abuse Testing Business." Business Communications Co., Inc. Report C-104. Norwalk, Connecticut. December 1988.

"Drugs of Abuse Testing Markets." Report No. A214B. Market Intelligence Research Company. July 1987.

"The Figgie Report on Fear of Crime: America Afraid." Part 1: The General Public. Sponsored by A-T-O Inc. Conducted by Research & Forecasts Inc. Willoughby, OH. 1980.

"Fighting Drug Abuse in Corporate America." *Special Report: The National Conference on Corporate Initiatives for a Drug-Free Workplace.* Hoffman-La Roche. Nutley, N.J. 1988.

Galvin, Deborah. *Biography for Security Trainers.* Academy of Security Educators and Trainers. Berryville, VA. 1989.

Harwood, Henrick, Napolitano, Diane, Kristiansen, Patricia, and Collins, James. Research Triangle Institute. *Economic Costs to Society of Alcohol and Drug Abuse and Mental Illness: 1980.* Chapel Hill, NC. June 1984.

Holzman, Harold and Mueller, Julia. *Maximizing the Effects of Deterrence as a Control Strategy for Internal Theft*. Centers for the Study of the Causes of Crime for Gain. School of Criminal Justice. Rutgers University. Newark, N.J. 1982.

The Joint Council of Law Enforcement and Private Security Associations. Chicago, IL. Minutes. August 21-22, 1986.

Lavarkas, Paul and Rosenbaum, Dennis. *Crime Prevention Beliefs, Policies, and Practices of Chief Law Enforcement Executives: Results of a National Survey*. National Crime Prevention Council. Washington, D.C. February 1989.

McDonald, William, Rossman, Henry, and Cramer, James. *Police-Prosecutor Relations in the United States: A Final Report*. Washington, D.C.: Institute of Criminal Law and Procedure. Georgetown University Law Center. Washington, D.C. December 1981.

Pauley, Jane. "Off-Duty Cops and Moonlighting." *Today*. NBC-TV. March 6, 1989.

The Peat, Marwick, Mitchell Foundation. *How to Prevent and Detect Business Fraud*. 1981

Press Conference Fact Sheet. International Conference on Terrorism. November 20, 1986. Washington, D.C.

The Protection Officer Training Manual . Cochrane, Alberta, Canada: The Protection Officer Publications. 1986.

"Results of the 1989 Arthur Andersen Enterprise Survey." Arthur Andersen. November 1989.

"Security Products and Services." *Leading Edge Reports*. (Study LE 7203). March 1990.

Shearing, Clifford, Farnell, Margaret, and Stenning, Philip. *Contract Security in Ontario*. University of Toronto. 1980.

Sherman, Lawrence and Klein, Jody. *Major Lawsuits Over Crime and Security: Trends and Patterns 1958-1982*. Institute of Criminal Justice and Criminology, University of Maryland. September 1984.

Standards for Law Enforcement Agencies. Commission on Accreditation for Law Enforcement Agencies, Inc. (CALEA). Fairfax, VA. January 1990 ed.

Tafoya, William. "The Future of Law Enforcement? A Chronology of Events." *A Delphi Forecast of the Future of Law Enforcement*. Unpublished Doctoral Dissertation. University of Maryland. December 1986.

"Use of Drugs by Sworn Officers." Order No. D-18. San Francisco Police Department General Order Control Code (88-05). March 24, 1988.

Voelker, Anthony. *Starter Kit: APPL Program*. New York Police Department. 1989.

"Who Do We Trust." *Gallup Report*. December 1988.

Wolfgang, Marvin. *National Survey of Crime Severity*. Philadelphia: Center for Studies in Criminal Law. University of Pennsylvania. 1980.

INDEX

Abbott Langer and Associates,
156-157
Academy of Security Educators
and Trainers, 11
access control, 199, 202-208
accreditation for security
organizations and management, 251, 323
adjudication, private, 269,
296-302, 329-331
ADT, 253, 264-265, 288
Advance Security, 253
Advertising Council, 252
alarm companies, 177, 183-184,
192-197, 216, 324
alarm industry, 129, 167-168,
282-288
alarm personnel wages, 156
alarms, 199, 202-208
American Bar Association, 25
American Can Company
Foundation, 252-253
American Management Associations
(AMA), 25-26, 29-30
American Society for Industrial
Security (ASIS), 3, 6, 11, 77, 151, 165, 246,
250-251, 322, 325
American Trial Lawyers
Association, 36-37
Area Police-Private Security
Liaison (APPL), 262
Arizona Community Watch, 265
Arizona Public Service Company,
265
armored car services, 130, 177-
178, 182-183, 192-197, 216, 221
Arthur Andersen and Company, 59
asset protection, private
security role, 115-119
Athena Research Corporation,
38, 247-248
Baker, Michael, 25, 27, 34
Baltimore County Police
Department, 261
Bates, Norman, 36
Bennett, William, 53
bomb detection, 199, 202-208
Bottom, Norman, 115
British Security Industry
Association (BSIA), 152-153, 323
brokering protective services,
269-281, 319-320, 328-329

Brualdi, Les, 288
Buckelew, Alvin, 94
Bureau of Justice Statistics,
7, 18, 172
Burns International Security
Services, 253, 295, 300
business-ethics, 45, 47-51
Business Risks International,
82
Butcher, Brian, 112
Calder, James, 300-302
California Commission on Peace
Officers' Standards and Training, 39
Carter, Carl, 257
Central Station Alarm
Association (CSAA), 251-252, 265
Chaiken, Jan, 274-276
Chaiken, Marcia, 274-276
Citicorp Diners Club, 91
citizen crime prevention, 113-
114
Clark, John, 49-50
closed-circuit television, 198-
199, 202-208
co-production, 109, 112, 319
Commission on Accreditation for
Law Enforcement Agencies (CALEA), 153,
251, 323
Committee of National Security
Companies (CONSCO), 11, 280-281
Communications Fraud Control
Association, 70, 249
Comprehensive Crime Control Act
of 1984, 92
computer crime, 45, 60-77
computer crime, dimensions of,
67-70
computer crime, findings,
recommendations, and forecasts, 316-318
computer security, 45, 60-70
computer security and
shielding, 200, 202-208, 223
computer security, equipment
sales and service, 73-74
computer security industry, 71-
77
computer virus, 65-66
Computer Virus Industry
Association, 65
computers and industrial
espionage, 66

359

contract guards, 177, 184-185, 192-197, 216-219
contract security, 124-125
contracting out of police activities, 272-281, 283-288
cooperative programs, 243-266, 328
Corporate Action Kit, 253
corporate ethics, 49-51
cost of crimes against business, 23-25
counterfeiting and software piracy, 74-75
counterterrorism, 46, 79-97
counterterrorism, business of, 86-92
counterterrorism, definition of, 85
counterterrorism, findings, recommendations, and forecasts, 319
crime control, police role, 110-113
crime prevention, 19, 113-114
crime, price of, 2, 313
criminal hackers, 65-66
Crow, W.J., 38
Dallas Police/Private Security Joint Information Committee, 256-257
Data Processing Management Association (DPMA), 76-77
Datapro Research Corporation, 67
Dearborn Security Network, 260-261
Delphi Technique, 170-171
desktop forgery, 75
Dinitz, Simon, 21
Donovan, Edwin, 139-140
Downtown Detroit Security Executive Council (DDSEC), 257-259
drug abuse, 45, 52-59
drug abuse, findings, recommendations, and forecasts, 316
drug detection, 54
drug prevention, 45, 54-59
drug testing, 54-59
drug testing, police officers, 56
drug treatment, 45, 54-59
drugs in the work place, 248-249

Eastgate Security and Investigations, Inc., 278
economic crime, cost of, 28-34, 314
economic crime, definition of, 19-21, 313
economic crime, indirect cost, 32-34, 314
economic crime, liability and litigation, 34-38, 314-315
Economic Crime Research Center, 313
economic crimes, 17, 28, 45, 298
economic crimes, findings, recommendations, forecasts, and research needs, 312-315, 330-331
electronic article surveillance, 200, 202-208
electronic bulletin boards, 64-66
electronic intrusion, 45, 60-70
electronic security products and services, 208-209
employment, law enforcement, 227-237, 240
employment, private security, 196-197, 209-219, 227-237, 240, 324-327
Erickson, Rosemary, 38
ethics and values, findings, recommendations, and forecasts, 315-316
ethics and values, 47-51
Ethics Resource Center, 47, 49
FBI Uniform Crime Report (UCR), 17, 19, 29-30, 114, 330
false alarms, 269, 282-288, 329, 332
false alarms, findings, recommendations, forecasts, and research needs, 329, 332
Federal Aviation Administration (FAA), 91, 95
Federal Bureau of Investigation, 82, 84, 92, 94-95
Federal Express, 49
Federal Law Enforcement Training Center, 263
Federal, R. Keegan Jr., 36
findings, 311-330
Finney, Richard, 93-94
fire alarm equipment and services, 167-168

Florida Department of Law
  Enforcement, 67-68
Food Marketing Institute, 248
Ford Motor Company, 261
forecasts, 311-330
foreign ownership, private
  security, 219-220, 325
fraud, 28
Freedonia Group, 187, 222
Frost and Sullivan, 72-74
Gallup Poll, 48, 52, 57-58
general crime trends, 18
Green, Gion, 123-124
Grocery Manufacturers of
  America, 248
gross national product (GNP),
  18, 173-174, 203-204, 227
guard services, 128
Hallcrest Systems, Inc., 3-4,
  9, 11, 171
Harris Corporation, 51
Hoffman-LaRoche Company, 264
Hollinger, Richard, 49-50
honesty testing, 191
Honeywell, 288
Humphrey, James, 257
information security, 126-127
International Association for
  Hospital Security, 147
International Association of
  Chiefs of Police, 11, 153, 246-251, 247-250,
  277, 295
International Association of
  Professional Security Consultants (IAPSC),
  187
International Business Machines
  (IBM), 263
International Conference on
  Terrorism, 79-80
International Foundation for
  Protection Officers, 147
International Resource
  Development, Inc. (IRD), 72, 74
International Security
  Conference and Exposition (ISC EXPO), 144-
  145, 322
international terrorism, 46,
  88-90
International Trade Commission,
  74
Interstate Commerce Commission
  (ICC), 27

Jacob, Herbert, 114
Jenkins, Brian, 90
Joiner, Larry, 279
Joint Council of Law
  Enforcement and Private Security
  Associations, 246-247
Joint Economic Committee, 23
Jones, Lee, 219
Kakalik, James, 2
Kansas City Police Task Force,
  279-280
Kelling, George, 111-112
Kingsbury, Arthur, 109, 113
Klein, Jody, 36
Kostanoski, John, 115
law enforcement employment,
  227-237, 240, 326-327
law enforcement expenditures,
  237-240, 326
Law Enforcement Liaison
  Council, 250-251
Leading Edge Report, 73, 201
Lesher, Richard, 58, 270
Levy Security Consultants,
  Ltd., 278
liability and litigation, 34-38
Lineberry, Robert, 114
Lipman Report, 70
Lloyd's of London, 126-127
locksmiths, 130, 177, 188-189,
  192-197, 216, 221-222
Market Intelligence Research
  Company, 54
Maryland Chiefs of Police
  Association, 261
McCrie, Robert, 51
McDonald, William, 298
McPherson, Marlys, 115
metal detection, 199, 202-208
microtaggants, 96
Mobil Corporation, 51
Mobil Foundation, 263
moonlighting, police, 269, 289-295
Moore, Arthur Cotton, 91
Moore, Mark, 49, 294
Moore, Richter, 145, 147
Mountain Fuel Supply Company,
  265
Murphy, George, 263
narcoterrorism, 89-90

National Burglar and Fire Alarm
    Association (NBFAA), 11,
    148-149, 251-252, 265, 284, 286, 288
National Center for Computer
    Crime Data (NCCCD), 63, 68-74, 76-77
National Council of
    Investigation and Security Services, 11
National Crime Prevention
    Council, 113-114, 252-253
National Crime Prevention
    Institute, 114
National Crime Survey (NCS), 17
National Criminal Justice
    Reference Service, 3, 6
National Institute of Justice
    (NIJ), 3-4, 55-56, 68, 246, 274-276, 280-281
National Institute on Drug
    Abuse (NIDA), 52-54
National Organization of Black
    Law Enforcement Executives (NOBLE), 153
National Research on Security,
    2-11, 332
National Sheriffs' Association,
    153, 246
Neighborhood Watch, 19, 113-114
Northwest Protective Service,
    Inc., 278
Oatman, Robert, 93-94
Omnibus Diplomatic Security and
    Anti-Terrorism Act of 1986, 92
Operation Bootstrap, 248
Operation Cooperation, 250-251
ordinary crime, 21-22, 29-30
ordinary crime, definition of,
    40
original equipment manufacturers and distributors,
    206-208
Overseas Security Advisory
    Council, 64, 91, 254
patrol services, 128
Pauley, Jane, 293
personnel characteristics, 137-
    141, 320
personnel security, 127
physical security, 125-126
Pinkerton's, Inc., 175, 249,
    277, 295
Police Executive Research
    Forum, 153
police functions, 2, 117-119
police moonlighting, 269, 289-
    295

police tasks, transfer of, 271-
    281
political terrorism, 46
Post, Richard, 109, 113, 253
PRIDE, 259-260
private investigations, 129
private investigators, 177,
    185-187
private justice, 269, 296-302,
    329-331
private sector access to
    criminal records, 250
Private Sector Liaison
    Committee (PSLC), 247-250
private security
    revenues/expenditures, 237-240, 324-326, 331
Private Security Advisory Council (PSAC), 2, 9,
84, 150-
    152, 243-244, 289
private security components,
    127-132
private security, definitions
    of, 122-124, 323-324
private security employment,
    196-197, 209-219, 227-237, 240, 324-327
private security functions, 2,
    120
private security performance,
    120-122, 327
Private Security/Police
    Partnership Models, 251
Private Security Task Force
    (PSTF), 2-3, 9, 112, 116, 123, 142-146, 150-
    151, 154, 243-244, 289, 297, 322
privatization, 269-281, 319-
    320, 328-329
privatization, East Hills, Long
    Island, New York, 278
privatization, Kansas City,
    Missouri, 279-281
privatization, Tacoma,
    Washington, 277-278
privatization, Wynstone, North
    Barrington, Illinois, 278
Project Honest Broker, 250-251
proprietary security, 124-125,
    128, 209-216, 325
protection, dimensions of, 109
protective measures, 125-127
Purbrick, Anthony, 153

Rand Corporation, 9, 122, 137-
138
Rand Report, 2, 109, 112, 243-
244, 294, 296
recommendations, 311-330
Reiss, Albert, 293-295
research needs, 330-333
Research Triangle Institute
(RTI), 100
Rosetti, Joseph, 296
safes, vaults, and secure
storage, 201-208
Salt River Project, 265
Schaefer, Governor William,
248-249
Schultz, George, 254
Scott, Eric, 110-111
Scott, Thomas, 115
security and police
relationships, 243-245
security and terrorism
interface, 46, 78-97
security consultant services,
130-131
security consultants, 177, 187-
188, 192-197, 216
security continuum, 116
Security Education Employment
Program, 252-253
security engineers, 187-188,
192-197
security fencing, 200, 202-208
security industry product
sector, 173, 198-209, 223-224
security industry, proprietary
security, 173, 209-216
security industry, security
service sector, 173, 180-191
security industry statistics,
effect of large companies, 217-219
security lighting, 200, 202-208
security locks, 201-208
security manufacturers and
distributors, 131-132, 177, 189-191
security market, analysis of,
163-172
security market, employment,
173-176, 181-197
security market, key market
indicators, 173-180
security personnel "vicious
circle", 142-143

security personnel, 2, 137-158
security personnel, armed, 143-
144, 321
security personnel attrition,
142-143
security personnel, compensation, 156-158, 321
security personnel, education,
149-150, 322
security personnel, findings, recommendations, and
forecasts,
320-323
security personnel screening,
141-142, 320
security personnel, St. Louis,
MO, 138-140
security personnel, standards
and regulations, 150-155, 322-323
security personnel, Starrett,
NY, 139-140
security personnel, training,
144-149, 321-322
security service and
manufacturing companies, 195
security service and
manufacturing employment, 196-197
security service revenues, 191-
195
security services and products,
17, 19
security services and products,
findings, recommendations, and forecasts,
323-326
Shakley, Theodore, 93-94
Shanahan, Michael, 248
Shearing, Clifford, 301-302
Sherman, Eva, 36
Sherman, Lawrence, 36-37
Small Business Administration
(SBA), 23
Somerson, Ira, 49
Southland Corporation, 247-248,
252
Southwest Gas Corporation, 265
Spain, Judith, 36
Spain, Norman, 36, 147
Standard Industrial
Classification (SIC) Codes, 7
Stenning, Phillip, 301-302
Stewart, James, 111-112, 281
Support Services Group, 219
Sutherland, Edwin, 20
Systech Group, Inc., 171, 206

technoterrorism, 94
telecommunications fraud, 249
telephone security, 200, 202-
    208, 223
Tempest, government code word,
    75, 200, 223
terrorism, 46, 78-97
terrorism, definition of, 83-85
terrorism, effect on public law
    enforcement, 92-96
terrorism, findings,
    recommendations, and forecasts, 318-319
terrorism, "hype" factor, 79-80
terrorism, influence on private
    security, 86-87, 91-92, 97
Texize, 252
thermal neutron activation
    (TNA), 95-96
Thomas, Max, 50
Thurow, Lester, 180
Towers, Perrin, Forster, and
    Crosby (TPF&C), 157
Trojanowicz, Robert, 281
turf issue, public and private
    shift, 116-119, 319
U.S. Bureau of Labor
    Statistics, 7, 172, 174, 179-180, 221, 228, 240,
    295, 331
U.S. Bureau of the Census, 164,
    167, 172, 240, 331
U.S. Chamber of Commerce, 26,
    58, 270
U.S. Department of Commerce, 7,
    25-27, 29, 173
U.S. Department of State, 64-
    65, 79-80, 82-84, 89, 91-92
U.S. Department of Labor, 57-
    58, 173, 228
U.S. Food and Drug
    Administration, 47
U.S. International Trade
    Commission, 22
U.S. West Communications, 265
unAmerican growth of security
    industry, 219-220, 325
University of Illinois Police
    Training Institute, 140
Utah Council for Crime
    Prevention, 265
W.L. Gore Corporation, 49
Wackenhut Corporation, 295
WAECUP, 115

Walsh, William, 139-140
Washington Law Enforcement
    Executive Forum (WLEEF), 255-256
Washington Researchers, 67
Washington State Restaurant and
    Hotel Association, 249
Wasserman, Robert, 49
Watham, Thomas, 277
Wells Fargo Guard Service, 295
Westergren, Gene, 140
Western Burglar and Fire Alarm
    Association, 286
Weston, Alan, 25, 27, 34
White House Conference for a
    Drug-Free America, 52-53
white-collar crime, 21-22, 29-
    30
white-collar crime, definition
    of, 39
Wickersham Report, 110
Wildhorn, Sorrel, 2
Wilson, James, 110
X-ray systems, 199, 202-208